Nolan Patterson from Black Star

FRANZ ALEXANDER, M. D.

FRANZ ALEXANDER cannot be defined by his profession, alone. Not only is he one of our foremost psychoanalysts, who has had a great influence on the history of psychoanalysis, but he is also a reflective scholar, who —more than any other man—has united psychoanalysis with scholarship and medical tradition, keeping it free of narrow dogma.

Dr. Alexander's role as an innovator in his field is based, also, on his wide range of interest, which includes all aspects of human experience, especially in relation to the life of the individual. This broad perspective is no accident. Born in Budapest, Hungary, in 1891, the son of Bernard Alexander, a philosopher and educator, Franz Alexander grew up in a world of artists, philosophers, scientific theorists, and scholars dedicated to the humanistic tradition. Later, while studying medicine at the Universities of Budapest and Göttingen, he came to know a different approach, that of the experimental scientists. After receiving his medical degree in 1912, he started research in brain physiology (interrupted by his military service as a physician during World War I but later resumed) which led him to an interest in psychiatry, and from there to the works of Freud. He soon found what was, for him, the ideal synthesis of the humanistic and scientific approaches—psychoanalysis. He went to Berlin to study, became the first training candidate at the Berlin Psychoanalytic Institute,

(Continued on back flap)

dent of the American Psychoanalytic Association.

The Western Mind in Transition

AN EYEWITNESS STORY

by Franz Alexander
M.D.

RANDOM HOUSE : NEW YORK

FIRST PRINTING

 Published in New York by Random House, Inc., and simultaneously in Toronto, Canada, by Random House of Canada, Limited.

LIBRARY OF CONGRESS CATALOG CARD NUMBER 60-5565

MANUFACTURED IN THE UNITED STATES OF AMERICA

To my wife

ANITA VENIER ALEXANDER

Preface

We are living in a rapidly changing world. The speed of this change since the industrial revolution one hundred and fifty years ago has continuously increased, and during the past fifty years it has reached an unprecedented rate. In this, our growing mastery of natural forces—technology—is the most obvious factor. Technological advancements have created new means of production and a new socio-economic system which has profoundly transformed the ways of life in the west. Technological advancement, however, is the result of advancing scientific knowledge. If the world has changed, the human mind brought about this change. Historical materialists cannot refute this basic fact.

This is one side of the picture. Social changes which ultimately derive from the achievements of the human mind have a transforming influence, in turn, upon the mentality of man. Culture is a product of the mind, and the mind in turn is influenced by its own creation: the cultural milieu. The child born today faces a world radically different from the one into which a child born fifty years ago entered. Those who were born at the end of the last century and have had the privilege, or bad fortune, of witnessing our present era, do not need to consult books on social anthropology, sociology or psychology to learn about this change. And yet, no matter how striking the difference between today's youth and the youth at the end of the last century may be, when one tries to formulate this new personality and to describe how it differs from its predecessors, one finds himself facing a formidable problem. This book is an attempt to throw some—admittedly dim—light on this complex phenomenon.

The author's audacity in attempting a reconstruction of some of the most striking changes in the Western mind is prompted mainly by the fact that he was born in the last decade of the last century and had thoroughly absorbed the ideas of the Nineteenth Century in his home, in his schools and in his social environment. He participated in the First World War and saw the rapid disintegration of those ideas; he witnessed the Second World War; he became a psychoanalyst between the two wars and as such had a ringside seat in observing the changes in the conflicts, hopes and motivations of his patients during the past four decades. Even independent of the validity of his own reconstructions, an account of how these changes affected him may have some documentary value.

This book is an attempt to fit together the different sources of information and experience into a meaningful picture: the author's own early recollections, his participation in the intellectual life of half of a century, at first in Europe and later in the United States, and his observations as a psychoanalyst. It is an attempt to account for all these influences on his own development, which is only one typical example of many similar fates. In trying to reconstruct his struggles to preserve the continuity of his self against the disruptive impact of a rapidly changing world, to integrate often contradictory trends—the cultural traditions of the last century and the new currents in philosophical and scientific thought, literature and art—he hopes to make more concrete a central problem of current psychoanalytic thought: the complex phenomenon of psychological growth, the emergence of an integrated self having a sense of continuity and indentity. There is a growing conviction among psychoanalysts and social scientists that this growth toward an integrated self is more difficult in our turbulent era and is becoming one central issue of our times.

It is well-nigh impossible to account for all the ideas and inspirations the author received from the writings of some contemporary and some older authors, all of whom left their marks on his thinking. Some of these influences are of recent origin, some go back more than sixty years; of some he is conscious; some he cannot trace any more.

◇◇◇◇◇◇◇◇◇◇◇◇

History is seldom written by contemporaries who experience a period of history as a part of their own lives. I do not refer to autobiographies, which, no matter how valuable a source of material they may offer to the historian, mostly deal with the writer's personal development and fate, in which the contemporary cultural background serves only as a frame and is not in the focus of interest.

Successful attempts to reconstruct the history of people's orientation toward the world in which they live have not been numerous in the past or in the present. Such a contemporary account of changing ideologies is neither traditional history writing, nor is it the usual type of autobiography. It is a type of autobiography in which the hero is not the writer but the world in which the writer lives. It is history *in vivo*—history lived by the historian.

The author does not feel the need to apologize for attempting such an ideological reconstruction of the times in which he was born, grew up and reached maturity. Such a document reflecting the history of attitudes as lived through by the author, no matter how much subjective distortion it may contain, may contribute to the understanding of the period in which he lived.

The historian has the advantage of a detached point of view and can confront such subjective accounts with a host of so-called objective data which he obtains by the approved methods of his profession. This detachment and the fact that he has a more comprehensive, total picture of the times he describes is of great advantage compared to "subjective" personal accounts. Yet, if we want to reconstruct the emotional attitudes of persons, an account of history lived by the writer himself offers a first-hand experience for which there is no substitute. The more typically the recorder represents his times, the greater is the potential value of his subjective account. If there is such a thing as a history of human attitudes, it consists of the sum total of the ever-changing subjective experiences of those who participate in it as actors. When it comes to recounting of events, data obtained from various sources is indispensable. Yet, even in the history of objective facts and happenings, eye-witness reports are of significance. In second-hand information the subjective distortions of eye witnesses are multiplied by the distortions of those who receive the information from the eye witnesses. The understanding of changing attitudes during an historical period is, of course, a much more subtle and difficult undertaking. Here, second-hand information is of even less value.

The minute study of individual life histories in psychoanalytic work is one of the most valuable types of information about characteristic emotional attitudes of a period. Much can be derived also from the study of contemporary art, literature, science and politics. The value of artistic and literary products in reconstructing the spirit of a period can be well compared with that of dreams in the study of individual personalities. Art and literature as dreams are the products of fantasy. They reflect the desires and ambitions of an individual, his most intimate subjective reactions. They are often in conflict with previous ideals, which never completely disappear from the deep layers of the personality.

We know from psychoanalysis that what we consider as rational behavior is strongly influenced by unconscious non-rational or non-utilitarian factors. The aspect of rationality comes primarily from the fact that *post facto* we "rationalize" our behavior. In other words, we arbitrarily select the acceptable "logical motives" behind our actions, which allows us to overlook the irrational factors which sometimes are more important in determining our behavior than the so-called rational motivations. The rationality of behavior is to a large degree a self-deception of men of the scientific era. Consequently, all attempts to explain social events entirely by rational factors, as has been attempted by the English utilitarian philosophers, give only very inadequate explanations. The underlying emotional factors are often contradictory to self-interest

—which bears out the fallacy of those political theories which operate with the unrealistic concept of the rational "economic man."

Art and literature directly reflect the prevalent attitudes and motivations and their eternal changes. The artist senses the change and expresses it, but he never can escape the influence of his earlier experiences. Often he has had to revolt against the past to rid himself of its influence, as did modern painters after the turn of the century. The artist expresses his own era most sensitively, but he also reflects the past of which he was a part. In rapidly changing times such as ours, this he does often in the form of a denial of past values, and this conflict is an essential part of his productivity.

To some degree all this is true also for science, but the conflicts between past and present views are fought out, not on the emotional, but on the intellectual level. One spoke of a revolution in physics when the relativity concept displaced Newtonian principles. The transition, however, had not so much the aspect of a violent revolution, but rather of a correction. Newtonian principles remain valid for man-sized phenomena and need correction only when the spatial and temporal dimension of the investigated events becomes too large or too small in comparison with the phenomena observed in everyday life. Science has a cumulative character: previous knowledge becomes improved, but it is seldom entirely discarded.

While science itself is more evolutionary than revolutionary, its effects upon society are most radical. On the other hand, the influence of contemporary events upon scientific ideas is not obvious and is mostly neglected by historians of science. An adequate history of science can be written by demonstrating the steady immanent evolution of ideas by which man tries to formulate his knowledge and the improvement of his methods of observation and reasoning. Yet, scientific thought is part of the total personality of man. How man makes use of his rational faculties is in itself influenced by his whole orientation towards the world in which he lives.

A conservative adherence to past views exists, of course, also in science, but is less effective than in any other forms of mental activity. Basic ethical principles have remained practically unchanged in Western civilization throughout known history, but Aristotle's physics has no resemblance to modern physics. Science consists in a continuous improvement of observing and of understanding natural phenomena. Hence, science is the fastest advancing form of human activity. It is less influenced by social events, but its influence on social life is most revolutionary. Indeed, it is a commonplace that most of those radical social changes of the last fifty years, as well as the less spectacular changes of the previous three hundred years, are primarily the results of the advancement of science and its application to technology.

Art and literature can be considered the most delicate indicators of the emotional climate of an era; they register changes most sensitively, but they themselves have only a modest capacity for bringing about radical social changes. The artist with his greater intuitive sensitivity perceives changing attitudes sooner than others, and he may accelerate existing ideological trends.

In the latter part of this book, without aiming at completeness, I shall try to indicate some parallel changes in all these fields—personality structure, art, science—during the first half of this century.

ACKNOWLEDGMENTS

I am most grateful to the following for permission to quote material:

The Bulletin of the Atomic Scientists, for a sentence, in Chapter I, from Dr. Max Born's article, "Man and the Atom" (Vol. 3, No. 6, June 1957); The American Psychological Association, for parts, in Chapter III, of my article, "A Jury Trial of Psychoanalysis" (*Journal of Abnormal and Social Psychology,* Vol. 35, 1940); W. W. Norton & Co., Inc., for three paragraphs, in Chapter III, from *Twenty Years of Psychoanalysis* (ed. Franz Alexander and Helen Ross, 1953); in the American Orthopsychiatric Association, for parts, in Chapter VIII, of my article "The Role of the Scientist in Society" (*Orthopsychiatry 1923–1948,* 1948); the Cambridge University Press, for a quotation, in Chapter IX, from Sir Arthur S. Eddington's *New Pathways in Science;* Pantheon Books, Inc., for quotations in Chapter XII from Boris Pasternak's book *Doctor Zhivago* (1958); *The Psychoanalytic Quarterly,* for parts reprinted in Chapter XIV from my article "A Contribution to the Theory of Play" (Vol. 27, No. 2, 1958); *The Saturday Review,* for quotations, in Chapters XV and XVI, from Peter Viereck's article, "The Unadjusted Man" (November 1, 1958)

Contents

THE WESTERN MIND IN TRANSITION

Part One

THE NATURAL HISTORY OF AN INNER-DIRECTED PERSON

"I believe in the supremacy of the mind. I believe in progress, in evolution and that all this is implemented by thought. I believe in thought as the redeeming principle in the world. Some call this intellectualism and take refuge from it in the darkness of voluntarism in the vortex of irrationalism, where nothing can be seen with clarity. Yes, life is the source of all human values, and life consists in action. But the only sure guidance of action is thought, the highest of values, the clear conscious thought. . . . The real deeds are the deeds of thought. Through thought we elevate life. The *Weltratsel* is not found in self-preservation but self-realization. The essence of self-realization lies in thought . . . Therefore, we teachers consider our work sacerdotal. We are small, but serve a great cause."

BERNARD ALEXANDER

CHAPTER I

Foundations

Sun—King—Father

It was the year 1896. I was five years old. The rays of the afternoon sun drew a brilliant oblique streak of dancing dust particles in the living room. Fascinated by this phenomenon, I was about to discover the principle of ultramicroscopy formulated many years later by Zsigmondy: the ingenious technique of illuminating microscopic slides from the side to make small particles visible.

My contemplation of the dust in the air illuminated by the sun's rays was interrupted by a momentous event. It was the celebration of the "Millenium," the thousandth anniversary of the Kingdom of Hungary. We were waiting for the great and memorable parade led by the king, Ferenc Jozsef (Franz Joseph), who was followed by his equestrian entourage of the Hungarian nobility in their richly colorful gala uniforms. Each family had his individual "attilla," an ornate velvet uniform, purple, red, green, white, ornamented with jeweled buttons. The parade included the archbishop and other church dignitaries, the members of the government, and the leading families of the country, all bearing historical names. In the hierarchic order of the procession, official position often came second to the prominence of the family. The parade passed by our apartment building (called the New York

Palace because it belonged to the New York Life Insurance Company) on the Elizabeth Ring—named after the Queen—where we lived on the fourth floor, the top of the building. From the windows, crowded with guests and relatives, we had an unsurpassed view of the procession. The air was filled with pomp and dignity—no exuberance of spirit—more like a Mass than a worldly event. I do not remember any of the sounds; what stays in my memory is silent awe. The traditional long feathers of the velvet caps, matching the gala uniforms of the courtiers, were waving in the breeze. To see the king in the flesh was a truly rare and special event. He was more an abstract idea in my mind than a living person, similar to God, by whose grace he ruled over the country. Only one rank below him, to me, stood my father—a benevolent ruler beyond criticism. In my childhood days, up to my fourteenth or fifteenth year, he appeared completely infallible, wise and reliable. I was proud of his national prominence—he was the leading Hungarian philosopher and educator of the era—and could not realistically aspire to measure up to him. Like the sun, like God, like the king, he was beyond my reach, an immense source of security, an example to follow within my power.

The New York Palace

The building we lived in was inhabited by other pillars of society. Our next-door neighbor was a professor of literature, a highly erudite nobleman, Mr. Zsolt Béóthy, who traveled over the world and always brought back, mostly from Egypt, valuable archaeological pieces for his collection. On each occasion he gave a piece to my father, who was interested in archaeology. In exchange, Father gave him relics from Pompeii, which had begun to be excavated and where Father visited every year. Interest in archaeology was widespread and the great Schliemann, famous for his Greek excavations which he believed to be the remnants of Troy, was one of Father's great cultural heroes. Schliemann had died one year before my birth and Father's secret desire, I learned later, was to see me become an archaeologist.

On the third floor lived a famous professor of philology, a noted linguist of the Hungarian tongue, Simonyi, who initiated me in a playful manner whenever I visited his home in the art of reading and writing even before I reached school age. On the same floor resided the Minister of Education, Baron de Berzeviczy, a descendant of an old family and a man of the greatest integrity. His rigid countenance, which never expressed any emotion, prompted us to refer to him jokingly as the "marble ox."

Another neighbor was a prominent lawyer, Nagy, whose daughter was about my age; together we were given private tutoring instead of being sent to the public elementary school. We also took violin lessons together from the concertmaster of the Budapest Opera. These lessons started when I was seven years old and continued until I was twelve, the only real torture I remember during my early days. I was completely without musical talent and the daily lessons taught me only one thing: to dislike music thoroughly, something which wore off only gradually in later days.

On the first floor lived the Hungarian representative of the New York Life Insurance Company, the richest man in the building, who was eager to obtain social recognition by rubbing elbows with the other tenants, mostly of academic prominence. His large family lived in great splendor; the children had French and English governesses. Nevertheless, we, the children of the academic and professorial families, did not consider them quite our equal and seldom visited them. How this discrimination developed I cannot reconstruct, but obviously it must have been transmitted to us by remarks of the adults. It represented the prevailing attitude toward businessmen, who, in spite of financial success, came second in the social hierarchy to the representatives of science, education, religion, the arts, literature, and, of course, to the nobility.

The social stratification among the children inhabiting the New York Palace, separating the intellectual élite from the representatives of business, did not prevent some social contact between the two groups. Such an exception was the second day of Easter, Monday, when according to Hungarian folk tradition the boys would visit girls of their acquaintance with perfume bottles hidden in their pockets. Suddenly they would pull the bottles out and sprinkle the girls. This was supposed to be a surprise attack and the girls would scream, as was expected of them, and then, in return for the scented baptism, present the boys with an Easter egg. Some of these Easter eggs, usually made of chocolate and of pastries, were real pieces of art; their excavated interiors were often decorated with miniature religious scenes, usually of the Nativity. These Easter visits were great events and we looked forward to them with much excitement, competing for the most exquisite and the greatest number of Easter eggs. In the home of the director of the insurance company we always received the most fantastic eggs—which made us forget our snobbish feelings.

The New York Palace was a lavishly built, rectangular construction around a courtyard with a fountain. The apartments opened from a wide corridor with a marble floor and balustrade. It was our playground and there we spent most of our time. It was the arena of our ball games and group warfare. In the apartment we had to observe the formal rules of polite behavior, but the corridor—called "gang" (from the German word for "corridor")—was the realm of unrestricted freedom. There we lived in our self-created world of play—active and exciting play which had no place for the anemic boredom of today's children, whose imagination withers away under daily doses of television programs which deprive them of the free creations of their fantasy. Our games were largely influenced by contemporary world events and the then-popular adventure stories which left ample place for our own elaboration. We played the Russo-Japanese War; our sympathies being with the Japanese, Admiral Togo was our hero. The same was true when somewhat earlier the Boer revolution captured our imagination. We detested Lord Kitchener and in our fights we took out all our deeply repressed rebellion against authority by ferociously attacking the unfortunate playmate who was sentenced to play Kitchener's part. The actual father images being inviolate, we had to find other fantastic "bad fathers" in order to vent our aggressions.

A great part of my early memories are linked with the "gang." My earliest recollections, reaching back to my fourth year, are connected with this luxurious wide marble area, where I developed my first metaphysical daydreams about the universe. In these fantasies, the world appeared to me as a large pale blue balloon filled with fluid; it was a finite universe with a curved space, not too unlike that of contemporary cosmologists. This universe pulsated, expanded, and contracted like a gigantic heart. This image was not prompted by science fiction and was not populated by spaceships, supermen and technical gadgets. It was truly metaphysical. I spent hours alone in the corridor spinning out these cosmological fantasies, which I only seldom communicated to my most intimate playmates—and then only against solemn promises to keep secrecy. It was classified material; it was my own personal fabrication. After I became acquainted with psychoanalytic theory, it was not difficult to identify these reveries as intra-uterine fantasies, a return to the source of all life, the briny fluid of the amnion and the oceans. Their connection with the attachment to mother explains the need for secrecy. These reveries must have coincided (according to theory) with the peak of my Oedipus complex. Because the father image was so benign and so revered, the aggressive component of the complex had to be displaced and the wish for mother completely depersonalized. Bad father images, such as the Russian army and the brutal Kitchener, were the targets of hostility and the abstract and inscrutable universe was a substitute for mother. The whole murderous and erotic complex was stripped of all its personal connotations. The maternal principle was etherealized into a vague mystical longing for heaven. There is no doubt in my mind that it was not an accident that President McKinley's assassination is linked in my memory with the "gang," where according to my recollection I was playing when I heard of this event. A father image was murdered—the shock that such an event could happen was deeply upsetting.

Since I write about these autobiographical fragments merely to illustrate the attitudes and values imparted to me in those early days, I have selected only those which seem pertinent.

Vacations

Vacation trips played an important role in molding my outlook on life. As a university professor, Father had nearly as many vacation days as working days. In addition to long Christmas and Easter vacations, there was a three-month summer vacation. Christmas was usually celebrated at home or occasionally at a winter sports resort in the High Tatra. At Easter both of my parents or only Father went to Italy. During the summer our family, often together with my uncle's family and the family of the philology professor, went on a longer trip to the Baltic Sea in Germany or to a lake in Austria or Switzerland. These travels made deep impressions on me. They broadened my horizon by exposing me to different variations of the same theme: Europe at the end of the last century in all its splendor, its belief in the uniqueness of the individual, its playfulness and its solid unshakable confidence in a stable order of things.

The party participating in these summer trips consisted of thirteen children, six in my family, five in my uncle's and two in the philologist's. Several compartments on the train were reserved for the long trip. The emotional climate which these journeys over Central Europe brings into recollection is that of great security. The center of this security was my uncle, a man of the world and an industrialist with international connections. Father was a typical Nineteenth Century academician, a humanist of great devotion, thoroughly impressed by the philosophers of Eighteenth Century enlightenment, particularly Voltaire and Diderot. My uncle, on the other hand, who was successful in interesting French capital in his coal mining ventures near Budapest, represented the *fin de siècle* entrepreneur. In his home I met—as much as children were allowed to meet adult visitors—a French financier who was a celebrated playwright and who became even more widely known for his duel with another famous playwright. His worldliness, wit and elegance, the scent of his perfumed handkerchief, symbolized for me the great world beyond, Western Europe in all its splendor and sophistication. Uncle, too, was erudite and daring, worldly and authoritative, and endowed with unusual muscular strength. He was an inexhaustible source of assurance for everyone under his protection. On vacation trips he was in charge of all the traveling arrangements; he always had a sufficient number of compartments reserved on the train and the right number of fiacres and hotel reservations upon arrival at our destinations. In such practical matters he was infallible and was treated by railroad personnel, hotel managers and concierges with utmost respect.

One episode is firmly embedded in my memory. On one trip through Germany, while the three families were in the dining car, a tall bull-necked German, disregarding the "reserved" sign, entered our compartment and took one of the window seats. Returning from the dining car, Father politely explained to the intruder that the whole compartment was occupied, but he received only rude answers and references to foreigners taking the best accommodations. When my uncle entered and rapidly sized up the situation, he took the stranger by his collar and physically threw him into the corridor with a laconic "Out with you !" During the whole performance, however, he remained entirely unaffected and, even during his physical fight with the stranger, he remained a perfect gentleman. He remarked condescendingly to Father, "This type of people cannot be persuaded by a platonic dialogue. They respect only superior force."

Perhaps this uncle introduced in me the first unconscious doubts of Father's omnipotence, for he treated him during these trips as one would an absent-minded professor, with good-humored condescension. The two together, however, represented the great prevailing value systems, the intellectual-cultural aspirations of that age, the capitalistic virtues of daring and ingenuity in individual enterprise, and the emphasis on the natural sciences.

The Humanities versus the Natural Sciences

At this point a digression may be appropriate. By profession my uncle was a chemical engineer with a solid foundation in physics and chemistry. In my last year of Gymnasium (high school) I discussed with him my choice of a career and mentioned that Father had given me full freedom of choice, but somehow in an oblique way had let me feel he would like to see me become an archaeologist.

He talked to me about Schliemann's world-famous excavations in glowing terms and indicated that if he were choosing a career it would be archaeology, particularly of the Greco-Roman and Egyptian civilizations. His secret plans must have had an influence on me, although he never tried to direct my interests in an obvious manner. For years I was an ardent student of Latin—I was able to read Cicero and Ovid without a dictionary and to write my letter of congratulations on Father's birthdays in Latin. He showed his satisfaction by giving me help in my classical studies.

All this I discussed with my uncle when I was about to choose a profession. During our talk Uncle finally erupted: "For God's sake, why do you want to devote your life to finding out what kinds of chamberpots the old Egyptians used ?" I can still feel some shame when I recall that, soon after, I used the same drastic phrase about Egyptian archaeology in telling Father of my decision to choose medicine as my career. My uncle, after this discussion, presented me with Ernst Mach's classical book, *History of the Theory of Heat,* in which Mach proposed his principle of "economy of thought." The aim of science, Mach said, is to reduce the extreme variety of divergent observations to a minimum number of general principles. The permissible minimum is that number of independent statements which is sufficient to account for all observed facts; anything beyond this number is redundancy. Moreover, he said, a valid and elegant theory must be free of internal contradictions. The elegance and beauty of a theory depends on this economy. Science strives for the maximum amount of simplicity which does no injustice to known facts. Further simplification is over-simplification, which may make a theory appear even more elegant but is not valid because it disregards those facts which, if considered, would require a more complex formulation. At our present phase in theoretical physics we are witnessing such a struggle for a unified theory which combines the relativity theory and quantum theory into one universally valid formulation.

For years Mach's writings, particularly the *History of the Theory of Heat* and his more philosophical *Analysis of Sensations*, which I found in my father's library, had a strong influence on my thinking. A constant struggle for economy of thought and simplicity has always been an aspect of my thinking and has repeatedly exposed me to the criticism of having a tendency toward over-simplification.

The influence of Mach at that time consisted, however, in making me feel more and more critical of the older philosophers. Metaphysics became anathema to me. Philosophers, I felt, made their task easy by disregarding all disturbing details and trivialities, but thus constructed an image of the world which has little to do with the world we live in. They achieved a simple formulation of the universe and man illegitimately, by introducing general principles not concerned with the actual data of observation. I often discussed Mach and his philosophy of positivism with Father, challenging him in an adolescent fashion on the relative merits of science and philosophy. Finally I decided for science and announced my decision to Father. He did not show any reaction; he accepted it without comment, but I felt that deep down he was disappointed.

Only much later, in 1918, did I discover that Father himself went through a similar conflict in his early student years. I discovered this from letters he wrote to Cyrill Horvath, a Catholic priest who was his professor of philosophy in Budapest. The letters were written from Austria and Germany, where he had gone to continue his studies. The Piarist Order preserved these letters and returned them to my father in 1917. These letters reveal the characteristic relation between pupil and teacher in that era. It was a highly personal relationship, not at all resembling the merely professional teacher-pupil relation of our present days. Father's letters also reflect the great freedom of the student to choose teachers and studies according to his own interests and inclinations—a far cry from the regimented and statistically conceived credit systems of present-day education. From Vienna in 1868 he wrote: "Zimmermann (Professor of Philosophy) does not treat me at all as a stranger. I learn more from him in private conversation than from his lectures. Yet, I should like to spend next year in Berlin to hear Virchow and Helmholtz. . . ." The young student of philosophy described in these letters his most subjective reactions to his teachers in Vienna, Berlin and Göttingen: Zimmermann, Helmholtz, Du Bois Raymond and Lotze. He considered knowledge of the natural sciences a necessary preparation for philosophy. He wavered between choosing philosophy or natural sciences, and he must have even considered medicine as a career. In one of his letters to his Professor Horvath, this conflict is clearly indicated: "The medical sciences as they teach them here (Vienna) emphasize the practical aspects and are somewhat repulsive to me. To study a problem for the mere sake of understanding it, the only remuneration being the pleasure derived from solving the problem, is a deeply ingrained attitude of mine. Here, I mostly hear that this or that disease is not so important because it is very rare and therefore it is practically not important to understand it." In many intangible ways of daily contact over the years Father succeeded in imparting to me his high estimation of knowledge for its own sake and his distaste for what is only practically significant. I shall return to this conflict between practical applications and pure science in a later chapter.

I was serving in the army when Ernst Mach died and one of the leading daily newspapers asked me to write an article on him. I showed my manuscript to Father, who made a few editorial comments and suggested that I insert an appropriate quotation from Goethe. This great humanist wanted to have my dry positivistically oriented writing mellowed by some literary reference.

Looking back upon my intellectual development, the struggle to synthesize these two major interests, that in science and that in philosophy and the humanities, remained for long years a main problem in finding my own identity. Soon after returning from Göttingen to continue my medical studies in Budapest, I started to work in the laboratory of Franz Tangl for experimental pathology. An able proponent of the physico-chemical approach to physiology, he insisted that his assistants should first of all have a thorough training in physics and chemistry. Tangl was a great admirer of the American physiologist, Jacques Loeb, and adopted Loeb's requirement that medical students have a solid foundation in physics, chemistry and higher mathematics. After the earlier influence of my uncle, the chemical engineer, Tangl became for me another source of identification as the representative of the experimental approach. This was further reinforced by the influence of two of my peers who were also working in Tangl's laboratory. Both were former schoolmates. One was Michael Polanyi, a promising prodigy in physics who, while still a high school student, had written a theoretical article on the periodic system of chemical elements which was accepted for publication by a scientific journal. He shifted from medicine to physics, became a member of the famed Kaiser Wilhelm Institute in Berlin while still a young man and finally a professor of chemistry in Manchester. The other friend was the ingenious experimentalist, Ladislaus Berceller, who was the first to call attention to the great possibility of multiple uses of the soya bean. Early in his life, right after the end of the First World War, he made a great fortune from his soya bean patents, only to dissipate all his assets in litigation against the German and Italian governments, whom he accused of having stolen his ideas and patents.

During the early years after high school, my interests in the sciences gradually won out and increasingly I turned away from philosophy, psychology and the humanities. The earlier identification with Father's orientation, however, proved indelible and I was driven, without being consciously aware of it, toward finding a synthesis between the two. This synthesis I found eventually in psychiatry and, in particular, in psychoanalysis.

Luck, as in all human affairs, had its share in my finding this solution. Professor Moravchik, the professor of psychiatry in Budapest, became interested in my publications on brain metabolism and suggested that I become a research associate in the laboratory of the Psychiatric Institute of the university. Psychiatry is an ideal ground on which to unify scientific with psychological and humanistic interests. It studies man not only as a physico-chemical system, but also as a person who is aware of himself and who is a part of a society of interacting human beings. It is an ideal choice for a person with the type of conflict I had, one resulting from conflicting identifications. Psychoanalysis, in particular, is suitable for harmonizing the scientific and the psychologic-humanistic trends because it is consecrated to the goal which even today appears unattainable to many thinkers: the introduction of scientific methods and the principle of causality into the study of personality. In this area of intellectual occupation, my incentive was nurtured by my earliest identifications. Working in this field thus offered me the opportunity to find my own identity, which gave me a feeling of continuity between my past and present.

Early Travels in Germany

When I was six and seven years old, we spent two consecutive summers at a seaside resort on the Baltic, which gave me the first occasion to experience what Freud described as the oceanic feeling. Standing for the first time at the shore of the ocean, I clearly recognized the relatedness of this sensation to my fantasies about the pale blue universe: a feeling of oneness with the world, a paradoxical combination of loneliness and belonging.

Here the sandy beach replaced the corridor of the New

York Palace. The fine sand was most suitable for building fortifications with walls six feet high, which faced similar constructions built by the native German boys. Our whole summer consisted of continuous warfare, sieges, sorties and surprise attacks carried out between these fortresses. The German boys, raised in the military tradition of the great Clausewitz, were much better in organization and more familiar with the classical rules of warfare. We tried to balance this superiority in system and organization by personal daring, mobility, quick decisions, exploiting the enemy's weak spots as they evolved in the heat of the battle, and we often succeeded in upsetting their carefully blueprinted war plans by unexpected and sudden shifts of action, by commando techniques. Their victories were collective deeds, ours were individual exploits.

We remembered from history the successful surprise raid over the German border by the still pagan Hungarian cavalry upon the Monastery of St. Gall. We identified ourselves with that Hungarian cavalry and tried to emulate the success it won over the heavily armored German cavalry by sudden flanking attacks. The German horsemen, impeded by their armor and long lances, could not turn as fast as these flank attacks required. Panic-struck, they were massacred by the Hussars riding their small and mobile Asiatic horses, unarmored and equipped only with short sabers. We relived those early days of our nation with immense pride and complete self-abandonment.

This was the first time I had the opportunity to face and act out the conflict between collective organization and individual virtue, an issue which remained with me for the rest of my life. Later I learned that I was not the only psychoanalyst with this type of identification. In an early book review I compared a theory of Ferenczi with a bold cavalry attack upon the unknown, and Ferenczi wrote me how pleased he was by this comparison.

One early September morning, a few days before our departure, we found our sand fortress completely demolished and soiled with litter. Our chagrin, mixed with indignation, was immense. We felt the sneak attack under the cover of night was a blow below the belt, a violation of fair play, which was one of the cherished codes of our behavior.

The Baltic sea resorts were frequented by summer guests from Russia and Poland. We got acquainted with a highly erudite Russian publisher and his beautiful daughter, a girl of my age, who became my first "girl friend." Listening to the conversation of the adults, I learned for the first time of political persecution, censorship, and the struggle for freedom of the press which eventually led up to the First Russian Revolution. This publisher appeared to me a mysterious figure surrounded with the aura of secrecy and conspiracy—something quite alien to anything I had known before in the carefree liberal atmosphere of Budapest. Years later, we heard that he had been exiled to Siberia.

Here also I made my first acquaintance with Prussian militarism and felt its ominous significance. The spa was frequented by families of East Prussian Junkers. My sister was at the beginning of her career as a concert singer and her beautiful alto voice attracted the guests in the Kurhaus, where she practiced daily in the late morning hours. Each time the salon was crowded with guests attending her informal daily concerts. On one occasion a tall captain entered the room. There was no place for him to sit and he descended on me and harshly commanded me to vacate my place for him. Automatically I obeyed his order, but with an intense rebellion I could not express. A new bad-father image thus entered my life, and I can still turn on all my destructive inclinations if I conjure up this scene.

The first trip to Germany took place when I was only six years old, but even then I could clearly sense the different spirit of that country. The atmosphere was more serious and restrained; it lacked the ease, the grace, the hedonistic qualities of Hungary. The art of enjoying life was less developed, the food cruder, the people more matter-of-fact, the streets more functional, the humor more aggressive, and the women's extremities larger and heavier. It gave me a foretaste of that rationalization of life which has since then gained momentum all over the world. In Europe, Germany was one step ahead toward an industrial civilization which is now in full swing in producing the new species: collective man.

Years later, as a student in Göttingen, I learned to know the other side of Germany, the country of poets, musicians, and scientists—that cultural undercurrent which was gradually overshadowed by the militaristic spirit but which, for centuries, coexisted with the latter, fluctuating but never completely submerging. Long and tedious, and yet fascinating, visits to the art galleries of Berlin and Munich, where I was dragged by my father in the company of my two older sisters, had a deep influence on my later development. Looking back, the visits appear as a combination of physical exhaustion from walking through endless corridors with the first understanding of the values which were the driving forces of my father's generation and which they succeeded in imparting to us. But while he and his contemporaries were lucky enough to finish their lives without witnessing the decline of these values, the following generation experienced the collapse.

In the hallowed atmosphere of the galleries, Father and my sisters stood with religious reverence before the paintings of old masters. Some of Father's occasional remarks to us, interpreting the artist's message, are still in my memory. It was on a somewhat later occasion, in the Friedrichs Museum, looking at the portrait of an old man by Rembrandt, that he said, "Rembrandt accomplished the same in painting as Shakespeare in literature, to bring out in the truest sense the uniqueness of a person as someone different from everyone else, a unique combination of those same elements of which we are all constructed. In his days the cult of the individual reached its peak, only to decline gradually ever since. He liked to paint old men because in old age individuality comes more to the fore than in the young. All infants look alike. The older you get the more different you become from everyone else. Each wrinkle on a face has its history; it is an imprint of innumerable single experiences. In getting old you have all the time to be molded by life." "But are Flaubert, Balzac, Dostoievsky not doing the same in their novels ?" interjected my older sister. He answered, "Yes, the Nineteenth Century made a valiant effort to stem the tide. Maybe this is the last gasp of contemporary man to save his individuality." This answer impressed me because it was much less optimistic than I was accustomed to hear from him. Today I recognize its prophetic significance.

It is difficult to understand fully the spirit of the Nineteenth Century without having been exposed to it in one's own experience. This became clear to me a few years ago when a modern woman painter, who attended a lecture I delivered in Los Angeles on the emotional sources of contemporary painting, pointed an accusing finger at me: "You are still living in the Nineteenth Century." This artist must have sensed my spiritual roots, toward which she felt defensive and inimical. She did not respond at all to my detached explanation of the psychological sources of abstract painting, in which I avoided any esthetic evaluation; she merely resented my empathy with the spirit of Impressionism, for which she felt contempt. Indeed, if we would understand why the Nineteenth Century has become an object of scorn in our days, this would throw light upon our present era: why does it repudiate its predecessor so violently?

Knowledge for Its Own Sake

One day, in my early teens, I burst into Father's library: "Who was the greater scientist, Darwin or Newton?" Father, who was sitting at his desk writing, looked up with some disdain in his eyes and suggested that we take a walk to the Swabhegy (the Swabian Mountain). It was one of his favorite hikes—an 800-foot hill on the Buda side of the Danube overlooking the city.

It was a clear Sunday morning in the spring. We walked onto the Elisabeth Bridge over the Danube. I felt embarrassed and did not dare repeat my question. Halfway across the bridge, he began to talk. He said he would explain to me the absurdity of my question. It amounted to the following: "You can very well ask the question which one of two sprinters can run faster. It makes sense. But your question about Darwin and Newton is senseless; first, because there is no yardstick for measuring the greatness of a scientist, an artist, or a statesman; second, because science and art are not racetracks. Both Newton and Darwin made new discoveries, enriched our knowledge, developed theories which enhanced our understanding of the world around us. They worked in different fields. Who was greater is a senseless question, and even if it could be answered, it would be entirely beside the point. Why would you like to know who was the greater ? If you want to compete, play tennis or make money; if you beat your partner consistently, you are a better player, not necessarily a better man. If you have more money than your friend, you are richer than he, not necessarily better or greater, and you can accurately state that you are twice or twice and a half as rich as he."

It was obvious that he was irritated and became more so as he went on speaking, although did not express his anger openly. Yet, with my adolescent mentality, I was not satisfied by his answer.

"Yes, but why couldn't one measure the benefits derived from these new discoveries?" I insisted. He controlled his displeasure and patiently explained that when Newton developed calculus, he was not interested in its possible practical use. He did not even dream of its future application, that the building of bridges—like the one we were crossing—would require calculus. His mathematics and his laws of motion would have the same significance if they never found any practical use. Knowledge is a value in itself. If Newton had subordinated his idle curiosity to practical goals, he would never have made his discoveries. The same was true of Darwin. Paleontologists or archaeologists do not pursue any practical aims. Sometime in the remote future, perhaps, knowledge of ancient history may enable man to learn from the past and even learn to govern his own destiny. This most desirable goal, however, does not motivate the historian's work. He is curious to learn about the past for its own sake, without any practical motive.

Father went on in a lighter vein and told an anecdote about a professor of history who had received a dissertation from one of his students for the doctorate. A few weeks later, the student came to hear the professor's opinion. "Well, my friend," said the professor, "you wrote a fine essay, but I do not quite understand why you say that Ludwig Kossuth was the greatest statesman that ever lived. How do you know ? Maybe in America there lived a greater one. It would be the same if I would tell you now that you are the world's greatest oaf. Maybe in America there is a bigger one."

Only much later did I understand the real cause of his irritation. Unconsciously I was asking: Can I ever become as great as you are—or, perhaps, even greater ? And he answered with chagrin: My dear son, why do you want to compete with me ? We stood before a lonely ancient oak tree at the top of the mountain, the Norma tree. Legend connects it with King Mathias Corvin. From its powerful trunk, mutilated by lightning, barren branches were reaching helplessly toward the sky—a memento for all who harbor in their souls the primordial sin.

We changed subjects, but I was not in a receptive mood. Even the view from the mountain top appeared less magnificent than usual. I knew Father was right but, at the same time, I felt that I would not be able to measure up to him.

It was somewhat later—just as though I had fully forgotten this incident—that I asked him at the dinner table: Who was greater, Schiller or Goethe ? This time he did not sermonize. Contemptuously he snapped back, "I don't know—I didn't measure them." This time it really sank in.

The reverence for great writers, painters, and scientists to whom I was exposed at home prevailed also at school among my schoolmates and teachers. A new interpretation of a Shakespearean character on the stage, a new novel, whether published in England, France, Italy, Austria, or Hungary, which in the opinion of the experts was expected to enter the Pantheon of literature, was a great event, the central topic of discussion. It commanded our interest more than the outcome of political elections, sports events or new technical achievements. In the hierarchy of social prestige the creative artist and scientist ranked first, while the leaders of industry and commerce were rated mainly as potential financial supporters of cultural accomplishments.

This orientation was particularly pronounced at home. Every Saturday evening my parents held open house, mostly frequented by authors, newspapermen, artists and, particularly, actors. Father, in his capacity as a professor of esthetics (his main field was the history of philosophy), taught at the Academy of the Dramatic Arts, of which he was Director for many years. He was at the same time the *feulletonist* of a daily newspaper and was considered as one of the leading authorities in contemporary art, literature and the theater. He belonged to the since-extinct species of philosopher-critic in all fields of art, a universalist and not a specialist in any field. The Saturday evening events accordingly attracted many young and old representatives from all fields of cultural activity.

With the exception of my oldest sister, we children were not allowed to participate. Occasionally, however, one of the guests, an actor or a singer, performed and we were permitted to listen and to peek from behind a curtain. On one occasion, the later famous and at that time promising Shakespearian actor, Oscar Beregi (at present retired in Hollywood), was declaiming Hamlet's cemetery monologue. The next day, at the midday dinner table, Father commented on Beregi's performance of Hamlet at the National Theater. I could not remember the content of his remarks until recently, when I again met Beregi in Los Angeles and he told me that Father had discussed with him his interpretation of Hamlet, particularly the detail that Beregi in the first act held the mother's arm. Beregi intuitively understood Hamlet's Oedipal attachment to his mother, which was later expounded by Ernest Jones. This explains his hesitation in taking revenge on his uncle, a puzzle which aroused the interest of such great thinkers as Goethe, Brandes and many others. For Father, however, the sexual implications of Hamlet's conflict were unacceptable.

These scraps of recollection may help give a picture of the era in which literary and theatrical events absorbed our interest, as much as today's youth is fascinated by a baseball game or a prize fight. This attitude was not restricted to intellectual circles; it was the prevailing attitude of all more or less educated people. All this went with an unshakable optimism about human progress—not primarily technological, but spiritual. Technology was a means to an end and not an end in itself. The humanistic Gymnasium was considered of higher rank than the so-called Realgymnasium, which stressed the applied natural sciences and which was considered as preparatory for a career in engineering.

Unlike the American public today, educated Europeans at that time were not particularly excited about new technological achievements. They took the convenience of the telephone and the electric light for granted. Only accidentally, for example, did I learn that the first suspension bridge and the first subway were built in Budapest; the Metro of Paris and the London tube followed later. Progress in the basic sciences, however, filled us with pride, and the great theoreticians of physics, chemistry and biology enjoyed the same hero worship as do great inventors in this country. In the United States, while Edison and Bell became national heroes, the father of thermodynamics—the great American theoretical physicist, Willard Gibbs—remained unknown even among the best educated. This I discovered in the first year after my arrival in the United States. I was speaking with one of my new friends who impressed me with his broad interests and wide information. During a conversation I mentioned the name of Willard Gibbs, but he had no idea who Gibbs was. I told him that I would have been failed in high school physics for not knowing the "theory of phases" of Gibbs, considered a cornerstone in the evolution of modern physics. In Europe, during the same period, Faraday, Maxwell, Helmholtz, Boltzmann, and Planck were considered the great promoters of humanity. The search for truth for its own sake, regardless of potential usefulness, was the supreme goal. The inventors who applied this knowledge for practical uses were second-class citizens in the hierarchy of the world of science.

Apart from "absolute truth," the other deity of that era was "absolute beauty"—which contemporary philosophers tried to establish by the inscrutable laws of esthetics derived primarily from the study of the great masterpieces of architecture, sculpture, painting and writing. Lessing's essay on Laocoön was a typical example of the official esthetics taught in the high schools. The concepts of moral, esthetic and physical relativism were still remote in spite of the fact that Protagoras in ancient Greece and Hume and Kant in the Eighteenth Century had postulated that man can never find out how the world "really" is because all his knowledge depends upon the nature of his sensory organs and mind. That man himself is the measure of everything, of truth as well as of beauty—as formulated in the theory of relativity and complementarity in physics, in the concept of cultural relativism in anthropology, and in abstractionism in contemporary art —has become only in our present days an integral part of our outlook on the world. Our present era can only be fully understood when we are able to account for these profound ideological changes in the first half of this century from a world of absolutes to the present era of relativity.

I do not claim to have an explanation for this transformation of our outlook and values. I am satisfied to describe its most conspicuous features as I witnessed it during my lifetime, and possibly to offer suggestions concerning some factors responsible for this great metamorphosis.

One thing is certain: this change from the search for absolutes in knowledge, taste and morals (and for *the* best possible social system) to acceptance of the relativity of all human endeavors came about rather simultaneously in all fields—in physics, psychology, anthropology, the arts, literature, politics and national economy. Because of the universal, all-pervasive nature of this change, it must be the result of a large historical trend similar to the Renaissance and the Reformation, and it appears futile to try to identify any single ultimate cause responsible for it. It is not well imaginable that Einsteinian physics, which reformed our conception of the universe, of time and space, energy and matter, was responsible for the revolutionary new interpretation of space in cubistic painting, the so-called cultural relativism in anthropology, the departure from the gold standard in economy, or the rejection of the classical rules of diplomacy. It appears rather that Western man came to a dead end with the patterns of thought, feeling and acting in science, art and politics which had prevailed for three hundred years. The last fifty years have seen the first profound ideological revolution since the Renaissance. The beginnings of this great spiritual change preceded the First World War, which only gave the *coup de grâce* to Europe's cultural and political structure. Therefore, it is not admissible to consider this dramatic and drastic event as the ultimate cause. Rather, the political and economic collapse can be regarded as one of many parallel manifestations of an all-encompassing revolutionary change, a steadily spreading undercurrent of disillusionment in the whole of Western civilization, leading eventually to a reappraisal of all values. This disillusionment, latent for long decades, found only sporadic expression in the writings of a few philosophers, as Kierkegaard and Nietzsche, and a few dramatists, poets and artists, but it gained momentum during the first ten years of this century. The First World War found a society internally prepared for the changes to come. This can be most clearly demonstrated by an "experiment of thought." Without the internal fermentation gradually loosening the traditional ideological fabric of Europe, the same historical events would not have had the profound consequences they actually had. A Europe which still believed in its Nineteenth Century principles would, within a reasonable period, have regained its equilibrium and would have taken things up where they had been left before the war. Instead there was no serious attempt to return in economics, in literary and artistic expression, or in science (where return to the past because of the steadily progressing nature of science is never possible).

That European civilization was approaching a dead end was most clearly expressed in the literature of the decadence. Action was replaced by contemplation. In this "estheticism" the end of an era came to its clearest conclusion. As if Western man—who three hundred years before had boldly set out to explore the earth and the universe, the body and the mind—now felt that his work was accomplished and nothing else was left for him but the esthetic contemplation of the world, trying to extract from it refined and highly individual impressions and moods. Existence for its own sake, without any particular goals or aims, became the only sense in living.

The witty aphorism, the wistful poem and the impressionistic reproduction of nature were the appropriate expressions of this state of mind. Perhaps more characteristic than anything else were the long afternoons spent in aimless and endless conversation at the sidewalk cafés, where profundities as well as cynical witticisms vanished in mid-air, never to be recounted for posterity. Nobody would have thought to ask at the end of such a sidewalk-café analysis of world or local affairs what the practical conclusion should be, what should be done about it. Such questions appeared both vulgar and naïve, uninteresting and irrelevant. One did not try to influence the course of events; one took events as phenomena of nature, things to reflect upon and evaluate in a detached esthetic fashion. The present generation of our pragmatic era may consider it a schizoid trend, a kind of withdrawal from the world of practical realities. And yet, paradoxically enough, this impractical withdrawal toward idle curiosity and detached contemplation was responsible for most of the practical advancement to come in the next era, surpassing within fifty years all the technological advancement since the beginning of the Industrial Revolution.

The student of today, who is exposed almost every year

to a new application of theoretical knowledge of far-reaching practical significance, becomes accustomed to consider science as no longer an idle gratification of impractical professorial curiosity, but as a highly important matter, something by which man can enhance his comforts and security, reduce his efforts for existence, conquer diseases of the mind and body, and prolong his life—not to speak of the added power he gleans from scientific knowledge for rule over others. He finds it incredible that all the valuable knowledge accumulated in the last three hundred years never could have been acquired if the scientists were motivated in their work by these practical goals. He will hardly accept the thesis that as soon as science renounces its intrinsic aim, to achieve knowledge for the mere sake of knowing, and shifts its emphasis to practical aims, scientific advancement and new technology will have to come to an end, although the practical application of already acquired knowledge may last for a period.

Some readers may object to my statement that there is a growing shift in the scientific world toward the practical from a merely theoretical knowledge. They may say theoretical interest is as great as ever and that I am exaggerating this trend toward the practical. Can one ask for a better confirmation than a sentence from the pen of one of the founders of modern physics, Max Born, referring to his professional days in Göttingen: "Both of these men, Oppenheimer and Teller, as well as Fermi and other participants in this work, including some of the Russian physicists, were once my collaborators in Göttingen long before all these events, *at a time when pure science still ex-*

isted." [1] The physicists themselves are keenly aware that since the practical importance of their discoveries has become so blatantly obvious, their social prestige has grown. Politicians and military leaders curry their favor and, in the eyes of the general public, they are no longer queer specimens barricaded in laboratories, detached from the world; they share the fame of heavyweight champions and baseball stars as objects of public acclaim. Doubtless, those of them who still remember the period of *l'art pour l'art* of science, whether they were then students or professors, look back wistfully to those days as a Garden of Eden from which they were expelled by the events of our "dynamic era."

As a young student of medicine, before the First World War, I spent some time in Göttingen, mainly to become a student of the famous professor of physiology, Max Verworn. At the same time, my future brother-in-law, Geza Revesz, who later became one of the leading experimental psychologists in Europe, was a young *Privatdocent* working in the laboratory of E. G. Muller, in Göttingen, a pupil of Fechner. He and another young psychologist, David Katz, later to become well known for his studies on hunger, were inseparable and worked at that time on learning-theory, using chickens as their experimental subjects. As a side result they discovered that chickens have the same optical illusions as man. "Who the hell is interested in the optical illusions of chickens ?" a pragmatic friend of mine asked some years later when I told him

[1] Max Born, "Man and the Atom," *Bulletin of the Atomic Scientists,* Vol. XIII, No. 6 (June 1957). Italics added by the author.

about this discovery. This question appeared to me as a portent. Men of action, of course, always have taken small interest in such useless occupations as finding out how the world is constructed. But in those days in Göttingen and other similar university centers the cult of pure science was flourishing. They represented little universes in themselves where the great events consisted of new ideas, theories and scientific techniques.

Through Revesz and Katz, I came in contact with the younger generation of scientists. Göttingen was the Mecca of mathematicians and theoretical physicists. Nernst, the great physico-chemist, had just left Göttingen to accept another chair, but his contribution to thermodynamics (the so-called "Third Law") was still one of the favorite topics of conversation among students. Minkowski, the brilliant mathematician, had just died; his four-dimensional approach to time and space, in which time was treated symmetrically with the three space coördinates, was considered as one of the great advancements, an opinion which was soon to be validated by Einstein's theory. Zsigmondy's ultramicroscope, which made possible the direct study of Brownian molecular movements, was another of the scientific sensations.

All these events were discussed after the dinner hour at the round marble tables of the Café National, a meeting place of students and young *Privatdocents.* There I had the privilege of getting my first informal instruction into the second law of thermodynamics from Theodor von Kármán, who was later to obtain world fame as a leader in aerodynamics. The great mathematician Hilbert was perhaps the most revered man in town. I often heard autopsies of his lectures around the coffee house table and was impressed by the adulation he received from his pupils. There, and in other university centers, the human faculty of reasoning—the highest or at least the most complex of all human faculties—was perfected to a hitherto unknown precision and penetration.

Although I was a student of medicine I attended the philosophy lectures of Edward Husserl, the father of phenomenology, and indirectly through his pupil, Heidegger, of existentialism. The phenomenological approach, which he claimed was the royal road to the essence of reality, rubbed me the wrong way. The mind, to me, was a biological apparatus; hence, our perception of the world and our ideas about it must be determined by the biological nature of the perceiving and thinking mind. My professor of physiology, Max Verworn, who accepted me for his *privatissimum* (a course to which only a few students of the professor's choosing were admitted), had just about that time published his small essay on epistemology—"Conditionalism"—in which he proposed a concept which has recurrently appeared in the history of philosophy, first advanced by Protagoras, then by Locke, Berkeley, Hume and Kant. The essence of their teachings is that we cannot know how things are in themselves because our notions depend not only upon the absolute (transcendent) nature of the thing we observe, but also upon the nature of our perceiving apparatus, our sense organs and our mind. I submitted a short essay on this subject—I tried to express the thesis that our knowledge of a thing is the function (in the mathematical sense of the word) of the nature of the object as well as of the perceiving mind—to Verworn and received his whole-hearted approval. Then I gave this essay to Husserl. He gasped and declared that I was a hopeless case in philosophy and should stick to physiology. It was only natural that in that stronghold of mathematics I should have expressed my epistemologic formula in mathematical symbols. Husserl made a faint attempt to save my obfuscated mind. He invited me to visit him at his home one Sunday morning. For a student to visit a full professor was like having an audience with a king. In Sunday attire I appeared at his home. He explained to me that only because my father was a noted philosopher did he feel he should try to convince me of how completely wrong my approach was to the nature of human knowledge. I stubbornly refused to give up my basic position, namely, that the mind is an instrument of the living organism and functions according to the laws of physiology. He dismissed me by recommending private instruction by one of his *Privatdocents*. Only after the man designated by him had succeeded in reforming my ideas would I be allowed to return to his lectures. The *Privatdocent*, after only one meeting at the Café National, gave up the difficult task of my indoctrination in phenomenology.

Göttingen was an exciting and stimulating place for everyone with academic leanings. It was a university in its original meaning, a universe of its own, with its own code of values and mores, enjoying a great amount of autonomy and isolation, an ivory tower where much of the intellectual brew was concocted which changed the world into what it is today. It was, of course, only one of many centers where the heritage of three hundred years of pure science came to its ultimate fruition.

It is impossible to select from the complex fabric of factors responsible for the course of historical events a single cause. Yet, if one had to name the most important factor in shaping our destiny and leading to the present state of western civilization, the answer is not difficult. The opportunity and impetus which such centers of learning and research gave to the best minds, motivated by nothing but their undiluted curiosity about the world, was the principal factor. The achievements of the present are the creations of detached impractical minds who were not only allowed but encouraged to devote themselves freely and without outside interference to advancing knowledge and nothing else. This knowledge is the ultimate source of all the technological miracles which have made our world what it is today.

CHAPTER II

First Acquaintance with Radicals

The world was a good place to live in, and a safe and stable place. Time and space were still absolutes, and so was the family, the government and the economic system. For the present-day youth it is hard to believe that at the turn of the century the existing economic and political systems appeared to us as established forever. Gold was a solid basis for trade, four per cent interest on savings was a guarantee of future security, and moral principles and rules of social behavior were settled. Such critics as Shaw, Ibsen, Wedekind, Kierkegaard and Nietzsche had not yet found a public hearing and were considered to be eccentrics, neurotics or malcontents.

For a school contest at the Gymnasium I decided to write an essay on Ibsen's Nora. The fact that this middle-class woman had found her home unbearable and had left it for no good reason aroused my curiosity; the tragedy when the door of her home closed behind her forever moved me deeply. It was a hidden threat to the stability of our world, a question mark which I could not put out of my mind. I received praise in class for my essay, which the teacher considered exemplary in its attitude toward the sanctity of marriage. Perhaps the praise was deserved. The idea of my mother walking out on her family from sheer boredom was as unthinkable to me as that the acceleration of falling bodies could one day change.

Although the image of Mother is less concretely imprinted in my recollections than that of Father, she was the stabilizing factor of the family, its emotional center of gravity. Her memory is drawn in delicate pastel shades, a poetic esthetically inclined person, retiring and yet the invisible cohesive power. She was the antithesis of the driving, socially ambitious, organization-minded mother as she is caricatured in current psychological literature on "momism." She, as most of her typical contemporaries, shunned public life and expended all her emotional resources within the family. She was the one to whom we could always turn in necessity. I do not recall, however, any dramatic incidents of such "maternal regression." The constant awareness of the inexhaustible emotional bank account she represented prevented panicky flight reactions in adversities. The elusive but all-pervasive security emanating from the mother images of that period probably constituted the most fundamental emotional basis for all those "absolutes" which lent to that fortunate era a feeling of immutable eternity. Perhaps this made it so difficult for me to recognize, even in the first years of my psychoanalytic career, the child's ambivalence towards the mother image, which has become so blatant in our present days of socially busy mothers. The magnetic effect of Goethe's "das ewig Weibliche" [1] was more famil-

[1] "the eternal feminine."

iar in our generation. Ibsen's Nora was to me the first assault upon this maternal image.

Another essay I recall was one I wrote on Michael Kohlhaas by Kleist. The hero's fight for justice, an abstract idea for which he was ready to give his life, only confirmed my belief in absolute values, ones which are independent of all vicissitudes of history. If justice falls, I wrote, the human race as we know it must perish too. I made this thesis so convincing that the teacher commented on it in class and forecast privately to me that I would become a noted writer.

It was not much later (in what is the sophomore year in an American high school) that I had my first serious conflict with the school authorities. During a Latin class I was caught reading a new play of Frank Wedekind, *Frühlings-erwachen,* one of the first literary challenges in Central Europe to the complacent security of the first decade of our century. The play, about an adolescent boy's suicide, contained a tacit accusation against the prevalent sexual hypocrisy of those days. I was threatened with expulsion from school, not so much for the trivial offense of reading during instruction, but for reading that particular book. Only my good record and, particularly, consideration of my father's achievements and position, saved me from that disgrace. And it was perhaps no accident that the professor of physics and mathematics, a subject in which I excelled in those days, supported me. He did not take literature and literary offenses quite as seriously as did his humanistic colleagues. The cultural leaders, however, were already on the defensive and felt instinctively the distant rumblings of the approaching collapse of their world.

They held as their supreme duty the protection of the youth entrusted to their guidance from the corrosive influence of such cynics as Wedekind, Shaw and Wilde, who ridiculed all that they considered immutable values. It counted against me also that, just a day before, a young assistant teacher had seen me at a meeting of the newly founded Sociological Society, a liberal but more leftist organization under the leadership of Julius Pikler, the professor of the philosophy of law, which acquired increasing importance as an opposition group, challenging the conservative and highly nationalistic policies of the leading parties. I was suddenly looked upon as a rebel.

My father was deeply disturbed by this whole affair, not so much because of my reading Wedekind but because of my attending a meeting of Pikler's organization. Father regarded his colleague's teachings with great skepticism and considered him an amateur philosopher, ignorant as measured by his classical standards, of unsound judgment and of dubious patriotism. Since his early years, Father had devoted himself to participating in the task of helping to build a Hungarian national culture independent of the German-Austrian influence which prevailed during his youth in the middle of the last century. He was a devoted nationalist in the constructive sense of the word. The Sociological Society was politically on the left; after the collapse of the monarchy, its members played an important role in Count Károlyi's government, which the Old Guard considered as the liquidator of the Empire, and with it of all those values they stood for. For the Old Guard socialism was unpalatable; they believed in the sanctity of the individual; they were convinced that history is directed by a few exceptional individuals and that all valid progress comes from the accomplishments of devoted and gifted persons. In fact, they aspired for and in some respects approached a society which came nearest to Plato's ideal, a society led, although not ruled, by an intellectual elite devoted to the welfare of the State. Their striving for the advancement of the higher aspirations of man was effective in their time. It was a central organizing principle of their personality which they adopted without any internal conflict, just as the government and society adopted them as their own objectives.

Father, as a young and outstanding student of philosophy, had received a government stipend to travel to different cultural centers in Europe and to become acquainted with the prevailing trends in philosophy. Some of his experiences he reported in letters to his professor of philosophy, Cyrill Horvath. There are no letters preserved about his studies in Paris, but he often spoke to me of how deeply he was influenced by the concepts of Hippolyte Taine, the founder of the "social milieu" concept in history.

Indeed, Father and his contemporaries were in a truly enviable position. This was particularly the case in Hungary after 1867, when Franz Deak made his historic agreement with the Kaiser, Franz Joseph, for Hungary to become an equal partner in Austro-Hungarian monarchy. The Kaiser of Austria became at the same time King of Hungary to be coronated with the crown of St. Stephen, the first Christian King who received the holy crown from Pope Sylvester II in the year 1001. A national rebirth, both economic and spiritual, followed this treaty, and the liberal current of 1848, when the Hungarian revolution against the Hapsburgs was subdued with the help of Russian troops, could now be resumed with full force. Credit for this vigorous national-liberal development must go in the first place to an enlightened, highly patriotic group of the aristocracy who selflessly devoted themselves to the development of Hungarian culture in noble competition with Austria. The Hungarian Academy of Sciences was founded by Count Stephan Széchenyi and, until the recent Communist regime, was named after him. A college for outstanding students was founded by Baron Eötvös. The fact that Hungarian national culture developed in opposition to the aim of the Hapsburg dynasty to incorporate Hungary into the Austrian Empire with a prevalent Germanic orientation, is responsible for the liberal and progressive nature of the Hungarian developments. The recent Hungarian revolt against Moscow is a belated expression of this passionate dedication to freedom. Cultural accomplishments in art, literature and science were officially encouraged, the political leaders looked for talent and promoted it with governmental funds and soon Budapest became a flourishing cultural center.

I have often been asked, why, in spite of the smallness of the country, did so many Hungarians come into the limelight in the theater, in literature and in mathematics and the physical sciences. The answer is not that Hungary is a gifted nation. All nations—as most children, if not sick—are gifted. What happens to their native talents depends upon the influences they receive from their environment. Father's generation, and the next one, grew up in an atmosphere in which creativity and intellectual and artistic accomplishments were publicly and officially held in the highest esteem. Young people were not aiming primarily at a prescribed routine career or social role, but at development of their own unique endowments, an aim which existential psychiatrists have recently taken up as their principal credo.

In Hungary, after 1867, a parliamentary system was adopted which represented a kind of democracy of the upper and middle classes, similar to the political structure in England before the latter part of the Nineteenth Century. In 1848 the resurgence of the ideology of the Eighteenth Century enlightenment all over Europe coincided in Hungary with a vigorous national rebirth. This gave the Hungarian development an added impetus. My father's generation could without any doubts devote their lives to the realization of a progressive, enlightened national culture dedicated to fostering the spiritual qualities of the citizen, the Platonic Utopia of a society led by the intellectual elite. This was something they believed in without inner conflict. Lack of "ego identity," the present-day absence of an internally consistent value system as a central organizing and governing principle within the personality, was unknown to those born into that fortunate creative period of Western civilization. They absorbed in a harmonious way the prevailing trends of that creative century, a firm belief in the power of reason and in the unlimited possibilities of knowledge and, above all, a high regard for the individual's creative self-expression.

Nothing displays this orientation more clearly than the notion of *l'art pour l'art.* The artist is motivated by the urge to convey to his audience his subjective state of mind, his way of looking upon the social scene and nature and his emotional conflicts, no matter whether he uses the medium of poetry, the novel, the drama, painting, sculpture or music. He does not try to make his audience better or more moral or to influence their political attitudes. He has no aim except to convey his own state of mind to the reader, and to arouse in him the same emotions and experiences. He tries to communicate his mental content, no matter what it may be. What makes this self-expression artistic is the form in which it is communicated, not its content. Many people have had deep feelings, romantic experiences or, when impressed by a landscape, revelatory insights about life, but only a few are capable of expressing them in a way suitable to arouse the same inner experiences in the audience.

Like scientific discoveries, artistic techniques can be used for practical purposes, such as propaganda aimed at specific political or social goals. Industrial art, for example, makes technical products more attractive for the buyer. In the latter part of the Nineteenth Century and until the first World War, utilization of artistic techniques for practical purposes was looked upon as a kind of depredation, even a prostitution of art. This may have been responsible for the decline of esthetic values in building and in furniture, since they serve practical purposes. This deterioration of taste in architecture and internal decoration was in vivid contrast to the high quality of the purely creative art of the period.

This almost religious search for truth and beauty in the form of pure science and pure art went with a disdain for the utilitarian and practical, which had to be tolerated, of course, as a necessity. After all, one had to live and, if possible, to live well with little effort so that one could dedicate oneself to the worship and promotion of the real values of life: knowledge and esthetic refinement. To describe how that era of contemplation—with its struggle to preserve the purity of science and art in a sterilized esoteric seclusion and to protect them from pollution by the practical needs of life—collapsed and was followed by our dynamic pragmatic period is a task for the historian. Here I am trying only to identify this change in mentality without claiming that it meant deterioration.

We who grew up in the spirit of our fathers had little inclination to give serious hearing to Marxian concepts, which did not fit in at all with our optimistic faith in an evolutionary process by which the deficiencies and injustices of the social system would gradually be eradicated. Inequities among men, however, were not to be liquidated. The regard for the uniqueness of every person, the cult of the individual, was incompatible with a society aiming at conformity of opinion and status. I remember an occasion when Father was discussing socialism at the dinner table. He exclaimed with irritation in his voice, "Socialism they call a just order ! It means reducing the exceptional person to the status of a moron ! If this 'justice' would have been observed by nature, we would be still floating in the pond as amorphous amoebas !" What made the Marxian doctrine most unacceptable for that generation was the materialistic stress on economic factors completely incongruous with their idealistic, esthetic orientation and their indestructible faith in the higher spiritual forces of man. The Marxian emphasis on economy, its exaltation of physical labor and political violence, not only contradicted their concept of man and society, but violated their esthetic orientation in which intellectual and artistic achievements were the supreme values. They substituted for formal religion the esthetic, rational and ethical propensities of man as objects of reverence, a humanistic credo as professed by the great Humboldt. In discussing these matters, Father compared the national economy with the visceral functions of digestion and elimination, which are not the aims but the necessities of life. They serve only as the physical prerequisites of the *raison d'être* of civilized man, the free expression of his creative forces.

I cannot forget a scene when once again Marx was under discussion in the family circle at demitasse after dinner, which always was served in Father's library. Father, who seldom lost his temper, angrily exclaimed: "No one can ever convince me that the stomach rules the mind ! The economic understructure of society is like the rule of the stomach ! We do not live to eat and defecate, but we have to perform those functions in order to be able to live for those things which make us human beings. Who is responsible for our factories driven by electricity, the faceless many or Faraday, Ampère and the other great theoreticians ? All that we cherish is ultimately the accomplishment of the mind and not of ordinary but of exceptional minds. The economic understructure does not determine our ideas. Ideas are responsible for new discoveries and changes in economy !"

Father, therefore, had nothing to fear when the school authorities reported to him that I had been seen at a meeting of Professor Pikler's Marxist-oriented organization. I was too strongly protected against their doctrines by all the consistent influences he had inculcated into me since my earliest youth.

I can still visualize his library with tall bookcases against the wall. From their tops the busts of Aristotle, Plato, Kant, Spinoza, Voltaire, Diderot and Schopenhauer looked down on me. I was not yet six years old, playing on the floor in the library with one of the big volumes before me. Suddenly, I triumphantly exclaimed, "Diderot !"—one of the first words I had succeeded in deciphering with the help of my newly acquired reading ability. The golden letters on the spine of the volume are still before me and I am happy that I got acquainted so early with the name of this great man of enlightenment. He was one of my father's favorite philosophers, both on account of his rationalism and his all-encompassing encyclopedic knowledge. In contrast Father had little regard for the romantic Rousseau, a pet target of Diderot's criticism. Later, when Father read my study on criminal psychology, he called my attention to a statement by Diderot that small children would be dangerous criminals if they had the bodily strength of adults. In this statement the perspicacious French philosopher had anticipated modern psychoanalytic insight. Much later Father also reminded me that Diderot was quite aware of the existence of the Oedipus complex.

CHAPTER III

Freud Enters My Life

> "Men are strong so long as they represent a strong idea; they become powerless when they oppose it. Psychoanalysis will survive this loss and gain new adherents in place of these. . . . I can only express a wish that fortune may grant an agreeable upward journey to all those who have found their stay in the underworld of psychoanalysis too uncomfortable for their taste. The rest of us, I hope, will be permitted without hindrance to carry through to their conclusion our labors in the depths."
>
> S. FREUD

The Freudian discoveries were somewhat less disturbing to Father than political radicalism, but he received them with an initial skepticism and reservation. His belief in the power of reason was challenged by the demonstration of the irrational trends of man. His basically Apollonian world picture was shaken by the discovery of the Dionysian underground forces which were to be successfully mastered and subjugated by the civilized intellect. To some degree he was prepared for the Freudian views by his thorough knowledge of Schopenhauer and particularly Spinoza, whose views in an article later published in a psychoanalytic journal he compared with those of Freud. He pointed out that both considered their goal to be the mastery of emotions by the rational forces of the mind. Had it not disturbed their Victorian repressions, my father's generation was intellectually well prepared to assimilate the Freudian doctrine, which from a historical perspective was but the logical continuation of the rationalistic tradition: to understand natural phenomena, including those of the mind, on the basis of scientific principles. Moreover, the biological orientation of Freud's psychology, which considers the functions of the mind as manifestations of the living organism, ultimately subjected to the laws of physiology, physics and chemistry, was in line with the pragmatic view of William James, for whom Father had a great regard. Yet his attitude toward pragmatism, which emphasized the utilitarian function of the mind as an instrument of the living organism, could be characterized as ambivalent. He accepted the basic position, but at the same time this contradicted his deep admiration for the creative and non-adaptive aspects of the mind. When these non-adaptive manifestations were discovered to be the products of unconscious processes in which sexual fantasies were so dominant, he shrank back and adopted a skeptical wait-and-see attitude.

Father, as editor of the *Journal of Philosophy*, while I was still a young medical student, asked me to review Freud's *Interpretation of Dreams*, a new edition of which had been sent to the *Journal*. He gave this book to me with the words, "This belongs to your field. It is not philosophy. Read it and write a review of it." A few days later I returned the book to father with the contemptuous remark, "This may not be philosophy, but it is certainly not medicine."

My second encounter with psychoanalysis came later, after I had finished my medical curriculum. Upon my return from Göttingen to continue medical school in Budapest, I entered the physiological laboratory of Franz Tangl, a leading experimentalist in metabolism. Studying under Verworn in Göttingen had revived my interest in the mind-body problem, which constantly preoccupied me during my formative years. I was well acquainted with the philosophical approach to this riddle from reading and particularly from frequent discussions with Father. A new influence came to the fore from my acquaintance with Geza Revesz, who stimulated my interest in the empirical experimental approach to this age-old problem. I proposed to Tangl a study in brain metabolism. The project involved trying to establish differences in the oxygen consumption of the brain when subjected to powerful sensory stimuli. After expressing his reservations and trying to convince me of the futility of this project, Tangl finally consented that in collaboration with Revesz (who, in the meantime, had returned from Göttingen) I could undertake such an investigation. This study, and two others dealing with change in brain metabolism during narcosis which led to positive findings, was published before my graduation from medical school.

Four years of service at the front in World War I meant an interruption but no diversion from the path of a laboratory career. After the armistice I joined the staff of the psychiatric hospital of the university and spent much time in the laboratory without showing the least interest in the patients' personalities and psychological problems. Blood chemistry was then my only passion; toward such intangibles as mental symptoms I had only a deeply felt contempt.

The routine work of a psychiatric hospital, however, requires some acquaintance with clinical psychiatry. One of the schizophrenic patients entrusted to my care continuously pestered me by recounting his innumerable vivid dreams. I vaguely remembered that years ago, as a medical student, I had read Freud's *Interpretation of Dreams*. The book was crazy, but the patient was too; maybe, I thought, this crazy book might help me to understand this crazy patient. So I undertook the trying task of rereading this epoch-making book.

While rereading the *Interpretation of Dreams*, I became repeatedly involved in arguments with a young psychiatrist, a pupil of Freud, who was a visiting member of the staff, to whom the liberal-minded professor of psychiatry had given permission to study a few schizophrenics with the method of psychoanalysis. The presence of an unmodified Oedipus complex could not be denied in the case of my schizophrenic patient who related his dreams with such great predilection. The dreams were undisguised expressions of murderous wishes against the patient's uncle, with whom in his dreams he competed for his mother's favors. I made my first shamefaced retreat, having to admit that my previous supercilious criticisms—such as "unscientific speculation," "mere fantasy," "perverted imagination"—were perhaps somewhat exaggerated.

The pupil of Freud was a modest, well balanced, intelligent woman psychiatrist, not argumentative and not particularly eager to convince me. I felt, however—at first vaguely and then more and more clearly—that she knew infinitely more about the patients than anyone else in the hospital, and that she had a powerful instrument at her command. Her poised and genuine confidence in her approach made a greater impression upon me than her intellectual explanations about psychoanalysis, which I could only partially understand. I began to realize that the attacks to which this Freudian was daily exposed in the hospital were explosions of the powerless anger of a group of conceited ignorants who did not want to admit that an outsider knew something they did not know, that she possessed a veritable master-key to the understanding of psychopathological phenomena. While the physicians were arguing about the pros and cons of Freud's teachings, the patients passed judgment. To everyone not blinded by emotion it became obvious that the patients with whom she dealt simply ignored the rest of the staff. Instinctively they felt that she understood their problems and dealt with their real issues. I became more and more aware of the pitiful insignificance of all the printed examination sheets, psychological experiments, intelligence tests, orientation tests, and the awkward routine of history-taking, in comparison with the vital and centrally aimed approach of this Freudian. She had a psychological microscope while the rest of the staff did not even own a magnifying glass. Yet, I was still far from accepting the principles of psychoanalysis.

A dogged struggle followed to grasp Freud's writings. At that time his style appeared to me unnecessarily literary and tiresome. After I had been submerged for years in the mentality of exact sciences, it was almost physical pain for me to follow the vague and ambiguous mental excursions which seemed to hang in mid-air without solid foundation. And yet they offered unexpected clues. There was system in these writings, an intellectual edifice which reminded me somewhat of theoretical physics. I remembered the long struggle for the understanding of the principles of thermodynamics. These I could not refute so easily on the basis that I did not grasp them immediately; they were supported by authorities of the past and present: Carnot, Calusius, Mach, Boltzman, Planck and others. Here, there was only one thing to do—to learn it or leave it. Here, it was obvious that lack of comprehension was a weakness of the student, and I had to admit to myself that most probably now, with psychoanalysis, the trouble was with me and not psychoanalysis. I read Freud again and again, trying to understand patients from this new point of view. Finally I succeeded in working out the unconscious emotional etiology of a case of kleptomania. Some of the local Freudians began to welcome me as a prospective convert. And then I withdrew again.

The typical mentality of minority groups never appealed to me. In the conservative atmosphere of my home every rebellion had a distasteful connotation. Minorities always believe that they are the chosen people, become suspicious, withdrawn, provocative, narrow-minded. The fact that they are rejected gives them a feeling of justification in rejecting everything and everyone outside. They assume all the negative qualities of their adversaries. Science cannot be well pursued in a sectarian attitude. Clinical psychiatry may have been in a blind alley, but there were the great accomplishments of modern physiology which could not be suddenly ignored, no matter how ingenious and fundamental this new approach appeared to be.

Finally, it would be futile to deny the importance of another factor of great practical significance. To turn to psychoanalysis meant to give up every idea of an academic career, for which I had prepared myself since my early school years and to which I was predestined by family tradition. I might have disappointed my father by selecting medicine instead of a humanistic discipline, but at least there had never been any question about devoting myself to teaching and research. The practice of psychoanalysis was simply a horror in the eyes of the philosopher-father, an undignified and morbid interest in the morbid. For this admirer of the highest aspirations of man, interest in sexual phenomena, not to speak of their pathological manifestations, was plainly a descent into a spiritual gutter. This great Shakespearian student, who had devoted a volume of five hundred pages to the solution of the question of Hamlet's hesitation to take revenge on his uncle, did not dream that Freudian psychology had given the clue to that puzzle which had resisted the genius of a Herder and a Goethe. Once when I spoke to my father about Ernest Jones' essay on Hamlet and mentioned the Oedipus complex, the old man lost his temper. I felt that I was witnessing the tragedy of the clash between the best of the past with the best of the present in human knowledge. Then I understood what Galileo's *Eppur si muove* meant. Without bitterness or hate against the traditional orientation which was my own during all formative years, I began to feel that my intellectual destiny was to follow the new pathways.

I left my home for Berlin and, after some wavering, became a student of the Psychoanalytic Institute, which had just been founded. Indeed, I was the first training candidate of the Institute. With this move I gave up academic aspirations and resigned myself to what seemed inevitable, that the gap between my and my father's orientation would never be bridged. It was one of the happiest moments of my life, therefore, when about seven years later the unexpected happened. Spending a few summer weeks with Father in a small French town, Barbizon, the birthplace of modern painting, I finished the manuscript of my first book and gave it to him for reading. During a long walk under the giant trees of the ancient forest of Fontainebleau, my father told me that the manuscript convinced him that Freud's teachings were the beginning of the first real psychology. Proudly he added, "Your philosophical background enabled you to express those things more logically and simply." He also told me that he never trusted the experimental school and considered it a blind alley, a rudderless boat, an instrument running amuck after it had rid itself of the rule of the intellect. Maybe, he said, not philosophy, but this new empirical approach, psychoanalysis, will bring back to psychology that constructive point of view which the great old thinkers had, viewing the totality of the person and not only the fringes. Maybe psychoanalysis will enthrone again real understanding in place of fumbling, rule by thought in place of rule by gadget.

This happened several months before Father's death. He died in his sleep. On his night table there lay open the last issue of the *Psychoanalytic Almanac*, in which the old philosopher had published his treatise on psychoanalysis, which he wrote while staying in Barbizon: a comparison of Freud's repression theory with Spinoza's view concerning the rule of the intellect over the emotions. He was seventy-six years of age when he finally appreciated Freud's contribution. This encyclopedic mind had to overcome not only the usual emotional resistances but the intellectual heritage of two thousand years. In comparison, the traditions of experimental psychology appear negligible. Fechner published his *Elemente der Psychophysik* in 1860, only thirty-five years before Freud and Breuer's *Studies on Hysteria* appeared. And at present there is already a struggle between the older traditional orientation in psychoanalysis and a newer point of view. It will not be long before the traditional tendency of psychoanalysis toward isolation and the refutation of the need for experimental validation of its findings will yield to an increasing demand for greater conceptual clarity, for quantitative methods and the introduction of experimental procedures, and for the coördination of psychoanalytic findings with physiology and the social sciences.

Independently of its final validity, psychoanalysis was felt subjectively as a great menace by many academic psychiatrists who grew up in its condemnation and sometimes even made their reputation by repudiating psychoanalysis. There still are academic posts in which the fact that the applicant has not been contaminated by psychoanalysis is considered a definite recommendation for being employed. Not long ago, in most university positions, young psychiatrists considered it wise to hide the fact that they had been psychoanalyzed; and any interpretation smacking of psychoanalysis was carefully avoided or offered only in disguise.

The primary significance of psychoanalysis apart from its therapeutic aspect is that it has developed a method which is adjusted to the nature of the field of investigation: the human personality. Psychoanalysis, in contrast to earlier methods, has adopted the everyday method which everyone uses to understand the mental situation of other persons, and, as is the case in every science, has further refined and developed the everyday method. Everyone has a faculty of understanding another person's mentality. This is a complex faculty. Its chief instrument is a kind of identification with the other person, that is, putting one's self in the other person's mental situation. By observing the movements of another, the expression of his face, the tone of his voice, and particularly by listening to what he says, one gets an idea of what is going on in his mind. This understanding is derived from the fact that the object of observation is a being similar to the observer; both are human personalities. If we observe another person, we note his external behavior, but we also know from our introspective experience what we feel when we behave similarly and use the same facial expressions, words, and movements. Because we know our own reaction in a similar situation, we understand the other person's motives. In psychological observation the external behavior of the observed object is supplemented by direct or introspective knowledge of one's own person. This is possible only because observer and observed are similar beings. The similarity between observer and observed is what differentiates psychology from all physical sciences. The most important means of this understanding is the use of the same word symbols by the observer and observed. Fine understanding of another person's motivation without knowing his language is fully impossible.

In another place, I have summarized the way in which psychoanalysis has improved upon the method of verbal communication by which ordinarily human beings convey to each other their feelings, motives, and ideas, and how it has developed this everyday method into a more reliable technique for getting insight into another person's psychological processes.[1] The essence of the psychoanalytic method consists in the utmost utilization of communication by speech for the study and understanding of another's mental state.

Experimental psychology, however, has followed other ways. When Fechner introduced the experimental method for the study of psychological phenomena, he probably did not foresee the momentous historical significance of this step for the future development of psychology. No matter how much important detailed information may have been obtained by ingenious efforts to introduce experiment into the study of psychological phenomena, and no matter how significant such efforts may prove in the future, for a long time they had a retarding influence upon the development of psychology as a science of personality. In fact, they have made psychologists lose sight of the real scope of their field.

The experimental method has been taken over from the physical sciences, where it has developed in steady adap-

[1] "Psychoanalysis and Medicine," in the *Harvey Lectures 1930–1931* (Baltimore, 1931), p. 88.

tation to the nature of the observed phenomena. The adoption of this method by psychology was an extremely artificial procedure. It meant that there had to be selected from the complexity of psychological phenomena certain isolated functions which lent themselves to quantitative experimental approach. The natural course of development in every discipline consists in devising methods for the solution of pertinent questions. The introduction of the experimental method in psychology took place under entirely different conditions; the object of investigation became subordinated to the method. One did not look for a suitable method for the solution of a vital problem; one started to investigate anything which could be approached by the experimental method, without any leading ideas, working hypotheses or theoretical assumptions. The result was a chaotic development, the accumulation of non-pertinent data, and the loss of sight of the objective of psychology: to understand mental activity as the functions of a highly complex system of forces—the human personality.

It is no wonder that as a reaction to this planless study of isolated phenomena, the principle was formulated that the whole cannot be understood by the study of its isolated parts (Gestalt). But before Gestalt psychology ever existed, Freud had applied this theoretical postulate in practice. Whereas Gestalt psychology developed the theoretical foundations of this principle and demonstrated its validity in the field of sensory perception, Freud turned his interest not to isolated faculties or abstractions like memory, will power, perception, apperception, not even to man in general, but subjected the individual human being with all his hopes, sorrows, fears and desires to a systematic scrutiny. Thus psychoanalysis gave back to psychology its original meaning. In common language we call someone a good psychologist who has a good intuitive understanding of another person, or an author who correctly describes his characters and their motivations. Psychoanalysis made of this intuitive understanding of another person's mentality an empirical science. No question, it is a very young science, just about to outgrow its childhood diseases. Yet by the careful and patient observation of a large number of adults and children, psychoanalysis has come to the formulation of a tentative picture of human personality.

The fundamentals of this theoretical construct can be considered as having a high degree of qualitative validity. The recognition of the basic mechanisms of repression, rationalization, projection, identification, displacement, the turning of psychic tendencies against one's self, fixation, and regression form the solid basis of a new dynamic psychology which offers a novel and amazingly consistent causal understanding of human destinies, normal and morbid behavior.

With this dynamic approach Freud substantiated in detail Fechner's theoretically assumed stability principle, according to which the total functioning of the mental apparatus is directed toward maintaining a consistent level of excitation within the organism. Freud succeeded in describing the totality of personality functions (ego functions) as consisting in the reduction of internal and external stimulation (biological needs and environmental influences) to a constant level. This task the ego performs through its integrating functions in adjusting internal (biological) needs to the given external conditions. The ego can perform this by the help of its double perceptive function: by the registration of both internal biological tensions and external stimuli coming from the environment through the organs of sensory perception. It is most encouraging that physiology quite independently came to the same conclusions, as expressed in Cannon's theory of homeostasis.

It must be admitted, however, that all this gives only a qualitative picture. Freud postulated apart from this dynamic point of view also a quantitative (economic) one. Yet the merely clinical approach did not allow a satisfactory quantitative analysis of the observed phenomena.

In the present phase of development, the method of psychological experimentation is likely to assume an entirely different significance from that which it has had during the last eighty years. Now that psychoanalysis by methodical clinical observations has developed a preliminary view of the whole structure and function of the mental apparatus, those quantitative methods which have been highly refined during these many years of more or less unguided experimentation can be applied for the validation and quantitative exploration of the qualitative relationships and principles which psychoanalysis has worked out.

There is little doubt that we are approaching a time which is ripe for the systematic introduction of experimental methods in the study of personality. Fechner's attempt was a premature one. Yet the more or less unguided experimentation of eighty years was not wasted time: during this period the powerful instrument of psychological experiment has been perfected. Now the productive concepts which Freud introduced in this field will give the experimental methodology a really constructive use. Experimentation without leading concepts is like shooting in the dark. Psychoanalytic theory is certainly only a tentative construction, but even in a dim light, one is more likely to hit a target than in complete darkness.

In the last two decades, psychoanalysis has been facing a new problem. Once a neglected and bitterly contested marginal discipline on the borderline of psychiatry and the social sciences, it has now found in this country broad recognition and acceptance. The majority of young psychiatrists consider their training in psychoanalysis to be the most important part of their preparation for their practice. Certification of accomplished training in one of the recognized institutes of psychoanalysis and membership in the American Psychoanalytic Association lends great prestige to a psychiatrist in the eyes both of the general public and of his confreres.

To deal with this new situation, the psychoanalytic community had no preparation. The traditional attitude of a minority group still prevails among analysts and in their institutions. The memory of the heroic past, when a small group of psychoanalysts faced a critical and openly hostile world, still lingers on. Freud, after futile attempts to convince the critics with rational arguments, chose the only policy open to him; he withdrew into splendid isolation. It appears that psychoanalysts are not free from that central phenomenon, which is so important in psychoanalytic theory as a universal factor in psychopathology: fixation. Five years ago, in a publication, *Twenty Years of Psychoanalysis,* I tried to describe this situation. I could not do it better today.

> Whenever such a transition from leading an opposition to participating in government, from heroic fight to responsible teaching and practice, takes place within a short period of time, there is danger that the pioneers will not be flexible enough for the required emotional reorientation; that they may remain—as we psychoanalysts say—fixated to an attitude which has become outmoded. The result is the tendency to misinterpret the attitude of others, a Don Quixote fight against windmills. Every question is misunderstood as a sign of hostility based on resistance. Valid criticism provokes, instead of reconsideration and re-examination, violent counterattacks. Smug complacency can only partly cover up the inner insecurity which accompanies the new position of responsibility. Instead of progressive improvement of knowledge and practice, the tendency to rest on the laurels of the past appears in the form of dogmatism. Repetition of the common historical pattern of a once progressive movement changing into stagnant doctrinairism is imminent.
>
> The questions pertaining to psychoanalysis as a theory and practice must be met. They can be satisfactorily answered only by a self-critical re-evaluation of all that we can offer; else we must evade the answers by ignoring the questions. This re-evaluation necessarily leads to changes and requires improvements in theory and practice. The complacent reiteration of earlier achievements and the routine continuation of former practices result in sterility.
>
> In this country, with the general acceptance of the fundamental discoveries of psychoanalysis and of psychoanalytic treatment based on these discoveries, we have left behind the heroic era of psychoanalysis and have entered a new phase of responsibility. . . . In the present era of ac-

> ceptance of psychoanalysis our principal responsibility is to evaluate what we know and what we can offer in good conscience to advance both our theoretical and practical knowledge, to avoid dogmatic consolidation by emphasizing that psychoanalysis is a developing discipline and not a finished product. . . . In this era in which the medical profession, particularly psychiatrists, want to learn all they can about psychoanalysis, our responsibility is to open up our gates and to give all we can. Instead of working in splendid isolation, we must find ways and means to reunite with the medical community which Freud had to leave for compelling historical reasons. His conceptions and findings were too novel and revolutionary to be accepted by contemporary medicine and he was forced to take the course he chose: to build an organization of his own and with his own societies, journals, teaching institutions and press.[2]

The conditions which induced Freud to take this position do not prevail today. Psychoanalysis has become an integral part, in fact the most basic part, of the psychiatrist's training. The separation of this training from the rest of the psychiatric curriculum has no sufficient justification today. It is an example of cultural lag. The relative isolation of psychoanalytic training from the rest of medical and psychiatric instruction outside of universities is a residue of the past. It has no rational, only historical, reasons. The separateness of psychoanalytic training in autonomous psychoanalytic institutes is often supported today by such arguments as that many university departments of psychiatry are not yet ready to incorporate psychoanalytic training, or that the nature of psychoanalytic

[2] Franz Alexander, *Twenty Years of Psychoanalysis* (New York, 1953), pp. 17, 18, 23.

training has so many specific features—for example, the candidate's own personal analysis—that its incorporation in the regular training of psychiatrists in university departments would be most difficult, if at all possible. Undoubtedly, the first of these arguments has some validity; not all universities are ready for the assimilation of a psychoanalytic curriculum. The second argument appears to be a rationalization.

During twenty-five years as the Director of the Institute of Psychoanalysis in Chicago, my objective was to prepare the way for the final integration of psychoanalysis in the traditional places of medical training, the universities and teaching hospitals. Today it is not difficult for me to recognize that my constant efforts were motivated not only by their internal logic and rationality, but also by my urge to unify the deep loyalty I felt toward the academic tradition represented by my father with my later dedication to the cause of psychoanalysis. Such a unification of psychoanalysis with the rest of academic training would mark a milestone in the task which Freud set out for himself: to apply the same basic scientific principles which have been so successful in the natural sciences to the study of the human personality. The university is an institution dedicated to the cause of reason, science and knowledge which can be taught to others. Psychoanalysis has reached a stage today in which its principles, methods of investigation and their application to treatment can be transmitted to students in a planned curriculum, as other branches of knowledge are taught in universities. This conviction determined much of my activities after I came to the United States.

CHAPTER IV

Precursors of August 1914

"You arrogant European of the Nineteenth Century, you are raving! Your knowledge does not complete nature but kills your own. . . . Naturally, you are climbing over the sunrays of knowledge upward to heaven, but also down toward Chaos. Your way of walking, namely, to climb through knowledge, is your downfall; the ground under you slips away into uncertainty; for life you have no longer any guiding posts, only cobwebs, which get torn through any new grasp of your knowledge."

NIETZSCHE

Contemporary writers, no matter how divergent their interpretation of the present era may be, all seem to consider the outbreak of the first World War as a critical turning point in modern history. This was the visible end of an era of stability in politics and economy, followed by social upheavals, economic changes and international tensions on a global scale. It marked the beginning of the liquidation of several monarchies and colonial empires. But even though these profound changes were manifestly introduced by World War I, the conclusion would be fallacious that the war itself was responsible for the collapse of the political, economic, scientific, and artistic heritage of the Nineteenth Century.

While the War was still going on, one often heard explanations such as that the whole conflict was brought about by the steadily growing Serbian nationalism which erupted in the assassination of the Archduke Ferdinand. The more hard-boiled ones maintained that the real issue was the trade policies of Austria-Hungary, preventing the export of Serbian pigs. Those with even larger perspectives considered the main issue to be the challenge of rapid German industrial expansion under the protectorship of the powerful German navy to England's naval and economic leadership.

The final historical evaluation of all these politico-economic factors, of the minor local tensions between the Balkan nations and the Austro-Hungarian empire, and of the larger issues in Western Europe is a task for future historians.

The less tangible collapse of the spiritual fabric of the Nineteenth Century began, however, much before August 1914. The revolution in modern art, literature, science and philosophy preceded the military and economic events. Kierkegaard published his attacks on institutionalized religion between 1849 and 1855; Nietzsche's prophetic writings appeared between 1870 and 1888. The post-impressionistic paintings of Van Gogh and Cézanne, the Fauvist movement, Cubism and Dadaism preceded the major political and economic events. Einstein published his relativity theory in 1905. The fact that, after the war, Europe did not return to its old standards, beliefs and emotional orientation strongly supports those who ascribe to the war nothing more than a precipitating role. It may even be argued that the economic and political tensions which appear to us as the immediate factors may be the manifestation of the same basic discontent which earlier appeared in art, literature and science.

It is not my purpose to discuss the relative historical importance of material causes versus man's spiritual outlook and to revive the wornout arguments centering around the tenets of historical materialism. Marx and Engels clashed with each other at this point.

It is most revealing that in theoretical physics, in the area of the most precise reasoning of which the human mind has been capable, the mechanistic-materialistic orientation was in the process of yielding to a dynamic orientation. The unit of the universe was no longer the solid particle, but the "event." Mass and energy became interchangeable, and instead of matter the physicist speaks of matter waves; instead of strict causation, of "potentia."

A simple translation of the modern principles of atomic physics to human affairs is not possible. Yet, the fact remains that in all fields of human thought and creativity, the naïve materialistic-mechanistic preoccupation with the immediate, the visible and tangible yields to a preoccupation with connections, relations, tendencies, forces. We are witnessing a rather sudden widening of both our emotional and intellectual outlook. Man, in his commonsense outlook on the world until the last fifty years, dealt mainly with the man-sized world which appeared to him as space populated with tangible and visible objects. Our current cognitive categories are consequently patterned after this "naïve realistic" conception of the world. Access to phenomena of different dimensions has required that the physicist substitute for these materialistic categories new ones which are not based on the visible and the tangible, but abstract constructs, such as, for example, multidimensional space. For such concepts he has only mathematical symbols, although he is constantly struggling to find a verbal translation for them.

Not much different is the picture in the field of medical research. Nothing demonstrates this more clearly than the appearance of the psychosomatic orientation. Willy-nilly, the contemporary research man in the field of clinical medicine has to operate with such intangibles as psychological trends, wishes, hopes and anxieties and to study their influence upon the visible materially describable processes of the body. I do not want to discuss here the ancient body-mind problem of philosophy. My point is the contemporary appearance of a non-materialistic orientation in the field of medicine, paralleling a similar trend in theoretical physics.

Art also departs from the visible tangible world to an abstract symphony of forms and colors, and it shows a tendency to penetrate behind the obvious and visible to something which the modern artist feels to be the essences.

Also, in postwar economy the solid gold coin (or currency exchangeable into gold) yields to a more esoteric symbol, a currency which represents complex interrelationships between different economic yardsticks and which fluctuates as a sensitive indicator of changes of balance between production, wages and prices in the national and international markets, which more and more become interdependent. In science, as in economy and in art, the circumscribed, the immediate, the solid unit is replaced by complex interrelationships. In art, the particular visible object yields its place to relationships expressed by merely formal attributes.

Of greatest interest to contemporary man is that he, himself, as a distinct unit—a person—begins to lose toward his own self the feeling of a circumscribed individual in his own right and begins to feel swallowed up in relationships. He begins to experience himself as part of a larger system. His confidence in self-determination ebbs proportionately to the growing evidence that he is driven by forces operating in the larger social fabric. His social role or function becomes more important than the uniqueness of his own self, which in the past was for him the most solid reliable evidence of his individual existence.

This can be reduced to saying that in all fields of human orientation, the emphasis is shifting from the circumscribed unit—be it the visible material particle in physics, the "object" in art, the gold coin in economy, the individual as a separate self-determining being in social life, the nation as an autonomous unit in politics—all this shifts to intangible but yet bitterly realistic interrelationships. The concept of matter yields to force and field. The study of units and equations between two variables yields to the study of complex relationships in organized systems.

The subjective expression of this world trend is what we psychoanalysts recognize in our patients as the threat to their ego-identity. The same shift has been described most persuasively in socio-psychological terms by Riesman by the advent of the "other-directed" person, whose center of gravity is no longer his internal personal standards, an individual who is no longer "inner-directed" but yields sensitively to the rapidly changing, ill-defined, uncrystallized values of others, an individual whose center of gravity is not within his own structure but within the field in which he moves.

The beginnings of these parallel shifts in modern man's outlook toward the world and himself are clearly recognizable well before the outbreak of the First World War. After the war these cultural trends continued with renewed intensity. Much earlier the threat of abstract science to the unique concreteness of individual existence has been intuitively felt by existential philosophers. I shall return to this revealing chapter of philosophy later, but first, I shall try to reconstruct how all this was subjectively experienced by me at the outbreak of the war and during the post-war period.

CHAPTER V

After August 1914

> "I never loved that old earth more than in those last years before the First World War, never hoped more ardently for European unity, never had more faith in its future than then, when we thought we saw a new dawning. But in reality it was the glare of the approaching world conflagration."
>
> STEFAN ZWEIG

I was serving my compulsory year in the Austro-Hungarian Army as a young physician in a military hospital when war was declared. The first impact of this news is unforgettable. It was the sudden intuitive realization that a chapter of history had ended. There was no apprehension in this feeling, but a sense of finality. Since then, I have discussed this matter with some of my contemporaries and heard about it a great deal in my early postwar psychoanalytic treatments of patients. To my amazement, the others who went through the same events had quite a similar reaction. Certainly, their realization that a new kind of world was in the making was not the result of logical reasoning. It was not the result of any kind of deduction. It was an immediate vivid and prophetic realization that something irreversible of immense importance had happened in history.

In spite of the continuous military preparations which for many years took place before our eyes and which I witnessed at home and during my trips to Germany and even to England, we somehow lulled ourselves in the belief that in our age and in our kind of civilization war was an anachronism. As I tried to convey to the reader before, the prevailing mood of my youth was security and stability. I could think of change only as continuous consistent progress. The humanistic ideals were taken seriously; they became an integral part of our personality. War had no place in this outlook. It was a remote possibility, a theoretical idea which had no relation to our actual daily existence. Father occasionally spoke of the Franco-Prussian War of 1871, but it did not appear that this was an important event in his life. The Boer Revolution took place in a remote part of the world; it had no more meaning for us than a novel. The Russo-Japanese War could still be disposed of as something that happened in semi-barbaric countries. Our world was not yet One World. In Europe we felt apart from the distant regions of the globe, as if they did not belong to our world, which was secure and civilized, enlightened, steadily progressing toward better and better forms of existence. Today, in retrospect, I know that all this, no matter how important, does not fully explain the depth and the prophetic nature of our reaction to the news that a war was in the offing.

Being active in the army, I received my orders the day after the declaration of war. Today, I know that at that moment another illusion disappeared: the illusion, that we are the masters of our destiny, which was the dynamic axis of our personality structure. Naturally, one had always to comply with certain technicalities, pass certain examinations, serve one year in the army, go through with the prescribed steps in preparing for a professional career—yet, our basic conviction was that we were building our own lives according to our own choices. We are endowed with certain talents and interests which are entrusted to us as a capital to be used according to our highly unique personal inclinations. Our destination was to develop our knowledge, skills, and gifts and to use them not so much to benefit humanity, but to fulfill our own selves. This was the only honest way to serve progress and humanity. Our first obligation was toward our own selves, selves which were principled by highly humanistic ideals.

And then came the military command prescribing precisely what we had to do without any recourse to our own judgment. Nothing could have destroyed more brutally the illusion that we are self-responsible persons. The declaration of war hit us in the core of our inner-directedness. The autonomous self proved to be an illusion.

One should not confuse this first impact of the war with "conscientious objection" as it appeared occasionally in the United States at the outbreak of the Second World War. There was no objection in our reaction against fighting for our country. It was not a protest against war as such. There was no protest in it at all. It was simply a deeply felt realization that self-determination did not exist, and therefore we were entering a new era. Up to this point we had no reason to doubt our voluntary, spontaneous—nay, enthusiastic—participation in a rational progressing world, to which we would contribute by developing our own potentialities. We felt this war was an inevitable necessity, and we had to do everything to win it. Yet, it was not a personal decision, and, just because there was no choice, it demonstrated the illusion of self-determination. We became parts of something larger than ourselves. We no longer felt as individuals who plan and act according to their own values, talents and inclinations.

A sudden surge of an excessive, almost jubilant patriotic feeling swept the Hungarian cities with cheering crowds on the streets. It is not difficult to understand in retrospect that this outburst of patriotic participation served to convince us that we were going to war not because we were ordered, but because of our own spontaneous patriotic feeling. Thus we tried to save the illusion of self-determination. In spite of this last attempt to save our illusion by an almost self-hypnotic enthusiasm, when the news of the larger implications of the war appeared—Jaurès, the French political leader, was assassinated; Germany, England, France and Russia became involved—the feeling that powerful superpersonal historical forces were pulling the wires behind the world scenery and the feeling of the insignificance of the individual became irresistible. For the first time in our lives we had been sucked in as participants in world events, and our isolated personal life had ended.

The average human being needs such a drastic demonstration. Only rare hypersensitive individuals could have foreseen long before all this happened what was coming to our world. Most explicitly it was Kierkegaard and Nietzsche who gave verbal expression to the growing trend which threatened the spiritual foundations of the Western world: the sanctity of the individual. The newly emerging currents in art and literature at the end of the century meant mostly a protest against the steadily progressing envelopment of the individual in a rationalistic and materialistic orientation which was quite ineffectually mitigated by humanistic tradition. Those of us who took this humanistic ideal seriously and who were not directly exposed to the progressing anti-individualistic forces needed this rude awakening.

But, as I said before, for a while the first shock ceded to an enthusiastic patriotic participation in the war. For me this was a natural reaction. Father's whole life consisted in efforts to participate in the creation of an independent Hungarian culture. He devoted his efforts to developing a proper Hungarian language for philosophy by translating the works of great philosophers into Hungarian. He edited the first Hungarian *Journal of Philosophy* and the *Library of Philosophical Writers*. He was a nationalist in the ideal sense of the word. His nationalism was blended with the highest humanistic values, in which public education was foremost. Although, as I mentioned before, I was to some degree exposed to some of the local and European critics of our era, fundamentally I identified myself with Father's orientation.

During the four years of service at the front, I once had occasion to visit Budapest for two weeks. I did not sense any radical change as yet. Only after the collapse of the Italian Piave front in late October, 1918, when I returned from the front in a freight car for cattle with fifty rebellious sailors, whom my orderly persuaded to let me in their crowded quarters, did I realize the advent of a new era. The sailors tore the insignia of an officer from my uniform, but treated me otherwise with condescending friendliness. From them I heard of the assassination of Count Tisza, the Prime Minister. The Budapest revolution of the returning sailors and soldiers had just been liquidated by Count Karolyi, who became Minister-President with a cabinet of decidedly leftist orientation. The city underwent a thorough change of face. The working men of the suburbs invaded the elegant heart of the city and everyone felt that the moderate Karolyi's regime was nothing but another Kerensky cabinet and that the Communist revolution was only a question of weeks. Soon, with Béla Kun's Communist dictatorship, Hungary as I knew it disappeared. The period under Horthy's regime proved a futile attempt at restoration of the status quo.

Shortly after Béla Kun's ascendance to power, Father was discharged from his University position by the new Commissar of Education, who was his former student and protégé. Coming home from the faculty meeting, he briefly told us what had happened. It was the first time I saw tears in his eyes.

I left Hungary. After a few months in Vienna, I went to Berlin to continue the psychiatric studies I had started in Budapest.

CHAPTER VI

Under the Weimar Republic

When I try to reconstruct my experiences in Berlin between 1920 and 1930 which are pertinent for this writing, I find it a most difficult task. The outstanding impression is that of living in a stimulating chaos.

I lived in Berlin during the first ten of the thirteen years of the Weimar Republic. During these years Berlin became the center of an intellectual and artistic rebirth overtaking the leadership of Paris. All this took place under continuing economic decline and growing social tension. Many of the new cultural enterprises which are vital today started in those days in Berlin: the revolutionary new theater under the leadership of Reinhardt; the Bauhaus movement in modern architecture and interior decoration; a new kind of literary cabaret which made fun of the already dead or dying official attitudes in politics, social organization and literature; and a virulent modern movement in art, literature and music. The names of Heinrich and Thomas Mann, George Grosz, Richard Strauss, Paul Hindemith are closely associated with this renaissance of German culture. With Planck, Einstein, James Franck and Heisenberg, Germany took leadership in physics. An enlightened industrial and political orientation appeared under the influence of Walther Rathenau, and the first realistic ideas about the foundation of a Pan-Europa were advanced by Stresemann and Briand, inspired by the writings of Count Coudenhove-Kalergi.

Last, but not least, Berlin became the strongest center of psychoanalysis. The first well-organized Psychoanalytic Institute was founded there by Max Eitingon, one of Freud's closest friends and disciples.

I was the first student to matriculate in the new Institute. After two years of vacillation between the traditional organic and the new psychological approach to psychiatry, my fascination with the self-consistent system of psychoanalytic thought won out, particularly because of its solid foundation in actual clinical observation. In the following years I was completely absorbed in trying to master conceptually and technically this new discipline, which was so different from all my previous experience in biochemistry and clinical medicine. In a sense, however, it was familiar because of its basic rationalism and empiricism. It was conceived in the spirit of the "scientific method," although it was applied in a thoroughly novel manner. Its philosophical cornerstone was to understand psychological phenomena as sequences following the laws of psychological causality, something which today is called psychodynamics. Formally, it followed the principles of physical causality.

My almost complete concentration on the study of psychoanalysis is at least partially responsible for the fact that I could not follow with equal attention the exciting new cultural beginnings under the Weimar Republic. I lived in the ivory tower of psychoanalytic theory and practice, which may explain why I was unable to organize my impressions about the various rapid cultural developments under the Weimar Republic.

In 1921 the decision to become a psychoanalyst placed a physician outside the medical fraternity. By joining this marginal group he gave up the aura of prestige which surrounded the graduates of standard medical schools. His compensation for this lost official prestige was that he became a member of the International Psychoanalytic Association under the leadership of Sigmund Freud. This was his new spiritual haven; he became a citizen of a small but devoted community. In the early Twenties, in almost all cultural centers of Europe, local societies or groups of psychoanalysts were formed. Any recognized member of such a group found friendly acceptance by his confrères in other cities. We all knew each other personally, whether we practiced in Berlin, Vienna, Zurich, Paris, Budapest, Rome, Amsterdam or London. We were bound together by the conviction that we were all members of a militant group with a new message, not only for medicine but for the whole civilized world. We had no doubt that psychoanalysis would gradually change the outlook of contemporary man and reform all those sciences concerned with man, not only medicine and biology but the social sciences as well.

During those chaotic postwar years, during which old traditions were liquidated and new groping beginnings emerged, the psychoanalytic movement offered me an opportunity to continue where I had left off at the outbreak of the war six years earlier. It was for me the road back to a life in which I could devote myself to a cause which appeared to me of the greatest possible importance. No matter how revolutionary the method and theory of psychoanalysis was, it represented to me the continuation of the same rationalistic approach to knowledge, which was the strongest tradition in my life.

It is true that psychoanalysis was concerned with the treatment of emotionally disturbed persons. Freud's major emphasis was, however, on understanding the nature of mental diseases. His aim was to develop a treatment based on knowledge of the disease to be cured. This required a theory of personality. In contrast to most of psychiatry in Freud's days, his was not at all a method based on crude empiricism—considering a treatment good if it helps, even if one does not know why and how it helps. The only etiologically founded treatment in psychiatry was that of the postsyphilitic conditions, such as general paresis, where the cause of the illness, *spirochaeta pallida,* had been discovered.

The causal understanding of neuroses was the strongest motivating force in psychoanalytic work. This required a general theory of human personality, and this was the goal which attracted me and most of the early disciples of psychoanalysis. This aim required a new research method and a new way of thinking about human behavior.

Many modern thinkers, in evaluating Freud's contribution, consider him the one who pointed out most effectively the significance of the irrational—the unconscious—in human behavior. This, however, is only half the truth. Freud's main endeavor consisted in understanding the laws governing unconscious processes, in order to make them accessible to the rational mind. He succeeded in explaining the nonsensical phenomena of slips of the tongue, of dreams, of irrational neurotic fears and obsessional ideas in rational terms, in terms of psychological causality. He showed that these processes—which appear irrational and psychologically unintelligible—follow their own psychological laws, however different they may be from those which govern conscious rational thought and behavior. In fact, the theoretical edifice of psychoanalysis is the most consistent and rational system yet produced in the field of psychology. This aspect of psychoanalysis is what fascinated me, a new possibility of understanding in the terms of science that most elusive area: the human personality. To join the psychoanalytic group, therefore, meant for me not embarking on a new type of avocation, but continuing where I had left off at the outbreak of the war: research for its own sake, a new kind of exploratory activity, new only in its techniques and subject matter.

Psychoanalysis was the connecting link between my present and the past; it re-established the sense of continuity in my life and, most of all, it allowed a synthesis of two orientations—the scientific and the humanistic—which I had not been able to reconcile successfully with each other in the past. In my eyes, psychoanalysis represented the first successful attempt to approach with a scientific orientation the problem of the human personality, a subject which hitherto was the exclusive domain of the humanities. I intuitively felt that in our troubled era, in which the unconscious irrational forces of man openly intruded upon all walks of life, the scientific understanding of man as a person and of the society he built were the most crucial problems. This was the next logical step in the history of knowledge. Therefore, psychoanalysis supplied for me not only a continuity between past and present, but a meaningful goal for my future. It became the cement of my own identity.

All this was strongly supported by Freud's personal influence. When I first met him he was 63 years old and at the height of his leadership role. As is clearly evident from his biography by Ernest Jones, in Freud's own development an early phase of insecurity and searching ended when he found himself in his pioneering work. From that point on, his growth as a person could no longer be separated from the growth of his ideas, of the new territory he conquered for science. Nothing shows more convincingly than Freud's life history the significance of devotion to an outside goal for the integration of a personality. From Freud's personality emanated a rare combination of confidence and skepticism, of intuition and the faculty for critical analysis, of a humanistic interest in man as a person and the conviction that even that which appears most irrational in man, such as his dreams or neurotic symptoms, can be understood in rational terms. Freud himself for many years hesitated whether to choose for his career the natural sciences, until gropingly he found the goal to which he could dedicate himself without reservation, an objective which no one before him could ever realize successfully: to apply controlled observation and critical reasoning to the most obscure field, the human personality, which only the great writers' intuition had sporadically penetrated in the past. He found the synthesis between science and psychological intuition, which since my early years had been my own dilemma. He, as a person, and his work gave me the directive to resolve my own identity problem. His continuous encouragement and openly expressed expectations of me gave me a strong impetus and confidence in my work.

Deeply absorbed as I was in my work, one central fact could not escape my attention because it was conveyed to me daily through my patients. It became obvious to me that neither the Weimar Constitution nor the current cultural trends in Germany were deeply rooted in German tradition. The new Constitution seemed foisted upon a Germany which had lost the war; it was kept alive only by the moral pressure of the Western powers. The new cultural trends in art and literature were motivated primarily by protest against the old order, which had become thoroughly disreputable because of its failure.

The occasionally open, mostly hidden, scorn and contempt many of my German patients held for the new order was too obvious to be overlooked. Therefore, the later developments under Hitler, which meant for the Germans a throwing-off of foreign importations and a reassertion of their basic Teutonic heritage, was no surprise for me. Seen from a larger perspective, the national socialist movement—partially at least—was a rebellion against the Communist ideology of mass culture. It had its deepest roots in anti-rational German romanticism with a paradoxical emphasis on organization. It was at the same time pro- and anti-individualistic, which is revealed in its name: nationalistic and socialistic. It tried to expel Beelzebub with Satan by introducing the terror of a ruling minority which prided itself in seeking the Nietzschean Utopia of the *Ubermensch.* Its outstanding emphasis was on racial-national identity. It was a caricature of a rebellion against the growing cosmopolitan, levelizing super-national historical trend. In a sense it was a defense against losing personal identity by regressing to earlier, more primitive stages of ego development, where ego-identity still existed. It was a neurotic defense against loss of identity on a national scale. The Weimar Constitution was felt as something superimposed upon Germany by the Western powers—which would make Germany like the rest of Western culture—something alien to German racial and national tradition, forcing Germany into a larger orbit threatening its own original qualities, making it cosmopolitan and rational, something which was foreign to its history, in which Germany due to its middle-geographic position surrounded by inimical and alien powers had learned to defend its identity for centuries. The reaction was, on a national scale, what Erikson describes for the individual as seeking identity by regression.[1]

The stress on individualism appeared in still another form in both the fascist and national socialist movements: in the rule by an elite. The more literate Mussolini was strongly influenced by Pareto, who explained all history as a sequence of a recurring cycle: strong individuals come to power by courage, adventure and brutality and introduce an ideology for the masses to keep them in submission; when long in power the ruling elite becomes corrupted and effeminate and is replaced by reckless new adventurers emerging from the subject masses; this new elite

[1] Erik H. Erikson, *Das Problem der Identität, Entfaltung der Psychoanalyse* (Stuttgart, Germany, 1956).

again gradually becomes corrupted and weak, and the cycle starts again. Both Hitler and Mussolini were upshoots and fit well into this historical pattern, which can be applied equally to Communist dictatorships.

Under the surface, and in spite of these ideological eruptions, the inevitable social process was relentlessly progressing toward a mass civilization producing a new species—the communal man. It came to its strongest expression in the United States, where its development was not interrupted by dramatic ideological warfares and social revolutions. It is in process of producing the organization man, the other-directed person, the conformist, the man with a social role but without a well defined and subjectively perceived ego-identity. On the larger social scale, the same movement is seen in the trend toward a global organization of nations which threatens national sovereignty. In its deepest meaning all this is a growing trend toward an impersonal, rational, planful organization of life which threatens the particular, the irrational, the instinctual in man. It is a struggle of multiplicity, the different, the particular, the unique and concrete, against an abstract rational order in which the individual components must sacrifice all those particular features which make their coördination into a sensible statistically conceived system difficult. In such an organization each individual component can only participate in a role, in its similarity to others who fulfill a similar role. Only categories count and not individual differences. This large historical process toward organization and integration of individuals and nations into a sensible rational order gives us the common background from which the particular manifestations of this process, the conflicts which it causes in the life of individuals and nations, becomes intelligible.

It is against this historical process that Kierkegaard was rediscovered and existentialism revived. It is the most verbal, most conscious protest against mass civilization, a desperate attempt to rescue the individual as a unique being capable of self-reflection and creativeness.

First, however, I shall try to illustrate this process of relentlessly progressing organization and institutionalization as I experienced it first hand in my own field, in psychoanalysis. The authenticity of this account is enhanced by the fact that I myself, after I came to the United States, played an active role in these developments.

CHAPTER VII

Psychoanalysis Comes of Age

In 1930 I received from Frankwood Williams, a devoted proponent and organizer of the mental hygiene movement in the United States, an invitation to present my views and findings in the field of criminal psychology at the International Congress for Mental Hygiene to be held in Washington, D. C. This request was the outcome of a book in which Hugo Staub and I presented the results of our joint attempt to apply psychoanalytic concepts to the understanding of the emotional sources of delinquent behavior and to throw light upon penal procedures and the psychology of the judge and the jury.[1]

I was not fully unprepared for this trip. Since 1926, as a training analyst of the Berlin Psychoanalytic Institute, I had accepted a considerable number of American psychiatrists for training analyses. I found that these students differed from their European colleagues in their whole orientation. It was not easy, however, to find the common denominator because they represented a great variety of subcultural groups. In fact, they were a more heterogene-

[1] Franz Alexander and Hugo Staub, *The Criminal, the Judge and the Public* (New York, 1931; originally published in 1929).

ous group than the European students, although the latter came from different countries. There were New Yorkers of intellectual background, a few from New England, from the Middle West, first and second generation immigrants from Russia, Poland and Western Europe, and also native sons of long-established American families. In spite of this heterogeneity, there was a general, intangible congruity among them, which distinguished these American colleagues. With one single exception—a man who later became my collaborator in the United States—their interests were more pragmatic. Theory for them was an aid to practical, useful purposes and not an aim in itself. Emotional investment in abstract generalizations—the indelible heritage of medieval European scholasticism—was foreign to them. Consequently, they were more tolerant toward individual opinions and convictions. Some of them, after they became exposed to the often fanatical ideological warfares among their European colleagues, openly and naïvely expressed their amazement. They simply could not understand all the excitement about theoretical issues which did not seem to have any practical consequences. For them, as told to me by one of my students while free-associating, these issues were as meaningless as the medieval debates about the angels on the point of a pin. Had I known in those days the American cultural scene, I might have foreseen that these American psychiatrists, who came to us in Europe to be trained, were predestined one day to organize practice and teaching in psychoanalytic institutes and societies on a scale not possible in post-war Europe.

In those days I felt only vaguely the dynamic vitality

of this group, which was perhaps less sophisticated in abstract thought, less dedicated to search for truth for its own sake, but which was bent on action, development, and organization.

There is no doubt that the American genius for organization, together with the political upheavals in Europe, soon shifted the center of gravity of psychoanalysis from Europe to the United States, but not without justifying some of Freud's apprehensions, apprehensions which he expressed to me before I departed for the United States. This memorable conversation, however, would take me ahead of my narration; I shall return to it at a later point.

The American students of psychiatry who arrived to Berlin in growing numbers in the second half of the Twenties were not my only source of information about the United States. A number of visitors came to call on me and further aroused my interest in the New World. One day, Dr. Alan Gregg, the Medical Director of the Rockefeller Foundation, came accompanied by Dr. Philip Miller, a professor of internal medicine at the University of Chicago. The evening we spent in the then-famous restaurant, Schwanecke—the hangout of intellectual Berlin during the Weimar Republic—is still in my memory. Both of these learned men dispelled many of my preconceptions about the United States. Gregg's pragmatism was mellowed by his all-around erudition, particularly a profound knowledge of the philosophy of science. This and his selfless dedication to the advancement of medical knowledge made him a most suited emissary of the Rockefeller Foundation to support research and teaching all over the world and to scan the field of medicine for potential original contributors. He was one of the leaders of the American movement to help wartorn Europe in her cultural, particularly her scientific and medical, revival, a movement which was less advertised but just as significant as American aid to Europe for economic reconstruction. Gregg's companion, Dr. Miller, was a research man in pure culture as I knew it in Europe. Neither of these two eminent physicians corresponded to the stereotype of the dollar-minded, practical and superficial American current in Europe in those days.

One day in the late Twenties came Dr. David Riesman, the eminent internist from Philadelphia. When he visited our home in Berlin, he had already passed his sixtieth birthday. At the dinner table, when Dr. Riesman learned that my wife was a Venetian, the conversation shifted to the history of Venice. Riesman amazed us with his profound knowledge of the history of the Venetian doges as it pertained to my wife's family tree. From there, Riesman went on to speak about the history of the Popes and about John XX, who was a physician. This dinner conversation is unforgettable for me. Here was a practicing physician from Philadelphia who strongly reminded me of my father, not only because of his encyclopedic knowledge and interest in European history, but because of the whole humanistic aura which emanated from his gentle personality. "Are these exceptions ?" I asked myself. But my conception of the United States was already thoroughly shaken.

And then, finally, Dr. William Healy of Boston, Director of the famed Judge Baker Foundation and pioneer of the American Child Guidance movement, called on me to discuss the book on criminal psychology on which Hugo Staub and I had collaborated. He challenged our emphasis on the role of the superego in criminal behavior. He and his collaborator, Dr. Augusta Bronner, contended that crime committed as a result of guilty conscience—a mechanism which originally Freud and later Staub and I had elaborated as a common unconscious root of delinquent behavior—was rare in the United States. They maintained that this type of neurotic criminality was primarily a European phenomenon. Crime in the United States, they said, was not so much an individual act, the result of neurotic confusion, but rather a social phenomenon: organized crime, a part of the total social structure. Its understanding was more a sociological than an individual psychological problem. During this discussion, Healy expressed his desire and hope that I would sometime visit the States to convince myself from first-hand experience of the basic differences between European and American criminality. He assured me that such a collaborative study with him would be most revealing for the whole field of criminology.

It was less than three years later that this plan of collaboration was realized. Its results were published in a joint book, *Roots of Crime,* which partially at least substantiated Healy's contentions.[2] Healy was instrumental in my being invited to the Washington International Conference by calling my work to the attention of Frankwood Williams.

Healy had a flair for theory, but what impressed me

[2] Franz Alexander and William Healy, *Roots of Crime* (New York, 1935).

more was his lack of dogmatism and his keen interest in controlled observation. He had a sound clinical orientation. At that time, I sensed already that our field was beginning to lose the proper balance between theoretical superstructure and observational foundation. Theoretical abstractions were threatening to achieve hydrocephalic proportions without the necessary amount of supply of the life blood of science—factual data obtained by controlled observation. As a caustic friend of mind remarked, "Psychoanalysis begins to look like Vienna, a large cultural center without a hinterland."

From all this, it can be seen that I did not go to Washington fully unprepared. The Conference itself was organized on a monumental scale, the likes of which I had not seen before. It seemed to confirm the popular saying that in America everything is bigger: the land and its products, the corn, the chickens, the turkeys, the mountains and the plains, the winds and the rain, the floods and all the natural disasters, the office buildings and the hotels, the political elections, and crime. More than four thousand psychiatrists attended the meeting from all over the world. Apart from the size and the superb organization, the genuine hospitality, the people's avidity to hear new and different thoughts and approaches and, above all, the lack of dogmatic preconceptions, the readiness to try out new ideas, were all new experiences for me.

I found that many of the American psychiatrists had not only an open mind toward psychoanalysis but a compelling curiosity about it. This basic impression was not altered by the violent and emotional attack of my paper by Dr. Karl Menninger, who nevertheless soon after this first encounter came to me in Chicago to undertake his training in psychoanalysis. His intimate friend, Dr. Bartemeier, who also was present at the Congress, was friendlier and soon followed Menninger to Chicago to study psychoanalysis.

At the Congress I met many of the leading psychiatrists and became well acquainted with some of them, such as Smith Ely Jelliffe and William A. White. These men were strongly influenced by Freud's teachings and expressed their belief that American psychiatry was about ready to assimilate Freud's teachings. This attitude of the leading men in official psychiatry was entirely a novel experience for me. In Europe the gulf between university psychiatry and psychoanalysis was wide, and not even the first efforts to build a bridge were visible.

I could not accept entirely the explanation of this open-mindedness of American psychiatry which was current in Europe. It was attributed to a lack of discrimination, to superficiality and disinterest in essentials, and to the propensity to evaluate everything according to its usefulness, efficiency, potential mass appeal, and its business possibilities. White's interest was sincere and profound, and Jelliffe's enthusiasm for the psychological explanation of organic diseases not more uncritical than Groddeck's panpsychism in Germany. Healy's broadmindedness was due to his empirical orientation and had nothing to do with the crude pragmatic credo that if something works it is good. In 1930 there was in the States no bandwagon of psychoanalysis as yet, and even the most perspicacious psychiatrists could not possibly foresee the future victory march of Freud's views.

In any case, I evaluated the reception I met with in Washington differently, and attributed it mainly to genuine curiosity and to a refreshing interest in new ideas, and above all, to an empirical rather than a theoretical or dogmatic orientation, an outcome of the pragmatic heritage of this country. I thought at that time that this might serve as a most needed corrective influence against the static orientation in our field, which threatened to assume almost scholastic proportions. Nevertheless, I could not help but become aware of the utilitarian climate which pervaded all walks of life. It was obvious that knowledge in this new world was subordinated to the dedication to improve the general welfare of the people. This went with a greater social consciousness, with a greater interest in the question of how a new discovery might contribute to social progress rather than of how it independently of any immediate utility increases our basic knowledge about the world. While I knew that this practical orientation was not favorable for pure research, I felt that our field with more than fifty years of intense theoretical preoccupation, was well protected from being vitiated by this overly pragmatic attitude. We psychoanalysts in Europe were primarily interested in understanding the structure and functions of the personality rather than in curing, to do which efficiently we felt our knowledge was not yet far enough advanced. For us, treatment of patients was a source of psychoanalytic knowledge, which in the future could serve as the basis for improved treatment procedures. At the same time I became increasingly convinced that experimentation with new treatment procedures was more than overdue. Already at that time I suspected that the psychoanalytic treatment procedure was still strongly influenced by Freud's original research orientation, which at that time was most appropriate. Then the most urgent need was in research, the exploration of the genetic background of mental illness. I suspected, however, that eventually our by-now-respectable amount of theoretical knowledge would have to serve for finding improved techniques of treatment.

While attending the Congress in Washington, I received a telegram from Chicago signed by Robert Hutchins urging me to visit him to discuss an appointment to the University of Chicago, whose president he had just recently become. A young American psychoanalyst whom I had trained in Berlin drove me through the Shenandoah Valley to Chicago. On this trip the magnitude and youthfulness of the country further impressed me, and I arrived in a most receptive spirit to hear President Hutchins' proposition. He offered me a Visiting Professorship in Psychiatry of one year's duration to introduce psychiatry into the University's Medical School. My counter-suggestion was that I become a Visiting Professor of Psychoanalysis because I intended to teach nothing but psychoanalysis, or possibly psychoanalytic psychiatry. Moreover, to introduce psychoanalysis into a University was a never-abandoned dream of mine. Both President Hutchins and Dr. Franklin McLean, then the Director of University Clinics, hesitated about my title. Even for these two most progressive and experimentally minded persons, a Professorship in Psychoanalysis appeared quite a radical proposition.

I was scheduled to give a public lecture in the afternoon at the campus. My lecture attracted a large crowd, mostly faculty members of the Medical School and the Social Science Division. Some psychologists and some members of the Law School also attended. The ensuing discussion was a veritable surprise for me. Such a dispassionate discussion of an address on this contested field—psychoanalysis—would have been unthinkable at any European university. That evening we signed the contract. Hutchins and McLean accepted my title of Visiting Professor of Psychoanalysis. With this they created a historical precedent, the first university chair for psychoanalysis.

In the meantime, I received an answer to a cable I had sent my wife: "By all means accept invitation. Want to meet my infamous countryman, Al Capone!"

Later I recounted to Alan Gregg a free association I had when I signed the contract with Hutchins and McLean. I suddenly remembered a scene in Jules Verne's novel, *Journey to the Moon,* in which a group of New York businessmen gathered in their Club had consented to finance a European inventor's plan to fire him in a missile to the moon. This was indeed a country of unlimited possibilities, a country where people unimpeded by tradition were willing to try anything, even a university chair for psychoanalysis.

Only on the boat returning to Europe did I begin to question the soundness of my decision. Soon after my arrival I visited Freud to discuss with him my invitation to Chicago and to get his advice on how to approach this difficult assignment. Freud was most dissatisfied with my acceptance of Hutchins' invitation. He was skeptical about its outcome. I have preserved the details of this conversation in as much detail as I could recall in telling them to Dr. Edwin R. Eisler, who recorded them. The transcript of this reconstructed conversation is now deposited in the archives of the Library of Congress, to be opened a hundred years hence because there are references to persons still living. Freud's general attitude toward the United States and some of his prophecies, however, are of great interest, particularly in the light of the later events of the following twenty-nine years. These have largely disproved Freud's expectations. Yet he foresaw some pitfalls in future American developments. He deeply regretted my pending departure for Chicago. He thought that his teachings would be diluted in the United States. "They are interested primarily in material things; what you call genuine interest is highly deceptive," he said to me. He rejected all of my arguments; he said that I misinterpreted as open-mindedness what was merely lack of discrimination. "They are open-minded to everything which is not better than dogmatic rejection; moreover, it is due to a lack of emotional investment in genuine understanding." He was ready to admit that psychoanalysis might even become popular in the States, but it would be a different watered-down eclectic kind of treatment procedure, which would have lost sight of its essentials.

In 1930, the exodus of Central European psychoanalysts had not yet begun, but Freud intuitively foresaw that the lure of the New World would deprive him of the presence of his most faithful disciples. Rank had already left for Philadelphia. In 1930, in the same year I went to Chicago, Rado accepted an invitation to New York. A year later Hanns Sachs went to Boston, Herman Nunberg to Philadelphia, soon followed by Felix and Helene Deutsch to Boston, and later by Walder, Hartman and Kris. There can be no doubt that already at that time Freud considered the American interest in psychoanalysis to be a threat to the integrity of the Central European psychoanalytic societies, which followed him faithfully through so many years in his great scientific venture. His negative reaction to my Chicago invitation was at least partially determined by these only too human sentiments. Freud knew psychoanalysis only as a revolutionary force and could not well visualize its development and influence after it had become an integral part of contemporary culture and an accepted part of medical practice and teaching. He feared that in the United States psychoanalysis would be corrupted by opportunism and would abandon its principles in order to become more acceptable to the medical fraternity and the public.

Credit must be given to the rapidly growing community of American psychoanalysts that none of these expectations of Freud came true. The American Psychoanalytic Association, if anything, became overly conservative in upholding almost everything for which Freud stood, both in theory and practice. This was largely due to the influence of the European disciples of Freud, who, when they came to this country, knew only too well Freud's reservations. Forced by world events to leave their master, they compensated by leaning over backwards and by withholding sympathy from any departure, from anything which could appear as compromise or deviation.

During my memorable interview, Freud expressed his misgivings without any reservations. He intimated that I was too optimistic and even gullible. He said, "They took you in in Chicago. I know from my own experiences in the States that masterful way of giving lip service." He generously gave me credit for my insistence on being called Professor of Psychoanalysis instead of Psychiatry, knowing that this title would considerably increase the difficulties of being accepted by the University. This insistence of mine allayed Freud's fears that I might yield to compromise. Yet, his parting sentence was: "I hope America will leave something intact of the real Alexander." Later he repeated this sentence in a letter written to Chicago.

My first year in Chicago certainly seemed to justify Freud's predictions that psychoanalysis, if presented faithfully in its undiluted form, would not be accepted in the United States. Much of what I originally interpreted as open-minded acceptance turned out not to be too meaningful. Moreover, it was restricted to a small progressive group of social scientists at the University of Chicago, men like Ogburn, Lasswell, Schlesinger, Dollard, and a few philosophers and lawyers. The medical faculty as a whole was both uninformed and prejudiced. Their prejudice in a sense was more tantalizing than that of the European variety; it was based on complete rather than partial ignorance and was therefore unassailable by arguments. Psychiatry was not represented in the medical school and only existed in a most rudimentary form in the city. Therefore, I had hoped I might start with a *tabula rasa* and would not have to contend with correcting existing misinformation.

At the first staff luncheon of the medical faculty my presence remained completely unnoticed. By a curious coincidence I was seated between a neurosurgeon and a young neurologist from Yugoslavia. Franklin McLean, who sponsored my appointment, had not yet returned from his European vacation, and nobody spoke a single word to me.

After McLean's return I was notified that no lecture room had been assigned to me in the medical school and that I was supposed to give a lecture course in the Social Science Division on personality development. McLean quickly sized up the situation and suggested that I give an orientation course on psychoanalysis to all members of the medical faculty. He personally invited them in a circular letter.

As an introduction, in order to acquaint my audience with some factual evidence for the existence of unconscious mental activity, I began my first lecture by discussing Charcot's and Bernheim's experiments with hypnosis. In the discussion which followed my lecture, one young physiologist asked me whether psychoanalysis is an experimental science. I answered that I had not spoken as yet about psychoanalysis, but added that psychoanalysis is not an experimental science. It is based on clinical observation obtained through verbal communication. Whereupon he declared that psychoanalysis then is not a science and he was not interested in attending my course. Not waiting for the end of the discussion, he left the room followed by part of my audience.

Discouraged, I wrote to Freud about this episode. In his reply he suggested that I ask my audience at my next lecture whether they considered astronomy and paleontology real sciences, since one cannot experiment with the stars or with fossils. He was obviously more amused than irritated by the incredible epistomological naïvete of these doctors. However, his letter was not written at all in the spirit of I-told-you-so. He encouraged me to go through with this venture and to do my best. I certainly needed this encouragement because I was about ready to give up. Dr. McLean also urged me to continue the course, which from then on was attended by a small number of seriously interested physicians, mostly internists. Some of them have retained their interest in the psychological aspects of medicine into the present.

Concurrently with this course directed to physicians, a spontaneous group formed itself in the Social Science Division to discuss the sociological implications of psychoanalytic theory. This group consisted of some of the leading authorities in anthropology, psychology, social and political sciences and economy. Hutchins, Ogburn, Lasswell, Adler, T. V. Smith, Thurston, Dollard, Miller, Knight, Merriam attended these meetings regularly. This was the group which originally supported my attempts to introduce psychoanalytic thought into the university. Their comprehension of psychoanalysis was far advanced in comparison with that of the medical faculty, where I scarcely succeeded in making a dent. With the exception of a small number of physicians, the medical faculty remained at first aloof and then growingly hostile. In a campaign of personal accusations of fantastic nature which had been started against me, I received only lukewarm support from the university administration. Yet, in the third quarter a lecture room was assigned to me in the medical school. There were no further incidents, and my lectures on psychoanalysis were exceptionally well attended by senior medical students and a few faculty members. In the same quarter, the Law School asked me to conduct a seminar on Penal Psychology. Looking back on that venturesome year, I believe that, in spite of the resistance the medical faculty put up against psychoanalysis, I succeeded in arousing interest in this new point of view and in conveying some basic concepts as a seed for future developments.

My extension course of ten lectures which the University arranged for the laity in the large hall of the Art Institute was attended to capacity, and earned the university my whole salary for one year. Outside of the medical faculty, the rest of the university as well as the community at large was at that time just about ready to give sympathetic hearing to Freud's teachings and to assimilate their essentials.

In spite of a formal defeat—the experiment with psychoanalysis was discontinued by the university—I left Chicago with the conviction that even the medical fraternity was almost ripe for the incorporation of this new psychological avenue of approach to the study and treatment of the human organism.

I knew well the prevailing sentiments about psychoanalysis in Europe. The resistance I met in Chicago was of quite a different nature. First of all, in Europe the feud between Freud and the medical profession was still a living historical reality. Official European psychiatry, as well as the larger medical community, had to vindicate the initial, mainly emotionally founded rejection of Freud. They stubbornly refused to give a fair test to the

Freudian discoveries. Here in the United States all this was past history. The American medical community—with a few exceptions such as Bernard Sachs, the neurologist—never was involved in this feud. Even Adolph Meyer, before he turned his back on psychoanalysis, gave glowing credit to Freud's theory of delusions of persecution. The resistance of the medical men in America was based primarily on an astounding lack of sophistication in the philosophical principles of science in general. I felt that this was an easier barrier to take than the deeply rooted vindictiveness of the European physicians.

There was still another factor to be considered. In the United States, as in Europe, the fiercest and most stubborn resistance against psychoanalysis came from the medical community. Freud's teachings, here as in Europe, gradually penetrated literature, influenced the thinking of social philosophers, and the general public increasingly assimilated its fundamentals. Just as Darwin's theory of evolution or the Copernican system in astronomy in the past, now infantile sexuality, the theory of the "dynamic unconscious," the fundamental fact of repression, the explanation of psychoneurosis, dreams, slips of the tongue from unconscious unacceptable tendencies, the function of unconscious fantasies in artistic creation, became the common property of the intelligent layman. At least thirty years have passed since Freud by attacking Victorian repressions was "disturbing the sleep of humanity." This discrepancy between public acceptance and medical rejection of Freud's teachings prevailed both in Europe and in America, as can be clearly seen from the warm understanding I received on the part of the non-medical members of the university and from my rejection by the physicians. In America, however, public opinion has a different —a more powerful—influence even upon the professions. In Europe a professor in a university is an autonomous king, responsible only to his own conscience. The faculty likewise is impervious to the demands and pressures of the general public. Herein lies both the strength and the weakness of the European university. It is more autonomous, so far as public opinion is concerned, and can therefore pursue its academic activities undisturbed by outside pressures. Its weakness consists in the resulting conservatism. Governed only by academic tradition, new ideas can be more easily rejected. This is particularly true of ideas which blatantly contradict academic tradition, and which, therefore, sometimes are more readily accepted by outsiders—by the representatives of related disciplines and even by the enlightened public—than by professionals. This was also true of psychoanalysis, a discipline which deals with the problems of human existence, bordering on art and literature.

The first years spent in Chicago had taught me how energetically the general public demanded to be informed authentically about psychoanalysis. I knew that this type of public pressure would have—not as in Europe—a powerful influence upon the fate of psychoanalysis in the United States. I foresaw that the American public, which in political life has learned not to entrust its fate blindly to its representatives but watches them and influences them perpetually, would take the same attitude in the fields of education and even in public health. The so-called experts do not enjoy the same blind confidence of the people as in

Europe. I was ready to apply these insights to my policies.

After leaving Chicago I spent a year in Boston in collaboration with William Healy of the Judge Baker Foundation, whom I knew from his visit in Berlin. We subjected a number of delinquents to psychoanalytic treatment and used this material for reconstructing the roots of criminality in this country. In the meantime, in Chicago a young group of leading private citizens, businessmen, a physician, a lawyer, a professor of the social sciences got together. They did not accept the failure of the University of Chicago experiment with psychoanalysis as final and asked me to organize a Psychoanalytic Institute and to take over its direction.

Although I considered the University of Chicago experiment as a near miss, it nevertheless demonstrated to me that I was over-optimistic in hoping that the University was ready to accept psychoanalysis. The logical step was, therefore, to create for psychoanalysis a small university of its own, thus preparing the way for the eventual integration of this new discipline into a university setting. When Freud withdrew from the medical profession and created his own Society, his own code of practice, his own teaching institutions, his own press, he did all this with a sense of finality. When I accepted the invitation to found a psychoanalytic institute, I undertook this task with a different orientation. I considered the foundation of separate psychoanalytic institutes as something transient, an intermediary step leading eventually to the only logical goal, the integration of this new branch with the rest of medicine, taught to psychiatrists in universities as a fundamental part of their residency training. Inasmuch as psychoanalysis also applies to the field of education and the social sciences, its sociological and educational applications should be incorporated into the respective university departments.

I took as a model the Berlin Institute for Psychoanalysis, in the development of which I was active, first as a student and later as a teacher. However, consistent with my evaluation of the future of psychoanalysis in this country, I tried to introduce important modifications. These pertained principally to public relations, particularly to our attitude towards the medical profession in general. I believed that the era of "splendid isolation" was over. It did not make sense to me to assume here the same attitude which was determined by the history of psychoanalysis in Europe and did not fit into the American cultural scene, and to continue a feud with the medical fraternity which originated in Europe but which had no historical foundation in this country.

I decided to make the Institute an integral part of Chicago's medical community. Shortly after opening our school, I announced an orientation course in psychoanalysis to which key members of the medical profession were invited. Such leading personalities as Ludwig Hektoen, the Nestor of pathologists in Chicago, Morris Fishbein, Editor-in-Chief of the *Journal of the American Medical Association,* Peter Basso, eminent Professor of Neurology, and a considerable number of internists, gynecologists, dermatologists and other specialists came regularly to my weekly presentations. The psychosomatic interest of quite a few of these physicians originated in this lecture course, which called their attention not only to the psychological aspects of medicine but to psychiatry itself. It can be said without exaggeration that since its inception, the Chicago Psychoanalytic Institute has encountered no animosity on the part of the medical community, which readily accepted the Institute in its fold.

At the same time, we also remained in touch with the general public through our popular pamphlets, annual reports, public lectures and discussions. We tried to dispel any mystery and secrecy about psychoanalysis, and presented its fundamentals frankly and meaningfully. The growing staff adopted these policies readily as something natural, and the Institute developed without any internal dissension. The only major strife developed in relationship to Dr. Karen Horney, whom I had invited from Berlin to become my associate in the direction of the Institute. I knew her abilities from Berlin and admired her independent thinking. I did not know, however, the deeply rooted resentment she harbored against Freud. After a brief period of collaboration we severed our relationship and Thomas French became her successor. Horney's resentment against Freud expressed itself in her attempts to discredit some of his most fundamental contributions, with the ambitious goal of revising the whole psychoanalytic doctrine, a task for which she was not fully prepared. She had excellent critical faculties but did not succeed in supplying anything substantially new and valid for what she tried to destroy.

In addition to lecturing to the medical community, we arranged meetings with social scientists, an enterprise which gradually wore off. In fact, the social scientists needed us less and less as the analytical point of view penetrated their own departments. Some members of our staff, particularly Helen McLean, made significant contributions to the psychology of race relations and, in an informal manner, to the study of changes in public opinion.

The most significant deviation from the European psychoanalytic schools was our emphasis on research, which for years remained our principal objective. This emphasis was the natural outcome of the general orientation of our staff toward psychoanalysis. It can be said that we were more impressed by what we did not know in the field of human psychology and psychotherapy than by what we knew. Why this should have been so is not difficult to comprehend. While I may consider myself as belonging to the second generation of psychoanalysts, most of my collaborators in Chicago were of the third and even fourth generation. Some of them had come to Berlin for their training analysis with me, some of them I had trained in the States before the Institute was opened. The attitude of this younger generation of analysts was naturally somewhat different from that of the founding fathers. These original disciples of Freud were dazzled by the novel discoveries of their master, which opened up an entirely new world for them, the hitherto unexplored field of the unconscious mind. Almost all aspects of human behavior appeared now in a new light. All that seemed before to be irrational and hence unintelligible—dreams, neurotic and psychotic symptoms, impulsive self-destructive behavior—found plausible explanations. The irrational in man—and more is irrational than rational in him—suddenly appeared comprehensible. Spinoza's ideal, the subjugation of impulses and emotions to the rational mind, came in the realm of possibility. Moreover, this first generation of psychoanalysts felt the brunt of the total impact of a revolting kind of prejudice and thoughtless rejection. It was quite natural that they considered their principal function to be the defense of the severely attacked new truth. And there was so much to do, to apply the new fundamental principles to the understanding of the entire range of human activities. The defense of the newly won insight and its applications became their main concern rather than the further development of theory, not to speak of its critical revision. Advancement of knowledge requires the critical appraisal of existing knowledge. On the battlefield there is no time to examine critically the efficiency of one's weapons; one has to use them. Being consistently criticized and challenged does not promote self-criticism; it stimulates self-vindication and counterattacks. It is easy to denounce the attitude of this first generation as dogmatic. Being completely rejected, they were maneuvered into the position of the defenders of the true faith. And yet, what they defended was not faith but hard-won convictions based on thorough observations. Certainly this was true of the best of the first disciples.

In the history of human thought this is a typical cycle: new advancement in theory strangely enough has the tendency to make the erstwhile pioneers adhere stubbornly to their once viciously attacked achievements. The merits of the once-new discoveries having proved so great in the past, the average scientist, because of the inertia inherent in human thought, is anything but enthusiastic about changing them. Advancement of knowledge, however, means change; it necessitates the abandonment or modification of older theoretical concepts, their replacement with improved formulations.

The history of psychoanalysis demonstrates this universal pattern of thought development. Among the second generation of psychoanalysts there were several who had more inclination toward critical evaluation of the original theoretical concepts, although the majority still tried to perpetuate the heroic past in the undaunted faithful defense of the Freudian heritage.

The Chicago atmosphere of acceptance was eminently suited to encourage a more self-critical, more research-minded attitude. Our first and most important step was the organization of a collective research project in which different members of the staff were studying similar cases. They were constantly comparing their observations with those of the other members of the team. The observations were quite systematically—if not yet mechanically—recorded. In regular group discussions, the findings and reasonings of the individual investigators were tested against each other. In psychoanalysis this type of collaborative research was long overdue. By the very nature of psychoanalytic treatment, psychoanalysts are, scientifically speaking, lone wolves. Observation made during treatment is the main source of psychoanalytic knowledge. This highly elusive observational material, if not recorded, is lost for further scrutiny. Discretion is another obstacle for detailed exchange of findings with each other. Moreover, private practice isolates the practitioners from each other to a very high degree. Only work in an institution permits steady daily contact among the research workers and the type of exchange of findings which is an essential condition of any empirical research.

For many years I was attracted by psychosomatic problems. I was impressed by the fact that in other scientific fields, such as physics and chemistry, advancements in knowledge frequently occur in the borderline fields where techniques of two different disciplines aid each other. Borderline fields also give excellent opportunity for testing the validity of theoretical formulations obtained in one field but with implications for a bordering field. The same phenomenon being approached by two independent techniques allows checking the reliability of the original formulations. The modern achievements of physics and chemistry to a large degree took place in the borderline area between physics and chemistry.

Choosing the area of psychosomatics for collective research was further motivated by my lifelong fascination with the body-mind problem. Also, from the point of view of the Institute's policies, psychosomatic research was an excellent choice. It required collaboration with other physicians and thus favored the assimilation of psychoanalysis within the larger body of medicine.

Our teaching policies too were dictated by the overall orientation of the Institute. The original curriculum of the Berlin Institute divided the training into two subsequent sections: theoretical indoctrination was followed by clinical training, which mainly consisted of the supervision of the candidate's work with patients and of clinical seminars in which individual cases treated by the students were discussed. For the first few years I followed this pattern in the Chicago Institute, but soon we shifted the emphasis upon clinical instruction. We started the clinical training somewhat earlier so that it overlapped to a high degree with the theoretical instruction. The underlying philosophy was to teach theory on the basis of the students' own experience with clinical cases, instead of trying to impart to the students a rather rigid theoretical system which they should then apply to their cases.

My main concern was not to allow the teaching in the Institute to deteriorate into dogmatic indoctrination and to expose psychoanalytic theory to the students in the spirit of a critical historical evaluation.

As time went on the teaching program became increasingly organized and stabilized all over the country. Concurrently with the Chicago developments similar institutes sprang up in New York, Boston, Philadelphia, Topeka, San Francisco, Washington and Los Angeles, to be followed later by smaller study groups in other cities. The American Psychoanalytic Association began gradually to take over responsibility for working out "minimum standards" of training and to supervise the activities of the local teaching institutes. More and more I became convinced that Freud's fears that in the United States his teachings might be diluted were unfounded. In fact, developments tended toward the opposite direction. If anything, a growing standardization and organization aimed at the solidification of basic standards characterized the American developments. Many of the leading American psychoanalysts felt the danger that this new field would be a free-for-all for poorly or self-trained physicians and even for quacks, and that soon a distinction between the well-trained psychoanalyst and these pseudo-analysts would become impossible. To protect the development of psychoanalysis from such deterioration, they went to the other extreme, setting up strict regulations and minimum standards and insisting on rather uniform instruction all over the country. The majority of the leaders were unaware of the dangers which this policy entailed, namely, of freezing our field prematurely and interfering with much needed therapeutic experimentation and revision of theoretical abstractions.

There was, however, a strong minority group following the leadership of the Chicago Institute, which opposed this trend toward a rigid and uniform organization of training. They believed that in our young field progress would necessarily come from individual initiative, experimentation with different systems of training and treatment practices. Soon the psychoanalytic community was divided into two groups: those who were satisfied with the status quo in theory and practice, and consequently wanted to organize the training and stabilize its standards on this level; and a less contented group, analysts who keenly felt the need to advance and reëxamine theoretical views, and even more to test the validity of treatment practices which had been more or less uncritically preserved and perpetuated by habit. Many of us felt the desperate need to experiment with new therapeutic applications of the solidly established psychodynamic principles. This group wanted to grant greater autonomy to the local institutions and favored individual differences. We foresaw the dangers of prematurely freezing the training and treatment practices at their present level. We knew that the therapeutic factors of psychoanalysis were far from being precisely understood, that the therapeutic results were painfully unpredictable, that interminable analyses were not always due to the severity of the patient's disease but to the deficiencies of the treatment techniques and to our relative ignorance. Often we could not account for the reasons why certain patients improved while others resisted treatment or even reacted unfavorably.

It is revealing that this controversy soon crystallized itself around highly formal and not necessarily essential details. The two groups opposed each other on such issues as whether or not patients should be required to be seen at least four times a week. Another controversial issue was whether or not minimum length for a training analysis should be precisely required. While the status-quo party insisted on definite quantitative regulations—for example, a minimum of three hundred sessions for the training analysis of a candidate—the other group wanted to leave such technical and quantitative details to the highly varying exigencies of each individual case. They insisted that the therapeutic activities of training analysts should not be policed and controlled by rigid rules, that the conduct of the analysis of their trainees should be left to the conscience and judgment of the training analysts. One can follow the letter of the law and still violate its spirit. Many of us had a very strong apprehension that this type of uniformity and formalization of the training could not but lead eventually to its deterioration and even to a stagnation of the whole field, a field so badly in need of further advancement.

Together with a number of colleagues I had strong reservations about allowing this organization fervor to take the upper hand, foreseeing the dangers that rigid enforcement of existing practical rules—many of them sanctioned only by tradition and not by real evidence—might paralyze initiative and perpetuate our field at its present unsatisfactory state.

This controversy became more and more accentuated and began to threaten the unity of the American Psychoanalytic Association. On local levels several splits had taken place. Philadelphia and Los Angeles each had two societies, New York even more than two societies, divided mainly on this issue. In order to avert a split on a national level, I met in a private summit meeting with two outstanding members of the more organizationally minded group. The spirit of the times—the universal trend toward organization, standardization and uniformity—was on their side. Accordingly, at this meeting a compromise was worked out in which only little concessions were made to the policies which I have stood for. I accepted this compromise mainly because I felt that at this phase of its development the American Psychoanalytic Association could not well afford a split on a national level. Such a split appeared to me to jeopardize the undisturbed development of psychoanalysis in this country, which in spite of Freud's misgivings has taken over world leadership in this field. It seemed unavoidable to me to accept a temporary recrudescence of the conservative point of view.

The two parties did not oppose each other in their views about psychoanalytic theory nor concerning the basic principles of treatment. They differed in the degree of their acceptance of the present state of affairs, in the degree of their satisfaction with present-day practices and in their flexibility with regard to teaching and treatment.

I had still another reason for accepting this compromise, although it allowed only a very limited flexibility in teaching and treatment procedures. Those who insisted upon the general enforcement of minimum training standards had an important practical point in their favor. They argued that, because psychoanalysis developed outside the officially accepted academic institutions, it had no protection against self-styled psychoanalysts. The past dissensions which took place earlier in Europe were not encouraging. Jung's, Adler's and, later, Rank's deviations pertained to the very fundamentals of psychoanalysis, and by any scientific standards they constituted a regression from the few cornerstones of arduously achieved sound knowledge. The general public, however, had no ways of forming judgments about these particular "schools." The proponents of strict organization felt that it was our obligation to protect the public from all kinds of misrepresentations. This required tightening of the organizational structure of the Association, thus increasing its authority both towards the public and new students. They pointed out to me that, with my European background, I could not fully recognize the dangers of a wild and uncontrolled growth of fads in practice and thought. In this free country tradition and authority has a less restraining influence against wild developments, they said; the only remedy lies in strict organizational measures. They said they knew this country better than I and were afraid of an "anything goes" abuse of the slogan of freedom.

In our summit conference these practical arguments convinced me more than all the other more philosophical considerations, and I reconciled myself to the necessity to seeing the pendulum swing for a while in the direction of control, regulation and consolidation—until the time comes again for a turn towards greater fluidity and for advancement achieved by individual initiative and freedom.

The revision of our therapeutic procedures, nevertheless, appears to me imperative. This is an aspect of psychoanalysis in which it is most difficult to accept the policy of patiently waiting for the advent of a freer atmosphere. The current therapeutic procedure was developed by Freud primarily for research purposes. He justifiedly took the position that at first the nature of the disease one tries to remedy must be understood. It is lucky, he said, that in our field the aims of therapy and research run parallel. In order to be cured, the patient must learn about the genetic background of his illness, which is precisely also the goal of psychoanalytic research. By this argument Freud could convince himself that, while treating his patients, he could study human psychology and at the same time offer some therapeutic help. No matter how one may feel about the limited effectiveness and lack of economy of psychoanalytic treatment, even today it is still the best procedure we have.

The parallelism between the goals of treatment and research, as all scientific formulations, is only approximately correct. As time goes on, it is becoming clearer that the emotional experiences which take place during treatment are equally or probably more important therapeutically than intellectual insight. Many psychoanalytic patients become free of their symptoms and undergo deep personality changes without much intellectual understanding of the factors which were responsible for their becoming neurotics, and many others who acquire quite a penetrating understanding of the historic background of their personality problems do not change appreciably.

The practical conclusions from this fact have far-reaching technical consequences. If the proposition is valid that the most significant therapeutic factor consists in the patient's interpersonal experiences during treatment, many aspects of the treatment procedure must be altered. The challenge before us is to transform the psychoanalytic method of treatment, which in its original form was primarily devised for research, into a more effective, more economical, more reliable therapeutic tool. The response to this challenge appears at present in the form of persistent experimentation with so-called psychoanalytically oriented psychotherapy, in which both psychoanalysts and other analytically oriented psychiatrists are engaged. If the psychoanalytic institutes due to conservatism and inertia do not take up this challenge, they will soon lose their influence upon the development of psychiatry in America. The challenge is here, and if the institutes do not accept it, other groups of dynamically oriented psychiatrists will. This would be deplorable because no group other than the psychoanalysts themselves is more qualified to forge from psychoanalytic principles a more efficient therapeutic instrument.

The gap between the treatment procedure as practiced by experienced analysts and what is taught to students is rapidly widening. The institutes do not fulfill their educational obligations if they remain content with training their candidates in a procedure mainly devised for research and if they leave it entirely up to the students to find out on their own in the course of their practice how to become effective therapists. This is clearly reflected in the statement which a recent graduate of a psychoanalytic institute—who was considered in his school a prize student—made to me: "Now that I have finished my training and started my practice, I feel that I have to forget almost everything I was taught in the institute and begin to learn on my own."

I do not present these developments here as I experienced them during the past thirty years to justify the views and the policies I have adopted in developing the Chicago Psychoanalytic Institute. In the light of the events of the last thirty years, such a justification is not needed. I do not attempt in this chapter to prove the merits of my perspective on the future of psychoanalysis. I have taken the opportunity of demonstrating the general trend toward increased organization and uniformity in my own field which I know so well, in which I grew up intellectually, and in which I followed different pathways always to satisfy my own curiosities.

If I had any doubts about the all-pervasive nature of this worldwide trend toward organization and uniformity, the recent history of psychoanalysis in the United States dispelled them thoroughly. It is a most telling evidence for the universality of this cultural current that even psychoanalysis came so thoroughly under its sway—a field devoted to the understanding of the most individual features of every person, a field in which differences are in the focus of interest, a field which shuns the statistical handling of human beings and studies each on his own merits.

This trend toward uniformity is obviously a historically determined necessity. Yet it should not prevent those who oppose it in their hearts from preparing for a time of revival of individual initiative and expression. The world needs both kinds of minds: those who try to protect and conserve what we have now and those who are relentlessly driven toward new explorations.

Part Two

THE ADVENT OF THE STATISTICAL MAN

CHAPTER VIII

The Role of the Scientist in Society

"Philosophy separated itself from Science when it asked the question: What type of knowledge of the world and life makes man happiest? This happened in the Socratic schools. This point of view —happiness—ligated the artery of scientific investigation—and it does it still today."

NIETZSCHE

Perhaps nothing highlights more impressively the change in our outlook and values than the radical change in the scientist's place in present-day society. He has come down from his Olympian seclusion to teach man the secret of fire. In my own lifetime the emphasis has shifted from knowing as an aim in itself to building, producing, curing —advancing general welfare.

The profound influence of scientific discoveries upon social life can justly be considered the most outstanding fact of our times. This influence is all-pervasive. No aspect of life, spiritual or material, remains unaffected by the advancement of the natural sciences. It has changed our view of the universe and our social, economic and political relations. It affects our health, our life expectancy, our habits and comforts, our family relationships, and our feelings toward each other and toward ourselves.

Nothing demonstrates more impressively this unique influence of scientific advancement upon social change than the history of the last three hundred years. These three centuries, during which natural science in its modern sense appeared as a novel phenomenon, have been characterized by an unprecedented acceleration of social change. In contrast, the previous eight hundred years of the Middle Ages, during which scientific activity was at an almost complete standstill, were static.

A similarly static picture, characterized by slow gradual change, is typical of the so-called primitive cultures. In these cultures many highly developed creative activities can be observed, such as all kinds of art expression—dancing, sculpture and the decorative arts—but there is a complete absence of science in its modern sense. Their social institutions, economic procedures, habits and customs, and psychological attitudes show a conspicuously slow change.

The intimate correlation between scientific advancement and rapid social change has become most apparent during the last one hundred and fifty years, since the beginning of the so-called Industrial Revolution. If the expression "industrial revolution" refers to the revolutionizing effect of technological advancement upon society, the last fifty years deserve this description more than any other period of history. The influence of electricity, of the combustion engine, of electronics, and of atomic discoveries, together with automation and mass production, has completely transformed all aspects of our life. We are living in a time of constant and confusingly rapid change which leaves no aspect of human life unaffected.

To philosophers, historians, economists and political scientists, this profound social effect of the natural sciences has been known for a considerable time. It required the dramatic example of the atomic bomb, however, to impress this fact upon the general public. With a sudden stroke, the forgotten man of the laboratory came into the limelight and became Public Hero Number One, overshadowing the business executive, the entrepreneur and the political leader who had held the stage heretofore. Not only did the general public discover the scientist, previously known only from cartoons as an absent-minded professor, but the government also discovered him. The development of science became the concern of the government; federal subsidy, organization and planning of scientific research became the foremost topic of the first decade after the war. For the first time in history, the scientist appeared on the stage of national life in a new role: he appeared before congressional and military committees. The ivory tower of the scientist was liquidated almost overnight with the advent of the atomic explosion. The physicist all of a sudden appeared in the limelight. He had finally produced something tangible, the immediate importance of which for the fate of nations became obvious even to the least sophisticated minds. Physical research became public concern, and with this both the anonymity and autonomy of the scientists came to an abrupt end. The government and the armed forces rapidly began to take over direction, supervision and financing of research, which was largely applied rather than pure. Secrecy was introduced into a field whose lifeblood was free communication of findings and theories. In place of individual creativity, the practical applications of what is already known became the paramount concern, if not of the scientists themselves, at least of the political authorities.

In my analytic work I had repeated opportunity to observe the conflict which their new social role aroused in scientists. This new type of social prestige tempted many "pure scientists" into administrative or executive assignments and into committee work, and thus gave them an opportunity to share public esteem with businessmen and politicians. For example, a leading natural scientist, the son of a well-to-do businessman, in spite of his achievements and fame in the narrow circle of his professional confrères, always felt himself an outsider in his affluent family and among his friends. While still a student, he started his own business quite successfully, but his scientific leanings won out and he returned to his studies. During treatment he recognized that, even after he had become a leader in his field, he retained the predilection to mix with businessmen and appear as one of them. He noticed that he relied to a great degree on the traditional symbols of social status, having large expensive automobiles and giving sumptuous dinner parties. With some hesitation he gave in to invitations to join important administrative and political committees, and more and more of his time was spent in such assignments. Thoroughly as he disliked this type of work, he accepted it to satisfy his urge for social status, for he felt that in American society only success in business and politics gave social recognition. Now, at last, he became, in the eyes of his older friends and the general public, equal in importance to his father and younger brother. But gradually the conflict between his genuine scientific interests and his desire for social prestige assumed neurotic proportions and he sought psychiatric help. During treatment he spoke a great deal about many fellow scientists who had the same problem. They started out as promising and dedicated research workers but after attaining some reputation they yielded to the same temptation to become committeemen and administrators. He asked himself: Will this trend dry up scientific advancement if the best brains become thus deflected from their original creative careers ?

The repercussions of this trend appeared among scientists themselves around the issue of freedom of science. Creativity and freedom are inseparable. Science, bent on the exploration of the unknown, cannot be blueprinted as a factory which employs already acquired knowledge.

In spite of the new public interest in science, there is a widespread popular misunderstanding concerning scientific research and its influence upon society. Only one obvious fact is appreciated—the practical application of the basic sciences, mathematics, physics and chemistry—to industry. This, of course, is the most conspicuous link in the causal chain of those events by which science exerts its transforming effect upon society: it is on the surface and it is obvious. The cornerstone of Marxian philosophy is recognition of the all-pervasive influence of the forms and means of economic production upon all social life, including the so-called ideological superstructure. Unfortunately, emphasis upon a single obvious correlation in the complex network of interrelated phenomena very often becomes the source of fateful error and misunderstanding. Technological development itself is not the first link in the chain of events by which science exerts its influence upon society. The most important scientific developments take place before knowledge is converted into practical use.

The first century and a half of scientific development which began with the Renaissance, spreading from Italy all over Europe, had no great transforming effect upon society. The work of Galileo, Copernicus, Kepler, Newton and Dalton had no immediate application to technology and did not transform at all the private and social lives of the people. There was a long latency period during which scientific knowledge was advanced for its own sake and with no concern for its utility. Toward the close of the Eighteenth Century, as with an explosion, the theoretical knowledge of the pure scientists began to exert its cumulative effect upon society. It was put to practical use in the form of technology.

The same pattern remained true during the Nineteenth Century as progress in the natural sciences and in technology gained momentum. The non-utilitarian work of Faraday, Ampère and Galvani on the nature of electricity preceded the electric bulb, the telephone and telegraph and the dynamo. The purely theoretical research of Maxwell and Hertz in electrodynamics made possible the radio. Understanding of atomic structure and radioactivity, achieved by the completely detached investigation of such scientists as Thompson, Rutherford, Becquerel, the

Curies, Bohr and many other theoreticians, prepared the way for the atomic bomb. Construction of the bomb itself was mainly an engineering accomplishment, for it involved the application of basic knowledge which had been accumulated much earlier. Because of its dramatic nature, this engineering feat captured universal interest, but the general public overlooked the important fact that the knowledge which made the bomb possible was acquired by men who were exclusively interested in learning about the nature of the atom and who were completely unconcerned about any possible future practical technological usefulness of their investigations.

In our technological era, most people consider science to be primarily directed to the improvement of human comfort and welfare. They consider the scientist to be a man whose primary concern is to discover things which make life easier and healthier or to make war more destructive. Nothing is further from the truth. Such a view overlooks the most important phase in the series of events by which science achieves such a social significance, namely the creative phase, the detached search of the scientist for knowledge for its own sake. This completely non-utilitarian preoccupation of scientists with truth, motivated by nothing but the desire to increase their knowledge of nature, is the essential accomplishment. The later development and application of this basic knowledge for practical use is, in spite of its great value, only secondary. Overlooking the primary significance of the creative, non-utilitarian activity of the scientist causes a grave misconception of science and of the ways and means by which it can best be promoted. This misconception may lead eventually to a complete standstill of scientific development and, if it prevails, may profoundly influence the history of mankind at this crucial phase of its development. At this time, therefore, when the advancement, organization, and subsidy of scientific research have become central concerns of public interest, it is of utmost importance to understand the psychology of the scientist and the real nature of scientific research.

What makes the scientist tick is the crucial question. Let us turn first to the testimony of the scientist himself.

We take our point of departure from a recent controversy among British scientists over this very question. It arose from a movement between 1929 and 1933 in England which was directed toward the central planning of scientific research, applying to it the basic tenets of Marxian philosophy. This point of view has been most consistently expressed by Bernal in a treatise on science and its social function.[1] Bernal believes that science should be reorganized and centrally planned so that it can serve what he believes to be its true social function: the promotion of human welfare. He denies justification to the pursuit of science merely for the sake of discovering truth, independent of its practical value. He finds it absurd for any country to pay scientists just to search for truth.

It was not until 1939 that these attacks against the autonomy of science, which essentially attempt to apply to it the principles of Marxian philosophy, were answered by a Manchester professor of chemistry, M. Polanyi.[2] To

[1] J. D. Bernal, *The Social Function of Science* (London, 1939).
[2] M. Polanyi, "The Rights and Duties of Science," *Manchester Economist* (October, 1939).

defend the autonomy of research, Polanyi and other British physicists, chemists and biologists organized the Society for Freedom in Science. Since Polanyi's article, others have been published on this topic, one of the most outstanding being a book by Professor Baker.[3]

This controversy in England preceded by several years the construction of the atomic bomb. After Hiroshima it was revived in the United States and it is still an open issue. The need of scientists for autonomy in research and for the right to follow their own curiosities and inclinations freely, without any other aim but knowledge for its own sake, was challenged by the appearance of the atomic bomb. The bomb came as a *demonstratio ad oculos* of what dangerous results scientific research might produce. Considerations of national defense made it imperative that atomic research be put under some kind of public control. The violent controversy about the military versus civilian control is only one aspect of this whole issue. While all this took place, it was again completely overlooked that research in pure science and research in technology, although related, are by no means identical procedures; they are not psychologically related nor are their social implications the same.

This whole controversy centers on two fundamental questions: (1) the nature of research, both in pure science and in applied science, and (2) the social implications of research. On the one hand, men of science insist upon the highly individual nature of work in the pure sciences, which is directed toward increasing knowledge for its own sake. On the other hand, society, which has gradually be-

[3] J. R. Baker, *Science and the Planned State* (New York, 1945).

gun to recognize the far-reaching practical implications of the detached work of scientists, claims the right to direct and control scientific work, particularly since it has become so evident that science can be utilized both for advancing human welfare and for the destruction of civilization. The two views confront each other as the liberal versus the totalitarian interpretation of science.

Defenders of the freedom of science argue that practical achievements are based on research which originally had no practical utility as a goal. This type of pure research cannot be centrally planned or organized; it is highly individual mental activity of genuine investigators whose only motive force is curiosity. Only applied science, which consists of the utilization and application of what is already known to definite practical purposes, can be centrally planned and organized. The totalitarian view, which advocates the central planning and organization of science, if it were generally adopted, would defeat its own aim because further technical advancement would gradually come to a standstill. Nations adopting such a policy could live for a while on the basic discoveries of scientists in countries where science remains free; they could for a while find further practical applications of principles established elsewhere. However, this utilization of scientific truth for practical purposes would soon exhaust itself. In cultures where science remains free and in the hands of the scientists themselves, basic knowledge would increase and prepare the way for new practical applications.

These conclusions are valid only if the contention is true that fundamental research in the pure sciences must be left completely to the initiative of individual scientists, that it cannot be planned, organized or, in its preliminary phases, directed toward definite goals. Otherwise, one must postulate the impossible—an all-wise central body, composed of leading scientists, which could decide what specific research should be undertaken to promote human welfare.

Observing the current discussions in this field, it appears that there is a strong inclination toward the latter view in many circles. Their philosophy can be reconstructed about as follows. Even though in the past scientific research was arbitrary and chaotic and left completely to individual initiative, why should such a condition be upheld ? Can it not be different in the future —research streamlined, rationally planned, coördinated ? Can it not make use of the country's best minds for exploring and deciding what fields should be studied and what steps taken ? This view is strongly influenced by the spirit of our industrial era; it tries to apply to scientific research the methods and mentality of industry and large-scale business. The proponents of organized research, looking upon the past history of science as the "horse and buggy" era, ask why our concept of research should be fashioned by Newton's apple and Galvani's froglegs. Why should one rely on such silly accidents ? Why not replace luck and that overrated something called intuition or inspiration with rational calculation and planning ? They point to the wartime experience of industry in promoting scientific discovery in an unprecedented fashion. Under the necessity of defense we discovered radar, the jet-propelled airplane, the rocket and the atomic bomb. In medicine the use of sulfa drugs and penicillin was perfected. The psychiatrist, driven by the urgent need to help the numerous cases of combat fatigue, invented new methods of treatment, such as the use of drugs combined with psychotherapy; psychotherapy itself made great progress, became more rational and effective. All this took place under planned and systematic research. The protagonists of organized research feel that research has not been sufficiently organized in the past; they regard the Manhattan project as a model of planned and organized collective research. They tend to consider the defenders of autonomy of research as esoteric sentimentalists or "intellectual snobs."

Polanyi's point of view, diametrically opposed to that of Bernal, is representative of the view of most scientists. He says, "Science munificently showers gifts on all men when allowed freely to pursue its own spiritual aims, but collapses into barren torpor if required to serve the needs of society." He demands the right of the scientist to pursue truth regardless of society's interests. "If a policy of endowing research for practical aims were universally adopted," he maintains, "such benefit as any particular practical task now derives from the general progress of science would be altogether eliminated. Science would immediately come to a standstill and its practical applications would gradually become exhausted." Polanyi quotes Thomas Henry Huxley:

> In fact the history of physical science teaches (and we cannot too carefully take the lesson to heart) that the practical advantages, attainable through its agency, never have been, and never will be, sufficiently attractive to men in-

> spired by the inborn genius of the interpreter of Nature, to give them courage to undergo the toils and make the sacrifices which that calling required from its votaries. That which stirs their pulses is the love of knowledge and the joy of discovery of the causes of things sung by the old poet—the supreme delight of extending the realm of law and order ever farther towards the unattainable goals of the infinitely great and the infinitely small, between which our little race of life is run. In the course of this work, the physical philosopher, sometimes intentionally, much more often unintentionally, lights upon something which proves to be of practical value. Great is the rejoicing of those who are benefited thereby; and, for the moment, science is the Diana of all the craftsmen. But, even while the cries of jubilation resound and this flotsam and jetsam of the tide of investigation is being turned into the wages of workmen and the wealth of capitalists, the crest of the wave of scientific investigation is far away on its course over the illimitable oceans of the unknown.[4]

This quotation clearly reflects the humility of the real scientist toward Nature, the great unknown. This is in sharp contrast to the self-assurance of the industrialist or business executive who deals only with known quantities. He can organize and systematically plan a sales campaign or the production of industrial goods: he knows how to produce the goods and to whom he wants to sell them. Science, however, is a continuous groping in the dark. The scientist is in an unending struggle against an infinite object—the unknown—which he attacks with the Lilliputian power of the human mind. He develops an awe before the complexities of nature; hence the humility of the scientist.

[4] *Loc. cit.*

The industrialist or the business executive, in contrast, holds all the cards in his hand: he deals with elements he can master, he can promise results and he can keep his time schedules. But he often forgets that he owes his mastery to the patient spadework of scientists who furnished the basic knowledge for technology. Every scientific investigation is an adventure. No one knows where it will lead, how long it will last, or what it will achieve.

Baker cites the testimony of a number of other scientists, among them Einstein: "The satisfaction of physical needs is indeed the indispensable precondition of a satisfactory existence, but in itself it is not enough. In order to be content, men must also have the possibility of developing their intellectual and artistic powers to whatever extent accords with their personal characteristics and abilities." Baker quotes Humboldt, who says: "The higher enjoyments yielded by the study of nature depend upon the correctness and depth of our views."

These quotations are highly representative of the attitude of genuine scientists. Their consensus is that science has only one responsibility and that is toward truth. To increase knowledge is the only aim of pure science and this goal cannot be subordinated to any other without blocking the advancement of science itself.

As a contrast to this non-utilitarian concept, Baker quotes Hitler: "There is no such thing as truth. Science is a social phenomenon and, like any other social phenomenon, is limited by the benefit or injury it confers on the community." Bernal has much the same attitude when he says that outside of the Soviet Union scientific work is nothing but elegant pastime.

Polanyi, by contrast, remarks pointedly that all the practical gains for general welfare derived from scientific research ultimately came from progress in pure science by workers who pursued their own scientific aims quite oblivious to possible practical uses. Even if society is interested only in the practical benefits derived from scientific research, and not concerned in the least about truth for its own sake, it can best obtain these benefits by letting the scientists pursue their own curiosity and indulge their puzzle-solving passion.

It should now be clear that this controversy boils down to the psychology of the scientific investigator. Is it true that his work is so highly individualistic that it does not tolerate any systematic planning and subordination to practical goals ? To the general reader with no first-hand familiarity with scientific research, such statements may give the impression that the scientist is a strange and delicate species who is devoted to his esoteric hobbies and who must be handled as gingerly as one does a prima donna. In fact, the scientist's attitude seems comparable to that of the artist. As the artist gives creative expression to his fantasy from an internal creative urge, the scientist is motivated by a creative curiosity to understand those puzzles which nature offers. Satisfaction of this curiosity is an aim in itself; it is not subordinated to anything else. The concept of *l'art pour l'art* can equally be applied to science.

It is impressive, indeed, how often scientists compare the gratification they derive from their scientific activities with the beauty derived from art. Baker quotes Haldane: "As a result of Faraday's work, you are able to listen to the wireless. But more than that, as a result of Faraday's work scientifically educated men and women have an altogether richer view of the world: for them, apparently empty space is full of the most intricate and beautiful patterns. So Faraday gave the world not only fresh wealth but fresh beauty." In this respect I should like to quote a somewhat forgotten American man of science, the physicist Joseph Henry, a contemporary of Faraday who anticipated the great British scientist in many respects in the field of electromagnetism: "There is—so to speak—an imagination of the intellect, as well as of the emotional soul: . . . the Truth has its palaces no less gorgeous—no less wonderful—than those reared by fancy in homage to the Beautiful."

Close psychological scrutiny of those mental processes by which fundamental scientific discoveries have been made in the past gives the impression that systematically planned activity does not play an important role in discovery, but that scientific discoveries are frequently made unexpectedly as a result of a sudden insight, often called intuition or inspiration. A classical example is Kekule's discovery of the carbon ring, the cornerstone of modern organic chemistry. Our whole chemical industry would be unthinkable without this initial discovery. Let me quote him verbatim:

> During my stay in Ghent, Belgium, I lived in an elegant bachelor room on the main street. My study, however, was situated near a narrow alley, and, therefore, I had no light during the day. I sat there and worked on my textbook, but it did not seem to progress: my mind was occupied by other things. Therefore, I turned my chair to the fireplace

> and dozed off. Atoms began to tumble before my eyes. Smaller groups held themselves modestly in the background. My spiritual eyes trained by observing this type of groups gradually began to discern bigger formations of all shapes. Long, more cohesive rows appeared; they moved like snakes turning and twisting. And then suddenly one snake grabbed his own tail and twisted mockingly before my eyes. And as if struck by lightning I awoke and spent the rest of the night to work out my hypothesis.[5]

The snake biting his own tail was the carbon ring, the clue to understanding a vast number of unknown facts. This idea created a whole new branch of chemistry—stereo-chemistry. Kekule was half asleep when this idea came to him as a revelation. Of course, Kekule was obviously submerged at that time in ideas about the structure of organic compounds. The brilliant solution, however, came during a moment of complete relaxation.

Many other scientists give similar testimony. Helmholtz, one of the greatest of scientists, reported that his lucky ideas "crept into his mind" without his immediately noticing their significance and recognizing from where they came. He writes:

> They came without effort as an inspiration. They never came when my brain was tired—never when I was sitting at my desk. At first I tossed a problem over in my mind from all viewpoints until I was so familiar with it that I did not need to write it down. This, of course, required long preliminary effort. But then, in order to recover from this

[5] Alfred Winterstein, "Autistisches Erleben im Schopferischem Vorgang," *Die Psychoanalytische Bewegung*, Jahrgang I, 1929. Internationaler Psychoanalytischer Verlag, Vienna.

strain, I needed one hour of complete rest and relaxation before the good ideas appeared. Often it was in the morning after awaking, as Gauss also has observed. The most favorable condition for their appearance, however, was while strolling over the shady hillsides in sunny weather. The least amount of alcohol dissipated them at once.[6]

Another important argument for the inspirational nature of scientific discovery is the fact that discoveries are often made seemingly by accident. As America was discovered unwittingly by Columbus while in search of a direct route to India, many scientific discoveries are unexpected by-products of work originally undertaken for quite different purposes. A classical example is Galvani's accidental discovery of the electrical current while studying the behavior of muscle contractions. The recent discovery of penicillin, an entirely new principle in therapy based on the anti-bacterial effect of certain molds, was also made in an accidental manner. Dr. Fleming, an English bacteriologist, noticed that bacterial colonies on old discarded agar plates were disintegrating in the neighborhood of a mold, which often develops on old agar plates. Thousands upon thousands of bacteriologists and technicians had been exposed to these facts, but the creative act in this discovery was recognition of the relationship between the distribution of colonies and mold. That mold inhibits bacterial growth was an instantaneous insight of a mind trained in methodical observation and reasoning. Only after this basic discovery could systematically planned studies be undertaken to find certain strains of penicillium which yield more of the anti-bacterial sub-

[6] E. Mach, *Prinzipien der Wärmelehre* (Leipzig, 1923).

stance, thus making the basic discovery of wide practical use.

If one bears in mind that basic research is an exploration of unknown territory, all this becomes quite self-evident. A well known physicist, when asked what he thought about the possibility of planning and organizing research on a large scale, answered succinctly, "How can the unknown be planned and organized ?" New discoveries consist in the recognition of a hitherto unobserved relationship between already known facts. This recognition quite often is suddenly precipitated by an accidental observation. Such accidents, however, happen only to the trained mind which is in constant preparedness. This does not mean, of course, that scientific knowledge is not the result of the highly collaborative effort of many scientists. Its development, however, does not and, in the light of what has been said, cannot take place through systematic planning and organization.

The development of science should be compared with organic growth rather than with the fixed routine of following a blueprint. It takes place about like this. In France a scientist proposes a new theory based on a new observation. This arouses the interest of a research worker in England who needed just this new view to explain a puzzle he had encountered within his own field, perhaps a quite different field. Now he can make a further step in his investigative work, which in turn stimulates the studies of an investigator in America. Not always is the needed piece of information supplied by contemporary workers. A long-forgotten isolated observation may gain sudden significance in throwing light upon a newly discovered fact. Not always do the pieces of knowledge which are fitted together in this exciting jig-saw puzzle of science come from the same field. A new mathematical theorem may be the missing link which a physicist needs to solve a problem. A biological fact may throw light upon a problem in physics. The most fundamental principle of modern physics, the law of conservation of energy, was discovered by a medical man, Robert Mayer, through his observations of animal heat. Cross-fertilization between individual scientists and between different scientific fields goes on every day in the small community—the world of science. The media of intellectual cooperation, scientific journals and meetings, which have developed during the last century, would not be improved by more rigid organization. Collective research, on the other hand, by the mere fact that it brings many scientists into daily contact under one roof, undoubtedly stimulates creative thinking. This is one of the redeeming features of large modern scientific research institutions.

Yet it is preposterous to try to chart the steady unpredictable growth of scientific knowledge. No one who understands the nature of science can support such a naïve plan. There does not exist a single mind or a great group of scientists able to foresee the possible concatenations and mutual influences of individual observations and ideas and, as a result, coördinate and accelerate this organic growth by planned action. Each step forward is an individual act, a step into the unknown. Out of many such highly individual mental accomplishments, science becomes integrated by a complex process of interaction of ideas. Byproducts of an investigation frequently prove later to be more significant than the original aim. One need not be concerned about waste or worry that the same problem is being attacked at the same time at different centers. Such a concern results from confusing the methods of industrial production with those of research.

One must appreciate the magnitude of the task of deciphering the secrets of nature. There are not enough separate centers of research in which the same problems are studied. The frontiers of the unknown are unlimited and the chances of making a new step are increased by the number of individual minds working parallel, but separately, on the same problem. What one man might overlook the other might see. One must not disregard the creative act involved in every discovery. It is not a question of man-hours, and therefore not a question of wasting time. Only when it is to apply already well explored principles to a new use is economically planned and systematic organization of research possible and desirable. The atomic bomb is an example. The time was ripe for its construction because all the fundamental knowledge for its construction was made available by several decades of unorganized creative research.

No organization—not even the most efficient one—can force a single creative step into the unknown because such a step can be made only by individual brains animated by individual interests and curiosities. To impose organization upon research in a field not yet ripe for it is not only futile but retarding in influence. The real creative step is an unconscious process and requires neither planning nor goal-conscious effort, but a relaxed attitude. Not infrequently it takes place in sleep. The creative act is the greater part of research and occurs only in rare moments. The best promotion of science, then, is to create for the scientist an atmosphere in which this mental act is most likely to occur. Certainly, systematic teamwork geared for definite circumscribed aims, deadlines required by grants given for definite purposes for a fixed number of years—in short, any kind of external pressure diminishes the most propitious atmosphere for inspiration. This may sound preposterous in the days of man-hours and time-clocks. However, whether we like it or not, the creative activities of men cannot be regulated by such devices. The creative activity of man must be left free to follow its own course. If utility is stressed, research is deflected from its original aim of knowledge for its own sake and eventually it must perish. If, on the other hand, the free spirit of intellectual curiosity is encouraged, scientific progress flourishes.

Nature is so complex and possible interconnections are so infinite that only by intuition or by luck does the investigator stumble into a new discovery. Considering the countless number of chemical substances in nature, how could the anti-bacterial effect of penicillin have been planfully discovered ? Or, before the phenomenon of electricity was discovered, would it not have been nonsensical to sponsor a project to discover in nature a force by which light and heat could be generated for daily use by people? All this is not in contradiction to the fact that existing knowledge can be systematically developed for certain practical purposes. However, only experts can decide when a field is ripe for such organized and planned research—and even experts often differ in this regard.

Polanyi, for example, mentions cancer, in which planned research has proved relatively fruitless in the past. He says, "For all its practical interest, knowledge of cancer can advance only if and when the progress of physiology, biochemistry, cytology and other branches of science throws from time to time new light on one or other of its aspects—a process which cannot be appreciably hastened by the endowment of research on cancer." Accordingly, it would not be surprising at all if the next step in the understanding or treatment of cancer came, not from investigations within the restricted field of cancer research, but from research in the basic biological sciences.

Of course, a distinction between pure science and applied science cannot always be carried through rigidly because the practical and theoretical activities of scientists often overlap. But, in this connection, it is noteworthy that Irving Langmuir, whose discoveries in the field of electric lighting have had incalculable practical value, pointed out in a radio address to the public that the best policy in industrial research also is to leave the investigator free to pursue his own scientific curiosity without prescribing definite practical aims to achieve.

The history of the natural sciences and technology, then, as well as the testimony of the scientists themselves, supports the view so succinctly stated by Polanyi—that basic scientific research is an aim in itself and has nothing to do with practical aims, that it springs from the scientist's passion for knowledge for its own sake. This view contradicts the totalitarian interpretation of science proposed by Bernal, which subordinates science to the needs of society.

The argument that the scientist has an obligation toward society to concentrate his efforts on promoting welfare is fallacious and, if applied, would undermine the development of science. The scientist's main interest is to learn about the things he studies; if he helps society by it, so much the better. If other men use the discoveries of science for destructive purposes, it is not the fault of the scientist. No one can demand of the scientist that he discover only harmless and useful things. Discoveries in themselves are neither useful nor harmful. It is the others, the industrialists, the politicians, the diplomats, who make them useful or harmful. Without war, for example, atomic knowledge would never have been utilized for destruction. It is the threat of war which interferes with the free research by which nuclear forces could be harnessed for peacetime purposes. To hold the scientists responsible for the abuse of their discoveries is nonsensical. The punishment of Prometheus for teaching mankind the secret of fire was a miscarriage of justice. Not Prometheus, not the scientist, is the culprit, but mankind, which abuses the knowledge it receives from its intellectual pioneers.

CHAPTER IX

The Scientific Revolution

COLLAPSE OF THE ABSOLUTES IN PHYSICS

> "Rather suddenly determinism faded out of theoretical physics. Its exit has been received in various ways. Some writers are incredulous and cannot be persuaded that determinism has really been eliminated from the present foundations of physical theory. Some think that it is no more than a domestic change in physics, having no reactions on general philosophic thought. Some decide cynically to wait and see if determinism fades in again. . . . I cannot agree with those who belittle the philosophical significance of the change. The withdrawal of physical science from an attitude it had adopted consistently for more than 200 years is not to be treated lightly; and it provokes a reconsideration of our views as to one of the most perplexing problems of our existence."
>
> SIR A. S. EDDINGTON [1]

I have tried repeatedly to account to myself for the fascination I have always felt for the advancements in physical theory. I have found the answer in the fact that before the atomic era the propelling motive of scientists in these fields was completely detached from any practical consid-

[1] A. S. Eddington, *New Pathways in Science* (London, 1935).

erations. The far-reaching historical implications of their theories before the first atomic explosion were not yet evident. Pondering about the magnetic attraction of physical theory for me, I remembered Father's letter in which he described why he turned away from medicine, a field in which the practical aspects are emphasized. For him the remuneration for solving a problem consisted in the pleasure derived from solving the problem and not its possible practical application. In no other discipline is the problem-solving passion more detached from all practical considerations than in mathematics and theoretical physics. In my own field, psychological theory and therapeutic procedures are closely interwoven, but I have always had a never-conquered longing for a field in which the pure devotion to knowledge was not yet influenced by utilitarian considerations. To a large degree the emotional dilemma of contemporary physicists can be traced to the sudden shift by which the most abstract theory has proved its immediate convertibility into practical purposes of fateful significance.

If one consults the writings of leading contemporary scientists—Einstein, Eddington, Jeans, Whitehead, De Broglie, Heisenberg, and others—who have tried to inform the general public about advances in their fields, there is general agreement that the main developments center around three focal points: the relativity theory of Einstein, the quantum theory as originally conceived by Planck and further elaborated by Bohr, Heisenberg and others, and the indeterminacy principle of Heisenberg.

It is not my purpose to deal in detail with these theories. This has been done by experts in popular and semi-popular interpretation. One of the main peculiarities of these new theoretical concepts is that they are further removed from common sense than any product the human mind ever created, with the exception probably of modern abstractionist art. To a large degree, they are conceived in the terms of mathematics, and their translation into verbal terms is a most difficult task, even for the expert.

What concerns us here are the psychological aspects of these theories, how they express a profound change in the physicist's relation to the physical world. The psychological implications of these new theories are of particular interest because, in contrast with older concepts in physics, they do not deal with an external world detached from the observer. They introduce the observer himself into their consideration.

The pre-Socratic Greek philosopher, Protagoras, had already postulated the relativity of all our knowledge about the world. The nature of our own mind determines partially, at least, how we see and conceive the world around us. In modern times, Locke, Berkeley, Hume and Kant came to the same conclusion. The cornerstone of the relativistic concept of knowledge is a simple incontestable fact. The rose is not red in itself. It appears red through the complicated apparatus which consists of an optical lens, the perceptive retina and the optical cortex of the brain, the excitation of which is finally responsible for the color sensation of red in the observer. How the rose itself is, is a meaningless question because we can know the rose only through our sense organs, the nature of which determines the quality of the sensation. The same is true of other information we receive from the world around us, such as the warmness or the weight of an object. It is not warm in itself; the sensation of warmth is a result of the bombardment of our tactile sensory organ by fast-moving particles, the velocity of which movement determines the nature of our sensations, such as cold, tepid, warm, warmer and hot. This point of view came to its most logical conclusion in Kant's pronouncement that the *Ding an Sich* (the thing in itself) is beyond man's ken. His knowledge of the world around him is restricted by the nature of his mind because he can see the world only through his own perceptive and thinking apparatus. This apparatus does not give a photographic picture of things as they are; the notion of an object is determined by both the unknown "absolute" quality of the object and the nature of the perceiving apparatus. The absolute nature of objects and events is inscrutable because we cannot crawl out of our skin and we can only perceive the world through the perceptive functions with which we are endowed. An inhabitant of another plant, if his optical and nervous apparatus were differently constructed from ours, would not perceive the rose as red but something else. Whether the rose is really red or not is a futile question—it is red to us and "X" to another type of perceiving organism.

Philosophers, who have, with great consistency, worked out these inevitable conclusions did not go, however, quite as far along this line of reasoning as did Einstein in his theory. It was fairly easy to recognize that color, temperature, smell, etc.,—"the secondary qualities"—are dependent upon our perceptive apparatus. More difficult was the next step: that the shape of objects, their length, and the point of time when they are at a certain place—

the primary qualities—are not absolute qualities, but are dependent upon the perceiver's position and movement. Kant still retained time and space as absolute qualities (*a priori*) which are only determined by the world outside. Insofar as time and space are concerned, *a priori* knowledge, which is not dependent on experience, is possible because in this area the categories of the mind and of the world are identical. In other words, in regard to time and space, the human mind gives a true photographic picture of the world outside. The theory of relativity abolished the difference between secondary and primary qualities. All our notions about the world are determined not only by the occurrences which take place independently of the observer, but also by his position in space and his state of motion. Absolute lengths or an absolute duration between two events are meaningless concepts, since our results of measuring will differ according to our own position and motion in relationship to the object's position and motion.

The revolutionary consequences of this formulation as they affect the laws of motion as formulated by Newton do not need to concern us further. Our present interest is in the psychological meaning of this revised way of looking upon the world around us. First, however, the two other revolutionary theories have to be considered.

The essentials of the quantum theory are well known. In its full significance it can be adequately expressed only in mathematical rather than visual or verbal terms. The study of phenomena of radiation and photoelectric phenomena led to the irrefutable conclusion that energy could be emitted or absorbed only in discrete energy quanta.

This discovery was in contradiction to the classical concepts of physics, which were based on continuous changes. An even greater complication arose from the fact that the phenomena of light diffraction and interference made the conclusion that light traveled in waves inevitable, but this wave theory could not always be applied to phenomena of radiation. The scientists, perhaps the first time, were confronted with a seemingly insoluble contradiction. Certain aspects of light required the wave theory, others a corpuscular theory of light quanta.

While this contradiction has been solved by mathematical procedures, introducing probability functions concerning position and velocity of atomic particles (electrons), conceptually it was not yet solved. Bohr's theory of complementarity is an attempt at solution of this contradiction. It appears to imply an admission of the limitations of knowledge: the phenomena of light cannot be treated from a unified point of view; they require two kinds of description which complement each other. The ultimate consequences of this has been drawn by Heisenberg in his uncertainty principle.

Formulated by Heisenberg, the uncertainty principle revived the most fundamental issues of philosophy and led to a still-continuing controversy between scientists as to what is objectively "real" in these formulations and observations and what is due to the nature and limitations of our perceiving mind and the methods of our observation.

The result of every observation obviously must depend (1) upon the nature of the phenomenon observed, (2) on the technical nature of the instruments of observation and

(3) upon the nature of the perceptive and cognitive faculties of the mind. These three factors obviously have to be separated. About the first, one can only say that the absolute nature of a phenomenon cannot be ascertained. The second factor has the least radical philosophical consequences, namely, that when we observe such extremely small objects as electrons, the very process of our observation alters the observed phenomena. Our measuring instruments must necessarily consist of equally minute yardsticks which interact with the object measured and therefore must unavoidably have an effect upon the processes we are observing. This difficulty is more than a technicality and requires recognition of the necessary imperfections of observing extremely small events which have the same dimensions as the measuring tool. This imperfection can be successfully eliminated by the statistical approach.

Farther-reaching consequences has the contention of the indeterminacy principle that the intrinsic nature of sub-atomic phenomena requires a revision of so fundamental a tenet of science as causality, the belief in the strict determination of natural events by events which precede them. It suggests that we shall have to replace the concept of strict determination of natural events with the old Aristotelian concept of potentiality and the more quantitative concept of probability.[2] Atomic events have a tendency toward certain states which can only be predicted statistically. The kinetic theory of heat has already shown that it is not necessary to know each molecule's actual behavior but only their average distribution to make ac-

[2] Werner Heisenberg, *Physics and Philosophy* (New York, 1958).

curate predictions as to their behavior *en masse*. The statistical approach to the phenomena of thermodynamics, however, did not postulate a fundamental impossibility of knowing each particle's behavior. It was assumed that the actual behavior of these particles followed the classical Newtonian laws of mechanics. Heisenberg's principle of indeterminacy is of a different nature. It maintains that quite apart from our technical inability, the nature of atomic phenomena itself precludes even a theoretical predictability of these minute events in nature on the basis of causality. Where an electron will be in the next moment cannot be predicted, only the probability of its position. The velocity and position cannot be ascertained simultaneously. The limits of our knowledge (predictability) are not only due to a technicality that the observation disturbs the observed event—but to the nature of reality itself.

Heisenberg maintains that our usual categories of thought, which are contained in ordinary language, are not suited to describe the sub-atomic world. Consequently, the conceptual contradictions inherent in atomic physics can be resolved only by using mathematical symbols—they cannot be resolved by translating them into ordinary verbal expression. This new area of physical exploration increases the already existing gap between the common-sense concept of "nature" and the "nature" with which science deals. New scientific techniques have permitted exploration of segments of nature which are not within our everyday perspective. Electricity, for example, led to the development of such concepts as the electrical field, which cannot be visually conceived. With the study of sub-atomic phenomena, this gap between common sense and the scientific outlook became even more obvious. This part of nature can be explored only by complex techniques and the results of these explorations can be represented only in mathematical terms and no longer by visually conceived and verbally expressible relationships. To these only mathematically representable objects or events one cannot attribute real existence in the same sense as we can to the world of our senses.

Atomic science thus increases the distance between man and nature, man's estrangement from nature, which Kierkegaard deplored more than 100 years ago as the ultimate effect of science on man's mentality.

In this new area of sub-atomic phenomena, the relativity of knowledge, its dependence on man's observing and reasoning faculties—something which should be a self-evident axiom of any epistemology—has become more obvious than ever before. It demonstrates clearly—as Heisenberg formulated it so succinctly—that the mathematical formulations in which this knowledge is represented "no longer portray nature, but rather our knowledge of nature." [3] This, of course, is true for all knowledge, including our common everyday observations. That the content and quality of our sense perceptions depend on the nature of our physiological equipment for observation has been explicitly stated earlier. What now becomes clearer than ever is the limited applicability of scientific concepts. They fit only certain areas; other areas require different conceptualizations. This is the essence of Bohr's

[3] Werner Heisenberg, "The Representation of Nature in Contemporary Physics," *Daedalus* (Vol. 87, Summer 1958, pp. 95–108).

principle of complementarity. It is not surprising that the same principle which pertains to our sense perceptions is also valid for observations made by such highly complex techniques as the microscope and, later, cloudchambers, photoelectricity and cyclotrons. These techniques of scientific observation are in principle but extensions of our native faculties of observation. It is obvious that the nature of these techniques is one of the factors which determines the results of the observations. The disturbing influence of the techniques used upon sub-atomic phenomena must be added as a new factor which determines the outcome of the observation.

The principle of complementarity is well known to the psychiatrist. He deals with human behavior, parts of which can be described and understood only in physiological terms and parts of which require psychological concepts and methods. The muscular movements involved in opening a newspaper can be described only in terms of neurophysiology. The motivation of the person who opens the paper, his curiosity about current events, can only be described psychologically. Only the two descriptions together, the psychological description of motivations and the physiological description of the resulting muscular actions, give a full account of the observed phenomenon.

All this is but a consistent confirmation of Protagoras' dictum that man is the measure of all knowledge. Knowledge, no matter how obtained, depends on man's limited faculties for obtaining knowledge—not only upon the limitations of his senses and the techniques by which he augments his native perception faculties, but also upon the limitations of his reasoning faculties by which he elaborates the data of his observations. Mathematical reasoning does not constitute an exception. This also depends upon the nature and limitations of that complex computing instrument: the cognitive faculties of our mind. In other words, laws of nature as formulated by the physicist cannot be justly called the laws of nature; they are a combination of the unknowable absolute laws of nature with the laws of our reasoning apparatus, our mind.

I do not quite see why all this should raise an entirely new epistemological issue. If we accept Freud's theory of the ego, according to which the perceptive and cognitive functions of the mental apparatus are the results of adjustments to external reality, we need not be surprised to find that this adjustment is not a completely perfect one. The ego is the imprint of reality upon the mental apparatus. The mere fact that deductive logical syllogisms —which are functions of our reasoning apparatus—can lead to experimentally verifiable predictions makes it cogent to assume that our logical apparatus is in some way—though not with a theoretical perfection—adjusted to the nature of reality. The imperfections of this adjustment become manifest in Heisenberg's principle of uncertainty, which, if our view is correct, would not necessarily indicate that it is nature which is imperfect (undetermined) but that the correspondence between nature and our reasoning apparatus is imperfect. We must thoroughly abandon Laplace's belief that a superior intellect could, theoretically at least, predict every event in the world from the preceding ones. We must give up the notion of the omnipotence of science and replace it with a more humble attitude. Since we are participant observers of the world, our notion of the world must necessarily remain in this general sense subjective. We cannot, in observing the world, assume a vantage point which is independent of the "world process" of which we are ourselves a part. We are participant observers and, therefore, in all our scientific formulations, the nature of our own physiological and psychological equipment, our position in space, our state of motion, the disturbing influence of our observational techniques upon the observed phenomena and the limitations of our mind must be introduced.

It is inevitable that, as these theoretical notions are grasped in their full significance, they will gradually change our emotional outlook toward the world as well as toward ourselves. As long as we dealt with man-sized objects, all these "subjective" factors could be disregarded for practical purposes. Although in a philosophical sense we were aware of the subjective elements, they did not interfere with formulations of physics and even less with our everyday notions. We could act and feel according to the "naïve realism" of common sense that there is a world around us which is just about as we see it and experience it. As soon as new methods of observation and reasoning brought us into immediate contact with the microscopic and macroscopic areas of the world, we could no longer indulge in naïve realism. We became citizens of a larger, less parochial world which lies outside of our accustomed dimensions. The Copernican system terminated our notion of being in the center of the universe in a stable position. The new scientific advancements in physics went much further in the same direction; we lost our privileged position to a much greater degree. Our scientific parochialism yielded its place to a cosmopolitanism in our whole outlook toward the world. The Laplacian certainty principle was replaced by Heisenberg's uncertainty principle. All this terminated our exalted position by impressing upon us certain limitations of knowledge which cannot be surmounted.

There is, however, another side to this picture. By acknowledging explicitly the limitations of causal knowledge, it became possible to improve the accuracy of predictions.

The uncertainty principle does not preclude precise predictions obtainable by the statistical approach. It is true that an electron or quantum potentially can be at any place in the universe, but the probability of its being at a certain area is so great that we do not need to be further concerned with this limitation of our knowledge. For practical purposes, we can tell where an electron is. Knowing the degree of probability of an event, for all purposes, is equivalent to knowing the actual course of an event, as Laplace hoped we might know about all events in nature. The behavior of large numbers of particles approaches the statistically predicted model. We can replace Laplace's goal of knowing the precise causal chains in all events in the universe with determining their probabilities, and we need not give up our hope to predict all possible events. After we recognized our limitations, we learned new techniques of mathematical analysis and can now do just as well with this refined instrument. Yet, we have to admit the limitations which prevent us from ever acquiring absolute knowledge. The emotional effects of this admission are what interested us in this writing.

Admitting that we cannot account precisely step-by-step for each event as it takes place as the unavoidable result of previous events is an acknowledgment of ignorance. Statistical knowledge can never emotionally substitute for it. Knowing only the frequency of a certain occurrence implies that our knowledge is limited. If a physician can say no more than that a certain patient has a 30% chance of survival, this is considered a most unsatisfactory statement. We want to know whether the particular patient belongs to the 30% who will survive—and we want to know why this is so. This requires, however, more than knowing the crude empirical fact that, in counting large numbers of similar cases, more die than survive. The uncertainty principle, emotionally at least, is a similar blow to the hope of omniscience, that is to say, to the hope of a precise knowledge of all causal sequences which occur in the universe. Naturally, we care less about knowing the fate of every individual electron than we do about the welfare of our fellow men. What difference does it make if we only know statistically the fate of electrons ? It is different with human beings. The patient, his family and his friends want to know the fate of this particular person—not the representative of a sufficient sample, but an individual who is different from all others. And although we care little about individual electrons, yet, the limitations of causal knowledge in atomic physics has a deep emotional impact. It is one of many similar blows which, in this last phase of Western civilization, have altered contemporary man's outlook on the world and society.

Unfortunately, the statistical approach so effective in physics is winning out also in the arena of social life. It is needless to point out and document in detail how in our society, in the field of employment and education, the individual approach cedes it place to the statistical. Every person is becoming the carrier of a paper form which identifies him by measurable quantities—height, weight, age, educational achievements (quantifiable by the number of credits obtained in school work), hours of work, dollars earned in the past, length of employment, race, nationality, religion and other statistically manageable items. He is judged not as an unique combination of these and other more important, non-measurable factors—for example, individual creativity—but by statistical averages of measurable data. This trend seems to indicate that we are giving up our hope of being able to deal with each individual on his own merits and are resigning ourselves to dealing with him statistically.

What made us change? It is obvious that the increasing number of people participating actively in the social process makes individual judgments impossible. The progressive differentiation of social functions is another factor; we have become more interested in social functions and roles than in the unique characteristics of persons.

It is difficult to consider the simultaneous occurrence of the statistical attitude in science and in social life as mere coincidence. Yet, no one would claim that statistical physics influences our statistical way of dealing with fellow human beings or that the social mores prepared the way for the new physical discoveries. The fact that parallel manifestations have appeared at the same time in other fields, such as social science, contemporary art, and personality organization, may indicate that all these changes are manifestations of a basic underlying trend.

CHAPTER X

Revolution in Art

"The Greeks praised Zeuxis because he painted cherries so faithfully that the sparrows came to pick them. This only shows that sparrows are not art experts and have just about the same understanding of art as the general public."

BERNARD ALEXANDER

It is not astonishing that the revolt against the mercilessly progressing juggernaut of rationalization of life has been most successful in art and literature. These are those preserves of the mind where fantasy can most freely detach itself from the exigencies of the serious business of living. While the scientist, because of the portentous practical significance of his discoveries, is in the process of losing his extraterritorial status and the autonomy which goes with it and is becoming "socially responsible," the artist, at least in western societies, has not only retained his freedom but flaunted it in the face of a bewildered public, defying convention and reason.

Products of art can be looked upon from two different points of view: the aesthetic and the psychologic. The aesthetician and the art critic try to evaluate artistic merit.

The psychologist is not primarily concerned with what is a good or a bad painting; he considers the works of artists as valuable personal documents which throw light upon the personalities of their originators. Like dreams or day-dreams, works of literature, painting and sculpture are products of the creative fantasy which reflect the psychology of the artist. The psychological study of art products may serve not only for the study of the artist as a person, but also for the study of the emotional climate of a historical period. Because the work of an artist is a reflection of his personality as well as a reflection of the spirit of his times, the literature and art of a given period are most important documents for the historian of culture. I am primarily concerned here with the question: In what way does contemporary art express the spirit of our era, as Byzantine art expressed the mentality of the Middle Ages or as impressionism did the outlook of the second half of the nineteenth century ?

To answer this question, one must first of all establish the characteristic features of contemporary painting. As in every past historical period, there is at present a great divergence in subject matter and technique used by different artists. In spite of these individual differences, there are fundamental similarities. It is not difficult, even for a non-expert, to recognize Byzantine paintings or to distinguish a Renaissance product from a nineteenth-century impressionist picture. Obviously, there are certain common features which are characteristic of a period, although it is not always easy to define them precisely.

Earlier art historians have tried to explain these common features primarily from the point of view of the techniques used by the artists. It is only recently that some cultural historians have attempted to understand the style in art characteristic of a period from the cultural climate to which all persons living in a given time and place have been equally exposed. Naturally, there are always exceptions—artists who do not represent the current trend. In trying to define the characteristic features of contemporary painting, we shall disregard those works which are not representative of our times. An artist of today may try to paint in the style of Rembrandt or Titian, but such an exceptional case must be explained on a highly individual basis. It may offer a most interesting opportunity to study the psychology of such an atypical artist, but it is not suitable for reconstructing the prevailing ideological trends and spirit of our times.

What are the most basic common features in contemporary paintings ? One basic similarity is the complete absence of real objects or their radical distortion. This trend is referred to as non-objective, or abstract, art. There may be a lack of any reference to real objects, as in some paintings of Mondrian or Klee. Or the objects may be fragmented into their constituent parts and reassembled in different perspective, as in cubist paintings. It is sometimes well-nigh impossible to recognize the fragmented object, the product often resembling a piece of a picture puzzle. In still other paintings, the object may simply be distorted but recognizable, or it may be reduced to its most elementary formal (often geometrically simplified) and color components.

Another feature is the distortion of the spatial configuration without fragmentation of the objects—by placing disconnected objects side by side. Another type of distortion consists in emphasizing aspects of the object which are commonly considered unpleasant; this may result in grotesque, ugly, or fear-inspiring effects, as in many of Grosz's drawings. In the use of such an expression as "ugly," I do not refer to the artistic merits of a painting. To represent ugliness is just as legitimate a function of art as to represent something which may be called pretty. Othello's deed was certainly ugly, yet it is the subject of a great piece of literature.

Another frequent feature in modern products is the tendency toward the fantastic, the eerie, the mystical, and toward dreamlike symbolism, as in certain paintings of Chagall, Miró, Dali, Tanguy, and others. Still another feature is the tendency to use primitive perspective or to mix different perspectives, presenting an object from all sides at the same time. This is not to be confused with the primitive way in which different perspectives were used by some early Renaissance painters.

All these characteristics, from the point of view of psychology, can be interpreted as manifestations of a central trend: withdrawal from the world as perceived through the sense organs, and substitution for it of a newly created, different kind of world. Of course, almost every artist, unlike a photographer, substitutes for the mere reproduction of the world of senses his own interpretation of his object. The mildest forms of this practice are simplification, omission, and emphasis, utilized to a greater or lesser degree by artists of all periods. Reinterpretation, however, goes much further in contemporary painting than in the works of most great masters of the past. The great freedom of reinterpretation of the environment as perceived by our senses is characteristic of the contemporary painter. Everything which appears ephemeral and non-essential is omitted and certain fundamentals are emphasized, as in the post-impressionist painting of Van Gogh or Cézanne.

The next step in this direction is abstraction, which may go as far as reducing the object to its simplest geometric outlines. Or the negation of the real world of senses may manifest itself in distortion. This is usually not a simple negation of the world as it is; it often has a hostile component and expresses an angry denial of the world as it is commonly perceived. For the psychologist this emphasis on the grotesque, or what one ordinarily would call unpleasant, is a clear confession of resentful rejection. Even stronger rejection is expressed in the completely objectless paintings, where only the very basic components of the visual universe are retained—color and line, light and dark. From these elements the artist creates a new view of a spatial world which contains no real objects. The cubist revolution contained both trends: the denial of the world as it is, along with an even stronger motivational force to rearrange the fragmented parts of objects in a new, seemingly wanton but really highly consistent manner.

As I said before, every artist creates his own world. The question is, how much does he retain of the actual elements as perceived by the senses ? Most contemporary artists go much further than their predecessors, with the exception of some primitives, in utilizing only the most basic elements, such as lines and colors, and in disregarding what might be called the incidental combination of lines, forms and colors as they appear in the environment.

It is like transposing a melody from one key to another. The great contemporary painters, such as Braque and Picasso, use the same artistic skill with which the old masters represented the real world we live in, to transform this world according to a consistent formula of their own. In the work of one of the forerunners of the era, Modigliani, the re-creative urge is the strongest. He is really not so much a revolutionary as a reformer. Modigliani gives expression to his reforming urge in a consistent, longitudinal distortion of proportions and bilateral symmetry. This has sometimes been misinterpreted as a mannerism. In reality it is but inner consistency in distortion. Otherwise Modigliani retains much of the technique of the old masters and even has a flavor of the Renaissance in his work.

Denial and radical re-creation of the world of the senses is one of the all-pervasive keynotes in contemporary art. The "re-creator" of the world sometimes uses technological motifs, as does, for example, Léger. It appears as if the artist envied the engineer who has actually succeeded in reshaping the surface of the globe and in superimposing upon the work of nature a new, technologically created, man-made world. Another way of creating a completely new world populated with dreamlike symbols is to be seen in the work of Miró and Tanguy.

We see, then, that the denial of the real world of objects is a well-nigh universal characteristic of contemporary art. It is not merely a reinterpretation of the world—this is universal in every art—but a fundamental transformation combined with an aggressive denial of the objects in the form in which they are commonly perceived. The ways and means of this re-creation are widely different, according to the inclination and personality of the painter. The emphasis may be more on either denial, rejection and ridicule or on magic re-creation. In some non-objective painters—for example, Mondrian—the nihilistic rejection of everything which even reminds one of the real world is the main issue. Ridicule of any order or reason is outstanding in Dadaism, as if the more unexpected and the more random the juxtaposition of the elements, the better the collage. Since everybody retains in himself a residue of childish revolt against the obligation to be orderly and sensible, this repudiation of order and reason has a secret appeal similar to Freud's explanation of the so-called nonsense jokes.

The question arises: Is this trend in contemporary art—to reject and to remodel the surrounding world—unique? Some students of aesthetics will have a ready answer. These features are not at all characteristic of contemporary art alone—they are present in every form of art and literature. No *real* artist ever tries to give merely a faithful reproduction of reality; the specific creative art consists precisely in the artist's attempt to re-create in his own manner the surrounding world. This re-creative urge may manifest itself in many different ways and is present even in the realist painter and writer. It has often been emphasized that the great artist reproduces the essence of the subject. A Rembrandt portrait of an old man, while it represents one specific person, at the same time condenses into the work the universal features of all the old men who ever lived and will live in the future. The presentation of the universal, the timeless, the essential, has long been considered one of the main accomplishments of the artist. The conventional formulation of aesthetics—that the writer and the artist express the universal through the specific, the abstract through the concrete—applies also to impressionist art. The meadow in an impressionist painting is not a meadow in general, but a meadow at 3:30 P.M. in June.

Another creative accomplishment of the artist is the condensation into one concrete example of the significant interrelationships among the objects depicted. A street of Paris by Pissarro is more than the representation of one special geographical location in the metropolis; it reflects the spirit of contemporary Paris through the fleeting impression made upon the onlooker. The ensemble, the tree-lined sidewalks, the advertisements, the color and attire of the milling crowd—all together have a common denominator expressing something essentially characteristic of the city. The artist's creation is to condense all this in one composition, not merely photographic, yet a faithful reproduction of one fleeting impression. In a sense it is much more realistic than a photograph because the visual impression is a highly selective act which emphasizes, distorts and omits various details. The camera can never show how reality actually reflects itself in the onlooker.

When technical terms enter into common usage, they have a tendency to lose their original meaning. After they are in use for a while, the terms begin to live their own lives, gradually developing new connotations and thus becoming a source of confusion. This is precisely what happened to the words "impressionism" and "expressionism." Nothing is further from the truth than the saying that the impressionist represents the outer world, the expressionist his inner world. The impressionist expresses something extremely subjective just as does the expressionist painter. Both represent, although in very different ways, the manner in which the world affects them. Both express their relation to the world. Negation of the world is as much an expression of a relation to the world as is acceptance. The real difference between the two schools lies in their acceptance or rejection of the world. The impressionist painters of the Nineteenth Century had a warm attachment to the world. Their pictures express more than acceptance—they express both curiosity and adoration. And this adoring love extends not only to sunshine, but to the rain, the fog, the meadow, the city street, the *boîte*, the stage, the delicate ankles of the ballerina, and the robust petty bourgeois in the garden restaurant. What the impressionist represents is not the real world of objects but his warm acceptance of this world to which he trustingly exposes himself and which he takes in faithfully and lovingly. To be sure, the primary interest of the impressionist era was in the man-made world—the street, the park, the sidewalk café, the dance hall, the beach with umbrellas—and not so much the forest, the wild mountain peak, or the stormy sea—not unadulterated nature, which was the preferred topic of the romantics. The confident, urbane Western European looked with love and pride upon his own creation. Paris became a principal theme as the pinnacle of an individualistic, enterprising world—of a world which believed in unlimited progress and in reason and science, and of a world in whose hierarchy of values art, literature, and music, the basic sciences and philosophy, as in Plato's *Republic,* occupied the highest rank. The intellectual elite had its own exclusive society, which it exposed to the masses in the café and the literary cabaret. The public, particularly the well-to-do middle class, participated vicariously in this life, looking through the peepholes of literature, painting, and the stage. Their own preoccupation with industry and commerce, which supplied the material foundation of this progressing world, appeared to them a humdrum existence, the main purpose of which, at least in theory, was to make this exalted aesthetic hedonism of the spiritual elite possible. In practice, of course, this existence mostly was meager indeed, but in theory material wealth was there to serve the spiritual progress of knowledge, art, literature, and the art of living; money was not an end in itself.

Then suddenly in the summer of 1914, in a Balkan slum district, the fatal explosion took place and the bubble of this aesthetic culture burst. The European's rude awakening was a sudden and overwhelming one. The real forces of the world—industry, the military machine, and diplomacy—which, at least for a while, had modestly and silently remained in the background and ceded the arena of public life to art, science, the stage, and literature, took over the scene of history overnight. "Blood and gold" are ruling the world, lamented the poet Andreas Ady, the Hungarian Verlaine, who sipped his absinthe in the sidewalk cafés of Paris and Budapest and was one of the most sensitive exponents of decadence. With one stroke the painters and poets showed themselves to be nothing but the luxuries of a wealthy, carefree, and peaceful era. And the exponents of the aesthetic ideology, thus deprived of their *raison d'être,* turned and revolted against a world which showed up the futility of their esoteric existence. Their answer was at first angry indignation and scorn, and then total rejection of the world which now so convincingly disclosed its sordid realities. "The real world is ugly, not worth while—why give it the consideration to depict it as it is ?" Not the pleasing superstructure but the ugly skeleton became the popular subject. "We, the painters and writers, shall show you how repugnant and ridiculous the world is and we shall rebuild it according to our own magic formula." It was not said in these words, but this is what the Blue Riders in Munich, the Futurists in Italy, the Dadaists in Switzerland, the Bohème of the Café du Dôme professed. The Futurist Marinetti, who also invented the symbol of fascism, announced at a demonstration in Paris: "Destroy syntax ! Sabotage the adjective !" And in Berlin, at the opening of a fall exhibition of paintings: "Destroy the museums ! Burn down the libraries !" [1] Now the aesthetic vibrations of the moment, so removed from the actual brutal facts of life, were no longer a worthy subject of art. Now the desperate efforts of Schnitzler's Anatole to endow his love affairs with suburban ingenues with the esoteric illusions by which this anemic Vienna playboy tried to enrich his uneventful life suddenly belonged to the era of yesterday, which had lost all its meaning in the dynamic present. To continue to indulge in the sentimental contemplation of the boulevard, extracting

[1] W. Mehring, *The Lost Library: The Autobiography of a Culture* (New York, 1951), pp. 129–130.

from it all shades of subjective variations of mood, was no longer appropriate in a Paris which had just recently been saved by its taxi drivers from military invasion. Impressionism, the hedonistic exploitation of the leisurely moment, became just as incompatible with the spirit of the day as a dance band at a funeral. And thus almost overnight, in the second decade of the twentieth century, this loving acceptance of the world changed into its opposite, into an angry rejection.

All this, of course, did not come as suddenly as it would appear at first sight. About the turn of the century the suspicion of having been double-crossed began to grow in the European mind. At first only the artists and writers, the forerunners of their time, gave expression to a change of attitude. What the artist anticipated by presentiment, the rest of us realized a few years later. For us it was in August of 1914 that this period of Western history came to an end. For the insensitive it appeared as a sudden collapse; in reality, it was a gradual disintegration. Indeed, the collapse of Nineteenth-Century ideology, its confidence in steady progress, its aesthetic, hedonistic value system in which the arts, music, literature, and pure science occupied a supreme position and, above all, the unquestioned loving acceptance of the world as man made it, was not as sudden as it appeared to the average man. The signs of decline, presaging the apocalypse, were numerous and steadily growing. The truth that every development contains the germs of its own destruction, and that these latent destructive forces increase as the trend approaches its pinnacle, can be demonstrated in the literature and arts at the close of the century. In literature it appeared as the decadent movement. In the poetry of Verlaine, Hofmannsthal, and Rilke, the enjoyment of the moment was mixed with a bittersweet melancholy, a wistful preoccupation with yesterday, an undertone of futility. Hauser characterizes this decadent component in impressionist literature which was prominent in Vienna:

> The Viennese represent the purest form of the impressionism which foregoes all resistance to the stream of experience. Perhaps it is the ancient and tired culture of this city, the lack of all active national politics, and the great part played in literary life by foreigners, especially Jews, which gives Viennese impressionism its peculiarly subtle and passive character. This is the art of the sons of rich bourgeois, the expression of the joyless hedonism of that 'second generation' which lives on the fruits of its fathers' work. They are nervous and melancholy, tired and aimless, skeptical and ironical about themselves, these poets of exquisite moods which evaporate in a trice and leave nothing behind but the feeling of evanescence, of having missed one's opportunities, and the consciousness of being unfit for life.[2]

In England the literary witticism, the provocative aphorism which challenged both reason and Victorian complacency, were virile portents of the same ideological revolt. In Sweden Strindberg, and in Germany Wedekind, were exposing the less savory features of man.

The detachment from the world of reality and the turning toward the mystical symbolism of the unconscious is seen also in the symbolic poetry of Mallarmé and the sym-

[2] A. Hauser, *The Social History of Art*, Vol. II (New York, 1951), p. 908.

bolic paintings of Redon. The first signs of the urge to replace the world with another more consistent than the old, but still retaining the semblance of reality, appear in the post-impressionistic paintings of Van Gogh and Cézanne. The new Rousseauism of Gauguin, his return to primitive culture and unimproved nature, is another form of repudiation of the Western world. The most revolutionary event in these ideological developments, however, came just about the turn of the century, when Freud proposed his theory of the unconscious mind.

In both art and literature, the estrangement from the world was progressing relentlessly. With his emphasis on essentials, on the skeletal structure of the body which is the same in everyone, the contemporary painter tacitly expresses his scorn for the credulity of the impressionist, who was so easily taken in by the pleasing surface, by clothing, by facial expression, by the skin and the muscles. These only hide the basic realities of the body, the viscera and the bony structure which can best be reproduced by simple geometric configurations. All the surface manifestations of the world, all the aesthetic bric-a-brac by which the ferocious animal, man, tries to hide his real nature were to be disregarded. Blood and gold, and we may add, the blast furnace, are ruling the world. The hypocritical and anemic aestheticism of the last century was a self-deception in which the decadent bourgeois could for a little while indulge himself, so long as he was not challenged by the underground forces of society. As soon as the great masses of humanity became mobilized and clamored for a place in the sun, this decadent aesthetic bubble disappeared like the foam on a wave in a stormy ocean. Writes Ortega y Gasset, the visionary Spanish philosopher:

> The mass crushes beneath it everything that is different, everything that is excellent, individual, qualified, and select. Anybody who is not like everybody, who does not think like everybody, runs the risk of being eliminated.[3]

In the dynamic world of Hitler, Mussolini and Stalin, and in the era of industrial mass production, the impressionistic and individualistic cultivation of the moment had no place. This is a century of action and not of idle contemplation. From illusions, from the ever-changing, evanescent impressions of the moment, we must return to the basic essentials, not only in social life but also in art and literature, no matter whether they are pleasing or not.

This is what the artists and writers of the early Twentieth Century express not in so many words, not in theory, but in their own medium of communication. And yet it was difficult, if not impossible, for the artists and writers to change their outlook at a moment's notice. They came into conflict with themselves, having to repudiate everything they professed yesterday and to reject a world in which they grew up. This was, after all, the only world they knew, the world in which they themselves were rooted. The most significant features of contemporary art and literature can be understood only when one realizes that the proponents of expressionism, abstractionism, and surrealism belong to this generation of transition. Their deep-seated conflict, their division of soul, accounts for those features with which the psychiatrist is so well acquainted

[3] J. Ortega y Gasset, *The Revolt of the Masses* (New York, 1932), p. 18.

and which are reminiscent of psychopathology. They could not merely reject the external world because this world had already made a deep imprint upon their own personality; they had to repudiate a part of the self, that part which psychoanalysis calls the rational conscious ego, which is nothing but the imprint of the external world upon the original unorganized mass of impulses and desires which Freud called the id. The conscious ego is the internal representative of the world of reality as against the original basic instinctual forces. It is the ego which demands the adjustment of the subjective impulses to the world. Since the rational ego of this generation was the heritage of the nineteenth century, their rebellion forced them to disavow this part of their own self. "The ego must be extirpated from literature," demanded Marinetti in Milan.[4] The result was an elemental breakthrough, from the unconscious, of the primitive disorganized impulses of the id. And this is why the unconscious mind as it manifests itself in dreams, in psychopathological symptoms, and in the uncontrolled train of thoughts during free association became the dominant note of contemporary art and literature. The unconscious broke through most clearly in the symbolism and dreamlike products of surrealistic paintings. The unconscious reveals itself directly in dreams, and dreams are primarily products of visual fantasy. Therefore surrealistic painting is a most appropriate representation of unconscious mental activity.

Rejection of reality and rebellion against it, however, do not constitute a static mental condition; they represent

[4] Mehring, *loc. cit.*

no final solution. Not even a psychotic can remain in a state of unrelieved revolt. He rejects the world but he must rebuild it according to his own imagery in the form of illusions and hallucinations. Every person does the same in his dreams and daydreams. In fantasy we can correct those aspects of the world which we are not ready to accept and which interfere with our subjective desires that are not adapted to reality. The similarity between the mental processes of the psychotics and the dreams of normal persons has long been recognized. Psychotics in a sense live continuously in a dream world; a healthy person indulges in such wishful distortions of reality only for a brief moment when the organism withdraws from the environment and is relieved from the strenuous task of conforming to the unalterable and sometimes very disturbing facts of reality. Every dream is a rejection of the undesirable aspects of the world, but it is also an attempt to make the world more acceptable. In order to accomplish this, the dreamer regresses to more primitive forms of mental activity. Rational thinking is expressed in words and is a highly advanced form of mental activity which is adjusted to reality. Everyone has to acquire the ability to think rationally during the process of intellectual maturation. In order to return to wishful thinking, the shackles of conscious verbal thinking must be discarded. In the dream one resumes the more infantile forms of mental activity which are characterized by magic and wish fulfillment. In dreams the ordinary rules of logic are abandoned, the unconscious does not know the limitations of time and space. The unorthodoxy of space relations in contemporary drawings and paintings most appropriately expresses not the empirical space conveyed to us by our senses, but the type of space which appears in our dreams. The role of symbols is similar. Pictorial symbols are often based on vague similarities and are therefore in sharp contrast with the precise distinction of meaning conveyed by words.

This affinity of contemporary art to the unconscious mind, particularly dream life, explains certain similarities between paintings of schizophrenics and those of contemporary artists. This similarity has been noted by various psychiatrists and also by artists. Some of them, like Dubuffet, derived great stimulation from studying the drawings of schizophrenic patients. The schizophrenic also withdraws his interest from a world which has become unpalatable and replaces his realistic perceptions with the wishful creation of his own fantasy, his delusions, illusions, and hallucinations. In dreams, as in the fantasy products of schizophrenics, the unconscious mind reveals itself in its full nakedness.

This comparison of contemporary paintings with the products of schizophrenics should not be interpreted as an evaluation of their artistic merits. There are gifted psychotics just as there are gifted neurotics. If Lombroso was right in maintaining that between genius and insanity there is only a narrow dividing line, insanity certainly does not exclude artistic talent. There are several examples of great artists suffering from major psychiatric conditions. Neither does this comparison mean that modern artists are mentally disturbed. To my knowledge, the mental health of modern painters is no different from that of older masters. We find among them mentally healthy persons and neurotics as well as borderline psychotics. Their mental health or illness certainly cannot account for those features in their work which I am considering here. The similarity is based on the close affinity of contemporary art to the deep unconscious layers of the personality which both contemporary artists and schizophrenics reveal directly. In addition to these similarities there are also great and significant differences. The good contemporary artists attempt to communicate their unconscious processes in an organized fashion. The psychotic's paintings, on the other hand, show disorganization, mostly a flight from the world, with much less constructive effort to recapture the lost contact with the world. The attempt to negotiate a new kind of relation to the world is the main striving of the modern artist.

The withdrawal from the realistic world of objects and the return to the non-rational magic world of symbols and wishful distortions is unavoidably accompanied by confusion and anxiety. Disturbed by confusion and anxiety, the individual tries to recapture the world by reshaping it in fantasy. As we have seen, contemporary art attempts this in a radical way by magic and symbolism and by return to the basic elements of line and color. Some of these paintings express little more than utter confusion, but mostly there is an attempt to bring order into chaos. In cubistic paintings both trends are there: the first impression is that of complete disorder but, on further contemplation, gradually a fascinating and novel principle of organization can be discovered. In other contemporary paintings, as in Mondrian's work, the confusion is completely avoided by offering a simple geometric configuration and the harmony of pure colors and lines. But the artist can achieve this perfect order and harmony only by ignoring the rich variety of the world that surrounds him. This is an orderly but badly impoverished world. The artist tries to recapture mastery over the very little which remains after he repudiates reality. A white square on a black background exhibited by Malevitch in 1913 in the Armory Show was the ultimate logical consequence of this defeatist trend to ignore the surrounding universe, which had become so unpalatable. What a contrast between this geometric art, essentially a defeatist attempt to master the nothing, and the magnificent attempts of a Cézanne or a Van Gogh to introduce into the real world new principles of visual organization !

As mentioned before, in every art the world is re-created to some degree, but the artist mostly attempts a more or less realistic re-creation. In contemporary art the re-creation is more radical than in any previous cultural era. It is the diametric opposite of impressionism, the last and most advanced phase of a cultural development which started with the Renaissance, when European man became liberated from the medieval restrictions of free inquiry and began to discover the world around him. The uniformity and rigidity of Byzantine paintings gradually gave place to a hitherto unknown freedom to see the world as it is. The background, as well as the facial expression and the body, became more and more realistic. In all fields of mental activity the trend was the same. Man began to explore the earth, then the celestial bodies, the animal and human organism, and finally the self and the society in which he lives. In art this same trend toward exploration and mastery of the world remained consistent until the end of the Nineteenth Century. The realistic representation of distinct objects was followed by the impressionist discovery of how to reproduce the medium between the objects. Light and air and the representation of the world in its totality, in the interaction of all its constituent parts, became the aim of painting.

Hauser, in his *Social History of Art,*[5] maintains that the first real ideological revolution since the Renaissance occurred in the Twentieth Century. The consistent trend toward the exploration and acceptance of the world was not interrupted until our present era, in spite of the fact that many of the innovations in science, art and literature were accepted only after a period of repudiation. Yet Kepler's astronomical theory was only a step further in the direction initially taken by Galileo and Copernicus, and Einstein's physics was a step beyond Newton's. In art, impressionism was at first violently rejected, and yet it was but the last step in the same consistent trend toward the pictorial discovery of the world which started with Giotto.

The first actual reversal of trend against this steadily progressing realism and rationalism is what we are witnessing today. It appeared in literature as a revolt against reason in the use of words according to their acoustic qualities instead of their meaning, in irrational and symbolic stage productions, and finally in Joyce's direct representation of the unconscious in free association. In painting it appeared as the withdrawal from representing the world of reality, in the distortion of spatial relations

[5] A. Hauser, *The Social History of Art,* Vol. II (New York, 1951), p. 908.

and the objects themselves. The real revolution consists, however, in the repudiation of the loving acceptance of the world of reality and in the revolt against reason. In politics the same trend manifests itself in the fascist emphasis on irrational motivations, on violence, vengeance, and greed, on the praise of a dangerous life. It appears in the form of political adventure and the abolition of freedom of thought and inquiry. The philosophy of existentialism is another consistent repudiation of the predominant role of reason.

Indeed, looking upon current ideological trends from this perspective offers a gloomy picture. Is this, however, a precise interpretation of the prevailing cultural trend ? It is unquestionably true that this century began with a revolt against the Nineteenth-Century value system, which had remained essentially the same since the Renaissance. That this revolt in literature and art manifested itself in a repudiation of the world of the senses and of reason—which is man's weapon to master the world—is also true. That this revolt was followed in art by an attempt to recreate the external reality by archaic unrealistic and magic mental activities is equally valid. And there can be little doubt that the concurrent fascist and communist developments in Eastern and Central Europe are the manifestations of unbridled instincts in politics. They also have a regressive character and are basically irrational and reactionary movements. The question is how to evaluate all these disturbing facts from the larger perspective of history. Are we at the beginning of a new period of medieval obscurantism in which the individual will lose all his spiritual and political freedom and, in order to save himself as an individual, will have to be content with withdrawal into the archaic wishful imagery of his unconscious mind ? In his fear and confusion will he yield to some kind of tyranny and give up all further attempts to master realistically his environment and his fate by increasing his own knowledge, understanding, and reason ? Will he be satisfied with powerless protest, flaunting his contempt of reason, ridiculing the world, and retreating into a dream world of surrealistic magic?

One can also look upon these cultural developments in a different manner. The present trend in art and literature may reflect a new step in the exploration of the world: the exploration of the unconscious. For almost four centuries man turned his interest outward, learning more about the nature of the universe than in any other period of history; he gradually translated his theoretical knowledge into a technological mastery over the forces of nature. During all these impressive accomplishments of extroverted activities, he completely forgot the exploration of his own self. He knew of himself only as much as he wanted to. He built up the illusion of himself as a progressive, rational, basically benign, socially minded personality, striving for truth, the cultivation of beauty and the realization of social justice. This was taught in the humanistic gymnasiums of the European continent and in the public schools of England. Those writers, artists, and philosophers who challenged this rosy picture of man's personality were disregarded or ridiculed by the official academies of culture. And the parents and teachers, the intellectual leaders, were alerted and on guard against the repeated onslaughts against their own repressions.

Their chief enemy was the Viennese neurologist, Freud, ostracized by the medical society because of his revolutionary teachings concerning the role of sex and the unconscious mind in the causation of neurosis. With the outbreak of the First World War the self-deceptive, complacent ideology began to crumble. And after the war, with the collapse of the political and economic structure of Europe, everything which hitherto was considered safe and stable was swept away. The controlling forces of the personality, in order to keep in check the asocial and irrational forces of the unconscious, need reinforcement from the outside in the form of parental example, law and police, the authority of the state, the teachings of the church and the school. But the disintegrating political and economic structure of Europe could no longer supply these external reinforcements. The older generation had failed in the eyes of the young. They were held responsible for the fiasco of the old system, whether it was the constitutional monarchy, the four per cent rate of interest, the gold standard which appeared to be assured forever, or the conventional standards of the professors upheld by the academies of the sciences and arts. The external authorities, the living representatives of our internal standards, were discredited, and the unconscious forces swept through the barriers of the conventional code. The unconscious—with all its elemental forces, mysticism, and irrationality—arose to the surface. It became the principal object of psychology and the social sciences, of art and literature, and it dominated the internal political life of nations as well as world politics. Are we witnessing at this very moment a brief lull before the storm? Will man be able to bring these unleashed destructive forces under his control again?

The same question on a smaller scale confronts the psychoanalyst every day in his practice. With his therapeutic technique, he tries to bring the unconscious impulses of the patient to the surface. The traditional apprehension with which psychoanalysis was received, the fear that this procedure might unleash all the asocial propensities of the patient, and turn a hitherto harmless neurotic into a selfish, ruthless person has proven unfounded. We have learned just the opposite. Repression, denial, hypocritical self-deception have been inadequate defenses against the instinctive forces of man. The only remedy is to make the patient conscious of his deeper impulses. The barriers of repression must first be overcome before a new and more extended control over the self can be obtained. Not even in a well-conducted treatment does this process of self-revelation always take place without occasional dramatic episodes. When this happens we say that the patient is "acting out." From the point of view of history, the last forty years of Western civilization may be considered as a brief episode of "acting out." Who can tell, however, whether or not we are at the end of this dynamic but chaotic phase of cultural and political history ? One thing is certain: if and when we are able to develop new internal standards and a new relation to a world which has changed faster than our adaptive capacity, a wiser and more conscious humanity will arise. The chaotic eruption of the unconscious has already contributed new dynamic forces which gradually can be brought under the control of reason and utilized constructively. It has already opened up new avenues of artistic expression. From his acquaintance with the unconscious archaic layers of the mind, the artist, in the same way as the scientist, has gained new materials and techniques for expressing a new relationship to the world.

Freud was not only the discoverer of the unconscious but also the inventor of a technique by which the unconscious forces, after being mobilized, can be brought under the control of the rational mind. After the scientific mastery of the unconscious, its artistic mastery will follow.

In contemporary American art the trend toward reconstruction is more pronounced than the rebellious denial of the world which was so characteristic in the early European developments. In Europe the movement started as an open rebellion against the orderly and optimistic approach of the Nineteenth Century. Soon after the movement reached the shores of the United States—at the Armory Show in New York in 1913—it lost many of its bitter and revolutionary connotations and was influenced by the mechanical and reconstructive spirit of an advanced industrial civilization. The effort to bring the unconscious under rational control is conspicuous in the works of many American painters.

There is no time, however, for complacency. We are at a crossroads of cultural development. The complete collapse of Western civilization or a new positive acceptance of the world and the rule of reason are the alternatives. If the outcome is favorable, we will have to come to terms with the world around us. Revolt and rejection of reality are destructive reactions; they cannot represent a permanent solution. There is no choice—the road must eventually lead back to reality and reason. Life is dependent upon the environment. It is two-way traffic: we express ourselves but we also receive from the environment. Art expresses the relationship of the self to the surrounding world. Negation and re-creation of the world with the help of magic must eventually yield to a more realistic solution. Of necessity, this will modify artistic style and expression. The naked unconscious, as it often appears in contemporary art, is not a suitable way of communication. It must go through the prism of the organizing portion of the personality, the conscious ego, to become meaningful. The artist will eventually emerge from the surrealistic detour through the depths of the unconscious mind with a fresh point of view, richer, and with a new constructive message which he cannot express in this era of negation and confusion.

CHAPTER XI

Existentialism and Psychoanalysis

"Despair is a sickness in the spirit, in the self, and so it may assume a triple form: In despair at not being conscious of having a self . . . in despair at not willing to be oneself; in despair at willing to be oneself."
S. KIERKEGAARD

When I first became acquainted with the precursors of present-day existentialism, particularly with the writings of Kierkegaard and Nietzsche, I did not grasp their historical significance. The "organization man," particularly in my part of the world, had not yet emerged, and, lacking the prophetic genius of these philosophers, I set their writings aside as profound but exalted contemplations. Like the rest of the world, I understood their significance as a protest against the depersonalizing trend of our era only when they were rediscovered by contemporary existentialist writers.

It is customary today to point out that, while the structure of western society, its means of production, its technological knowledge and its political system have undergone a thoroughgoing metamorphosis, the basic psychological—not to speak of anatomical and physiological structure of man—has remained the same as far back as written history reaches. The instinctual drives, the aspirations and the conflicts of western man today appear not much different from what we can reconstruct from Greek, Roman or medieval literature. In all ages, people loved and hated, competed and cooperated, sought security and adventure, hoped and despaired, adjusted themselves to conditions and created new environments to live in. While these basic components of human nature remained unchanged, attitudes toward the universe, social behavior and values show well-defined, if not consistent, variations.

The ancient Greek's orientation is clearly distinguishable from that of the medieval person's, as well as from that of the Renaissance man, although the first and last may show certain similarities. In trying to define these changes in attitude, one should not attempt to construct a single trend—for example, a continuous progress toward greater rationality, humanism and enlightenment. Such a trend may exist for a limited historical period, but periodic revival of an older attitude is common. After 800 years of Dark Ages, the return to ancient rationalism and individualism was evident at the Renaissance. Now this three-centuries-old trend toward rationalism is being challenged. Man has begun to doubt the omnipotence of his reasoning faculties and he is becoming more aware of the power of seemingly indomitable instinctual forces, of the fact that much of his behavior is determined by impulses of which he is not aware. The most perplexing feature of our present days is that, while the rationalization and the planned organization of social life is continuously progressing, at the same time there are growing signs of a deep-seated countercurrent within the human personality, signs of a protest against the rationalization and depersonalization of life, accompanied by fear and confusion. The existential philosopher calls this "existential despair," the psychoanalyst calls it "loss of ego-identity."

The liberation of the European man from the dogmatic conformity of the Middle Ages encouraged his curiosity about the world around him. Navigation and the discovery of unknown lands broadened his horizons and prompted him to investigate the unknown instead of believing blindly in authority. These were undoubtedly the precursors of the rationalism of our industrial age. Today we are witnessing in the existentialist movement in philosophy, literature and art a major reaction to this trend.

Extentialist writers regard Sören Kierkegaard as their spiritual father. For long years the writings of this Danish philosopher remained unnoticed by the professional philosophers as well as the general public. He was considered an emotionally disturbed man, a local figure, a religious fanatic in a world in which, according to him, true—not institutionalized—religion was rapidly losing its hold. In the perspective of today he is recognized as one of those highly sensitive individuals who react to intangible portents unnoticed by the majority. Had not the steadily advancing scientific rationalistic outlook entered its present-day crisis, Kierkegaard would have remained a relatively unknown philosopher. He was rediscovered when the antithesis between reason and existence, which was the essence of his own personal struggle, became a universal issue for the contemporary European.

There is no doubt that the most stupendous accomplishment of man consists in the perfection of the observational and reasoning powers of his intellect. Within an unbelievably short period he changed the surface of the earth, modified the conditions of individual and social life and is now in the process of penetrating outer space. All these triumphs, however, concerned the world around him. In the fervor of this extroverted mastery of the world around him, man forgot the mastery of his own self. He conquered the world and lost his own self.

This central fact is the axis of Kierkegaard's thinking. Reason became detached from the reasoning person; in this sense it became sterile. While looking for the stars, man allowed that which is nearest to him, his own self, to go into oblivion. "Everyone is farthest removed from his own self—we do not know ourselves," Nietzsche wrote later in his *Genealogy of Morals*. All this became an issue only when religion, the traditional caretaker of man in all his other than intellectual needs, lost its hold on the western world. Science displaced religious mythology and undermined its authority. Science could not, however, substitute anything in the place of religion to guide man in his own most critical decisions. It did not give him new morality, new faith, new answers for the essential question: What is the meaning of personal existence? Man as an individual being, different and separate from all others, was left alone in all those issues which concerned him most intimately in all the unpredictable vicissitudes of his own fate.

All this was for Kierkegaard a highly personal experience, something which has only today become universally felt in our western civilization. In this sense he anticipated coming events, and herein lies the explanation of his present-day influence. He dedicated his life to a passionate defense of the individual and desired as an inscription on his tombstone: "That Individual."

Kierkegaard's answer to the existential dilemma was to revive true Christianity as distinct from institutionalized religion, which according to him, had failed to fulfill its destination. Like Kierkegaard, Nietzsche was motivated by the conviction that abstract reason cannot solve the basic problems of human existence. "Reason," Nietzsche wrote in his *Thoughts Out of Season*, "is only an instrument and Descartes, who recognized only reason as the supreme authority, was superficial." He succinctly said that the true statement should read *vivo, ergo cogito* and not the Cartesian *cogito, ergo sum*. Reason is in the service of life, of the will to live. While Kierkegaard found the solution in original Christian faith, Nietzsche relied on the Dionysian principle, the dynamic power of life, the deep irrational instinctual forces which were corroded by Christianity. The common element in these two so opposite philosophies is their denial that scientific abstractions can solve the actual concrete problems of human existence. Both represent a reaction against the belief of three centuries that the eventual salvation of mankind lies in science. Both felt that by exploring the world around him, man has lost his own self. Both emphasized subjective experience, man's real concrete concerns about his own fate. This is why contemporary existential philosophers claim them both as their spiritual predecessors.

Nietzsche foresaw the perils of our "theoretical culture," which is founded on the "delusion" that causal understanding can penetrate to the essence of the world. To the latter, man has access only through subjectively experiencing his irrational Dionysian forces. Dionysian art permits him to feel most intensively his limitless passion merely to exist. Existence has no rational aims. When western man wakes up from his "Socratic delusions" and recognizes the aimlessness of existence, he will unavoidably become a victim of nihilism. The only escape lies in recognizing that existence itself is the ultimate value.

"In a remote corner of the universe which is forged out of innumerable scintillating solar systems," Nietzsche wrote, "there existed once a star on which clever animals invented knowledge. This was the most arrogant and mendacious minute in the history of the universe; and yet, only a minute." Intellect has no other mission than to serve life, which in itself is the ultimate value.

Morality, too, is subordinated to the passionate will to live. From here it is only one step to the idea of the superman who succeeds in freeing himself on the shackles of self-deceptive illusions and has the courage for full self-realization. Man will perish because of his conventional virtues. The sooner he disappears the better, so that the superman can replace him.

No other philosopher fought so passionately as Nietzsche did for the uniqueness of the individual. "If you have a virtue and it is your virtue, then you have it alone and you do not share it with anyone else." When one tries to express these highly unique idiosyncracies in words, they lose their uniqueness. "Therefore, one cannot clearly speak, one can only stammer about them: This is *my* idea of goodness; this *I* like; this pleases *me* completely; this is the only way *I* want to strive for goodness."

The same emphasis on subjective experience, of "being here in the world," is the point of departure for Heidegger's highly abstract, but at the same time subjectivistic, philosophy. Man is in the world, is a part of the world, the only one endowed with the faculty of self-awareness and of communicating this with others through language. Man's ability to interpret the meaning of his own existence historically gives him a key to the understanding of the world. Although Heidegger does not acknowledge this, his philosophy, in spite of its novel terminology and claim of transcendent validity, is still centered around the basic fact of self-awareness. He employs Husserl's phenomenological method, which attempts to describe with utmost precision the ever-flowing content of consciousness.

The evaluation of Heidegger's involved analysis, of "being in the world," of time and the meaning of truth, must be left to the professional philosopher. Much of his contributions appear to the psychologist as semantic restatement of old metaphysical, psychological and epistemological perspectives which are not always kept separate from each other. The impression of its novelty comes more from linguistic gymnastics and interesting etymological analyses than from conceptual content. Heidegger's profound meditations on death, which can occur at any moment and therefore should serve as a constant remainder of the stark fact of existing, had been anticipated by Nietzsche. Speaking of the effect of tragedy, Nietzsche wrote, "We should recognize that everything that came to be must be prepared for painful destruction; we are forced to look at the dreads of individual existence—and yet, we should not be paralyzed. A metaphysical consolation pulls us out for a moment from the chaos of ephemeral existence."

Nietzsche was much more a psychologist than Heidegger, and in many respects he anticipated Freud. It appears, therefore, paradoxical that the greatest impetus for development of existential psychiatry came from Heidegger's writings. Psychotherapy deals with the concrete facts of individual existences, while Heidegger's approach, although highly subjectivistic, remains in generalities. This is in striking contrast to the approach of Freud, who dealt with actual individual fates as they reveal themselves during a uniquely frank communication of a person with his therapist. Heidegger's philosophy does not offer any operational clues by which his profound insights can be applied to concrete cases. It does not provide that type of cumulative knowledge which is the essence of every science. Heidegger, for example, postulates that man should understand his being historically, but how to do this concretely he does not tell. Freud by his method made this philosophical postulate operationally possible; the psychoanalytic technique succeeds in historically reconstructing each person's highly unique genetic (biographical) background. Because psychoanalysis represents a body of growing knowledge, it belongs to the realm of science and not to philosophy, something which Freud emphasized in his frequent protestations that he should not be considered a philosopher.

Existential philosophers undoubtedly should be given credit for emphasizing the general principle that the *via regia* to the exploration of the world is self-awareness, because of the simple and basic fact that man exists in the world, is a part of the world and because of his faculty of a historical self-awareness which connects the past, present and the future, he experiences the "world process" in his own existence.[1] That natural science restricts itself to data of sense perceptions and deals with objects only, and therefore does not take advantage of man's ability to experience subjectively his own development as a possible source of knowledge, is equally true. But psychoanalysis went further than proclaiming the theoretical validity of these philosophical postulates; it translated them into a growing body of scientific knowledge. Herein lies its historical significance. Freud demonstrated that what Kierkegaard, Nietzsche and Heidegger considered unapproachable by the "scientific method"—the subjective world of man—indeed can be approached by improved and systematic methods of psychological observation and reasoning. In this sense, psychoanalysis is a complete repudiation of the "anti-scientism" of existentialist philosophers. It demonstrated that communicated self-awareness can be developed to become a systematic controlled method of inquiry into human motivations, a source of that type of growing cumulative knowledge which is synonymous with science.

For the psychoanalyst who is devoted to the exploration of the self, it is difficult to feel anything but amazement in witnessing the lack of understanding of Freud's

[1] This is essentially a restatement in psychological terms of Hegel's metaphysical concept of the "world spirit," no matter how emphatically existential thinkers repudiate Hegel.

work among many perceptive existentialist writers. They rediscovered Kierkegaard and Nietzsche as the saviors of Western man against the corroding influence of a completely outward-directed intellect. They turned to Heidegger's highly abstract elaboration of the same fundamental issues and overlooked the fact that Freud actually succeeded in applying man's most developed faculty, his reasoning powers, to the concrete understanding of his self. Psychoanalysis has demonstrated, in spite of all its present limitations, that the same faculties which made the natural sciences what they are today—systematic observation and reasoning—can be applied not only to the physical universe but to man himself. Freud has shown that the existential dilemma, the estrangement of reason from being, does not need to lead to anti-scientism, to a discrediting of the intellect. In fact, it is a challenge for psychology and the social sciences to complement the one-sided picture the natural sciences gave us by improving the most unique human faculty, that of self-reflection and verbal communication, for a concrete operational understanding of his own self.

Existential philosophy served its purpose by emphasizing the need for a change of focus from the world outside to man himself, who by his faculty of self-reflection has a most direct access to the understanding of the universe. Man is a part of the universe—a part which, in experiencing his being, has direct access to the "world process" of which man himself is one concrete case. Philosophy could not supply more than this basic insight. To show how self-reflection can be carried out in a methodical and controlled fashion was the contribution of Freud. From this perspective existentialism appears, paradoxically enough, as another defense against facing concretely one's self.

Some extenuating circumstance for the neglect of psychoanalysis by existential writers is found in certain recent developments in psychoanalytic teaching and practice. These developments can be summarized under four points:

First, an exaggerated emphasis upon technical details and upon often dogmatically stated rules of procedure. In the same way that pure religion became overshadowed by institutionalized religion, there are signs that institutionalized psychoanalysis is in danger of losing sight of its fundamentals, particularly of the fact that every person is a unique problem and his treatment requires a highly individual application of general principles. Increasing attention paid to formal aspects of the treatment has begun to overshadow the basic psychodynamic evaluation of the psychological processes which take place during the treatment. This trend may give some justification to the existentialist's reference to "methodolatry," emphasizing method and losing sight of the goal.

Second, regarding intellectual insight and its instrument, interpretation—instead of the patient's emotional experiences during treatment—as the most fundamental curative factor in psychoanalytic therapy. This is the result of confusing etiological research with therapy.

Third, the persistent emphasis upon the really non-existent incognito of the analyst, who supposedly functions mainly as an abstract objective intellect—overlooking the fact that psychoanalytic therapy is an interaction between two distinct and highly individual personalities. Existential psychoanalysts refer to this latter fact as "encounter."

Fourth, a growing emphasis on adaptation. The psychoanalytic concept of the ego does not imply such an emphasis. Freud conceived the ego's function as an integrative one: it reconciles individual needs and strivings with each other and with the existing conditions in the environment upon which the fulfillment of these needs and strivings depends. Freud, it is true, considered the ego as the representative of external reality, but at the same time even more as a representative of internal reality. Its primary function is to gratify subjective needs, which it can accomplish either by adapting them *as much as necessary* to existing environmental conditions *or by changing the environment creatively.* The neurotic ego cannot fulfill this task because it excludes by repression and other defenses those subjective impulses which it cannot harmonize with other impulses (superego demands) and with external reality. It sacrifices its own potentialities for the sake of an unsuccessful type of adjustment achieved with the help of repression and other defenses, and thus becomes impoverished.

To this the existentialist refers as the unauthentic self. Psychoanalytic treatment attempts to enlarge the ego's integrative scope by bringing repressed mental content into consciousness, thus allowing a person to be himself as much as possible under given external conditions. This is the same goal the existentialist calls finding one's authentic self. How to achieve this goal they do not say. The loss of ego identity is the result of the failure of this integrative function. Enlarging the ego's integrative scope by overcoming the defenses directed toward one's own impulses is the aim of psychoanalysis. This is far from a simple adjustment to existing conditions. It is a struggle for self-realization within the limits set by social reality. And these limits are not fixed. Man created social reality and is capable of changing it. To be able to change reality is probably the greatest accomplishment of man. Culture is a creation of man—as much as man is the creation of that culture which he himself has built. A one-sided emphasis on conforming to external reality which is considered as unalterable is far from the original concept of psychoanalysis.

Nevertheless, it is true, that the neglect of the creative activities of man is perhaps the greatest gap in contemporary psychoanalytic thought. The "unconscious" more and more is becoming a repertory of all that is repressed and "unadjusted," and thus equated with what is called neurotic. That the "unconscious" is the source of what is creative in man is forgotten. At least partially, Freud himself was responsible for this trend when he expressed his awe of artistic creativeness, something he did not dare to tamper with. This avoidance in his case, however, was entirely due to his immense reverence for the complexity of the creative act and not to overlooking its existence or to minimizing its significance in the human psyche.

Efforts to overcome the defenses of the ego which originate in the weak infantile ego's inability to deal with the powerful pressure of individual impulses certainly do not promote adjustment alone. Equally or more so, the creative possibilities of man are enhanced by restoring the ego's integrity, which it has lost under the impact of early experiences. Properly understood, psychoanalysis does not strive for conformity by adjustment and by sacrificing the unique self; it strives for self-realization.

Existential philosophy recognized the loss of the authentic self as a growing trend in our civilization. It did not offer any measures for combatting it. Philosophical insight and emphasis on the need for a vivid experiencing of the self are not sufficient. Psychoanalysis, by reconstructing the structure and dynamics of personality by arduous and systematic observation based on free communication between two persons, by a highly developed method of getting really acquainted with one's self, opens up the way to this goal. The existentialist's biased depreciation of operational knowledge and his exaltation of philosophical—no matter how profound—generalities can at best identify goals without giving signposts for how to reach these goals.

The main objection which can be raised against existential writings is that they often attempt to describe psychological realities in terms of philosophical generalities, many of which are taken over from scholastic tradition. This is the case in spite of the contention that the existential approach is based on the most concrete and immediate phenomenological analysis of all the data of self-awareness. Many existentialists, like Boss, for example, frankly admit that their actual therapeutic approach does not differ essentially from the psychoanalytic approach; what they offer is a new philosophical outlook and a comprehensive interpretation of the interview material, which they maintain is not in contradiction to psychoanalytic interpretations but in addition to them. Also, contemporary psychoanalysis puts the separate dynamisms, conflicts, the manifestations of transference and resistance in the perspective of the totality of the individual's unique personality. This is what analysts call "ego analysis." The expression "integration" seldom, if ever, appears in existential literature, but actually what they struggle with is the highest integrative aspects of self-awareness. Psychoanalysts consider integrative patterns as unique for each person, and to find this specific unity of each person is the true aim of the psychoanalytic approach. The experiencing of the self as an unique example of all possible combinations is implicit in psychoanalysis. Furthermore, the contention of the existentialists that every mental act, such as perception and memory—not to speak of striving and making decisions—is an active, nay creative, phenomenon has been stressed by psychoanalysts and by Gestalt psychologists. The old concept of the passive ego driven by the id, the super-ego and external reality is yielding to a more dynamic picture of the ego, the main function of which is the exquisitely active integrative decision-making act. Much of the existential contribution consists in restating this fundamental insight in old philosophical terms, which lack the clarity and precision of Gestalt psychological and psychoanalytical conceptualizations. This does not detract from the value of restating all this with a new emphasis, but the claim for novelty cannot be granted to the existentialist psychiatrists. Neither do I see much merit in revising old scholastic expressions, such as "potentia" for developmental possibilities or "experiencing existence and being" for self-awareness, or in reviving such scholastic pseudo-problems as the difference between "essence" and "existence," or in replacing with the poetic, visionary and passionate language of Kierkegaard and Nietzsche the more sober and better defined ideas and expressions of Freud, through which he tried to describe and interpret the same fundamental facts of self-awareness, which is the central issue in existentialism. Neither does it yield more profound insight to speak of the struggle of the neurotic to find his authentic self without explicitly acknowledging the fact that the most important factor in the fragmentation of the personality and the loss of ego-identity is the failure of the neurotic ego in its integrative functions, inasmuch as it excludes by repression, projection and other psychodynamic processes all that it cannot harmoniously reconcile within its unity. The role of multiple contradictory identifications is equally overlooked. The concepts of the dynamic unconscious and repression are circumvented by many existential psychiatrists, and it is difficult not to interpret this as an instinctive avoidance of the most basic discoveries of psychoanalysis, without which the "unauthentic self" of the neurotic remains a mere literary expression, or at best a general idea. The trend toward bombastic pathos in style, toward confusing value judgments and factual observations, the propensity to preaching instead of describing and explaining, is at least partially due to the fascination which the existentialists feel toward Kierkegaard's and Nietzsche's highly intuitive but unsystematic prescientific writings.

Yet the existential movement cannot be simply ignored as an inconsequential trend in modern psychiatry. While it has not yet reached the American shores with its total impact, it is one of the most influential currents in European philosophy and psychiatry. Primarily it is not a new contribution to the content of psychiatry or psychotherapy. It is a consistently formulated basic orientation. It is a vocal protest against the prevailing trend in our civilization to reduce the human individual to a cog of the social machinery. For such a society the uniqueness of the individual is useless; hence, it prefers to deal with him in his social role and not as a distinct personality with the specific mission of realizing his unique potentialities. Such a society emphasizes adjustment and utility instead of creativity, the polar opposite of adjustment. To be creative means to produce something which is not yet in existence; adjustment means to accept and to conform with what is already there. The existential revolution is inspired by the despair of the European man who feels threatened with being reduced to the level of the "faceless masses." It is a desperate cry for preserving the most specifically human aspects of man and his creative genius, his self-awareness as a unique being different from all others. Existentialism is the philosophical expression of this revolt, which manifests itself in all fields of creativity, above all in modern art and literature. More than in any other cultural era, the modern artist creates his own universe instead of depicting that which is around him; he creates his own space as the cubist, he reassembles the parts of the human body according to his own delight, he changes, he exaggerates, he omits, and in extreme he completely disregards the world as it presents itself to our senses. In literature the dread of estrangement from the world and from the self, what is called existential despair, appears most effectively in Kafka's, Rilke's and Camus' writings and in Sartre's nihilistic philosophy.

Psychotherapy is a natural medium for absorbing the existentialist outlook (not its nihilistic offshoot of Sartre). The way was prepared by psychoanalysis, for which every person is a unique problem who must be understood in his own unique world. Existentialists who emphasize this principle, that every patient must be understood in his own specific world and not in general terms, not in terms of universal mechanisms and conflicts, should not overlook the fact that the essence of Freud's endeavors as a therapist was precisely this highly individualistic orientation. One should not confuse psychoanalysis as a therapy with Freud's theory, which tries, as every scientific theory does, to formulate general principles and which has to be applied to each living being in considering all its specific features.

From this perspective one must welcome the existential emphasis because it counterbalances the prevailing trend to which psychoanalytic teaching (not so much practice) is in the process of succumbing, namely, to lose sight of the gap between theoretical generalizations and the individual patient, whose uniqueness of necessity requires a flexible application of general principles. It is also a needed correction of the trend toward replacing the individual approach to each specific person with rigid technical rules. This trend eventually leads to a deification of technique as an aim in itself, as the essence of psychoanalysis, instead of making technique a servant of its goals.

CHAPTER XII

The Struggle for Ego Identity

> "For the immediate man does not recognize his self, he recognizes himself only by his dress. . . . He recognizes that he has a self only from externals. . . . The whole problem of the self in a deeper sense becomes a sort of blind door in the background of his soul, behind which there is nothing. He accepts what in his language he calls his self, that is to say, whatever abilities, talents, et cetera, may have been given to him; all this he accepts, yet with the outward direction toward what is called life, the real, the active life he treats with great precaution the bit of self-reflection which he has in himself, he is afraid that this thing in the background may emerge. So little by little he succeeds in forgetting it; in the course of years he finds it almost ludicrous, especially when he is in good company with other capable and active men, who have a sense and capacity for real life."
>
> S. KIERKEGAARD

In my own field—in psychoanalysis—the growing threat to man's individuality became the focus of attention under the term "loss of ego identity." The writings of Erik Erikson and of Alan Willis are representative of this concern.

The most human faculty of man is the awareness of his

existence as a distinct person who exists in the continuum of the past, the present and the future and who, with a sense of self-determination, plans and shapes his own fate. Self-awareness is the most immediate of our experiences; it cannot be compared with any other experience, and, because it cannot be experienced but from the one single vantage point of subjectivity, it is so elusive. And yet, it is the most fundamental fact of our life. One becomes keenly aware of one's self in the morbid states of depersonalization, when a person suddenly feels strange to himself, or occasionally in hypnagogic states in the transitional stage between the waking state and sleep. Only when the feeling of identity is disrupted do we become aware of its existence. In a healthy state, we are aware of ourselves without being aware of the fact of awareness, just as we are not aware of the air we breathe until we are suddenly deprived of it.

We know from psychoanalysis that this feeling of personal identity is the result of a complex developmental process. Yet, we feel that it has always been there as far back as our memory goes. We feel that it is the same person who played on the floor as an infant, who was praised, loved, and rebuked by his parents, who quarreled with his brothers and sisters, who went to school, who chose a profession, who married and had children. This feeling of continuity in a mentally undisturbed person is not interrupted and starts quite early in life. Beyond this, there is no memory because remembering presupposes the existence of an ego which has the feeling of some kind—no matter how vague and primitive a form—of identity. A statement like "I remember sitting on the floor and playing with a toy" contains the crucial pronoun "I." Without an "I" there is no memory because there is no one yet who can remember. Patients occasionally report scraps of vague memories, events which have no subject but appear impersonal: "a colored window glass, a monkey on a chain," without including themselves in the picture. These are the precursors of memories which are registered and perceived in an isolated manner. In focusing attention on those isolated engrams, the patient begins to add such statements as: "I think the colored window glass was in a country inn; the monkey on the chain was in the courtyard of the inn to which my parents took me. My sister was standing beside me in the yard. This monkey once bit my sister." These additions point to the fact that there was already the nucleus of a self-aware ego, one that was aware of having a sister and of having parents. Sometimes there are retrospective additions of a later date. We may say, then, that before there is a synthetic awareness of sensations and experiences which belong to an "I," no memory is possible. Isolated conditioning experiences are probably present from the beginning of life, but these do not have the quality of memories which presuppose a simultaneous awareness of an "I" who experienced what is remembered.

It is evident that the emergence of this feeling of identity must be the result of a continuously progressing integrative process. Among psychoanalytic authors Erikson has gone furthest in attempting to reconstruct the major events of this integrative process. His reconstruction is partially based on the libido theoretical concept of distinct phases in personality development: infancy, early childhood, latency, adolescence, early adulthood and adulthood, each characterized by biologically determined changes in libido organization. He considers as equally significant the socio-psychological influences of the environment as they affect libido development. Each new phase of development is considered as a crisis requiring new integrative tasks to include the changing libidinal forces and the changing expectations of the environment upon the growing individual into a harmonious unit, which is perceived as the self.[1]

In adolescence, this crisis, known even in the pre-psychoanalytic era, is loudest. Adolescence, in fact, often appears as a transient neurosis caused primarily by the impact of the biologically reinforced sexual impulses upon a yet emotionally unprepared ego. These are felt as a foreign body which is not yet amalgamated with the rest of the personality. Suddenly a mature body almost overnight is entrusted to a yet inexperienced ego. At the same time, the adolescent is confronted with an environment which considers him as almost an adult, has new expectations of him about which, in lack of experience, he feels most insecure.

It is doubtful that in other cultural periods or in primitive static civilizations the continuously progressing integrative tasks during the process of maturation consist of a series of crises. Ego maturation under stable external conditions in which child care, as well as the social expectations, are routinized must be a much smoother process with less incumbent dangers of "diffusion" of iden-

[1] Erik Erikson, *Childhood and Society* (New York, 1950); Erik Erikson, *Das Problem der Identität, Entfaltung der Psychoanalyse* (Stuttgart, Germany, 1956).

tity. Crises during maturation naturally have always occurred in exceptional cases, in families with disturbed parents, or in cases of sudden social dislocation, such as emigration. The influx of foreign-born parents for decades was a consistent feature of the American scene, a factor which has been keenly recognized by such anthropologists as Margaret Mead as a particular hazard of psychological maturation. These second-generation children cannot take their parents as models to show them the ways of socially accepted behavior. They must find them alone and learn them from their peers. Today, on account of the accelerated speed of social change, in a sense we live in a permanent state of immigration from one social structure into a new one. Parental attitudes become outdated from generation to generation.

The universal hazards of libido development under stable conditions are by no means beyond the integrative powers of the ego and only at present—under the challenges of ever-changing social influences—appear as "crises," as a universal source of psychopathology.

Psychoanalytic literature, it appears to me, has mostly emphasized the role of identification with adults and peers and with prevalent ideological trends as the most significant factor in ego development. The other factor, the growing person's own groping experimentations to find acceptable behavior patterns, is less considered. Erikson, it is true, is fully aware of the significance of play, in which the child exercises his native and acquired faculties in an experimental manner and has opportunity to find his own individual solutions. The serious demands of life do not yet force him to be successful. He may try again and again to solve, so to say, "hypothetical" problems without grave consequences, should he fail. Successful identification with adults requires understanding and patient guidance. Encouraging play activities, on the other hand, puts the child on his own resources and allows him to complement identifications with adults with his own original solutions, by which within the larger framework of existing traditions he can freely develop his own uniqueness. Teaching and spontaneous learning do not go parallel. If, during growth, each phase of ego development is firmly consolidated before the next is undertaken, the phenomena of neurotic withdrawal and regression, identity diffusion, or shallow conformism need not occur.

The microscopic analyses of Erikson and other psychoanalysts are well complemented by Riesman's macroscopic picture of the emergence of the other-directed person.[2] According to Riesman, the inner-directed person is one who possesses a well-defined stable internal organization of principles and values which govern his behavior. This gives such a person a relative independence from the changing attitudes and expectations of others. It goes hand-in-hand with a feeling of identity as a distinct person who takes himself for granted and is not disturbed by constant doubts about his goals, values, internal problems and who is not preoccupied constantly with comparing himself with others. Such a person's attention can be fully absorbed by goals and strivings toward causes which lie outside of him; he can afford the luxury of healthy extroversion, devotion to things beyond his own personal concerns. He has successfully solved the problem of internal

[2] David Riesman, *The Lonely Crowd* (New Haven, 1953).

organization of his self by incorporating traditional values and integrating them with his own individual propensities. He does not need to be preoccupied with the ways of a good life; these were given to him partially in successive package deals through identifications with parents and peers, each corresponding to his chronological and emotional age. Partially, he acquired them in undisturbed play activities. He acquired them during a smooth, relatively undisturbed process of mental growth. This feeling of identity is an ever-present component of his self-awareness, without his being specifically aware of it. When he is mature, he takes his goals and values—and first of all, himself—for granted, and his energies can be directed toward things and persons outside himself. In psychoanalytic terminology, when he is grown up, he is capable of "object love"—his libido is liberated from its early self-directed position, which characterizes everyone during the childhood phases of life when he is engaged in building up his body and personality. After maturation he has a surplus of energy to spend freely.

If he is a creative individual he can use this surplus for acquiring new knowledge by which he can change his environment; or he can contribute to others by artistic and other socially useful activities. If he is an average individual he can raise a family and find his niche in the social machinery. Nowhere in professional literature have I found this as well expressed as in Pasternak's novel *Dr. Zhivago:*

> But what is consciousness: Let's see. . . . Consciousness is a light directed outward, it lights up the way ahead of us so that we don't stumble. It's like the headlights on a

> locomotive—turn them inward and you'd have a crash.
>
> So what will happen to your consciousness ? *Your* consciousness, yours, not anyone else's. Well, what are *you ?* There's the point. Let's try to find out. What is it about you that you have always known as yourself ? What are you conscious of in yourself ? Your kidneys ? Your liver ? Your blood vessels ? No. However far back you go in your memory, it is always in some external, active manifestation of yourself that you come across your identity—in the work of your hands, in your family, in other people. And now listen carefully. You in others—this is your soul. This is what you are. This is what your consciousness has breathed and lived on and enjoyed throughout your life—your soul, your immortality, your life in others. And what now ? You have always been in others and you will remain in others. And what does it matter to you if later on that is called your memory ? This will be you—the you that enters the future and becomes a part of it.[3]

Pasternak intuitively recognizes here a most significant factor favoring ego integration: devotion to an external object, be it love of persons or dedication to a cause. Such an outward-directed orientation serves as an axis, a crystallization point for organization, for the building of a harmonious system (ego identity). Persons find themselves in and through the cause to which they are dedicating their efforts. Jones, in Freud's life history, demonstrated this thesis with unparalleled clarity. An insecure, vacillating young man, Freud found in psychoanalysis meaning for his existence and grew into a leader. That people in a social group can best form a cohesive unit when they devote themselves to a common goal—for ex-

[3] Boris Pasternak, *Doctor Zhivago* (New York, 1958), p. 68.

ample, to defeat a common enemy—has been well demonstrated by the recent work of social psychologists. Showing the integrative value of goals which are pursued with the hope of success is the main contribution of Thomas French to psychoanalytic knowledge.[4]

We are observing in this phenomenon a kind of beneficial circle: the internal consolidation, the formation of a well-defined ego identity liberates energies for outward-directed efforts, and such dedication to external causes in turn promotes internal consolidation of the personality.

Paradoxically, the other-directed person is in a sense more introverted. He is constantly challenged to make instantaneous adjustments; in fact, his life is spent in finding his place; he can never accept himself as he is; he does not know who he is, since his self never was crystallized. Because he remains a problem to himself, his focus is directed inward, and yet at the same time he must constantly watch the others, since all his cues come from outside, having none of his own. He is always on the go, always searching without ever knowing what he is after. His energies are absorbed by the continuous, never-ending problem of adjustment, because no adjustment he makes is supposed to last for long in our dynamic society. His social mobility only adds to this difficulty. He lives without an internally determined long-term life plan. Because of his social mobility he continuously changes his jobs, his occupation, his marriages and his social environment. He depends more than the inner-directed person on chance and opportunities. Because his life does not follow a de-

[4] Thomas French, *Integration of Behavior* (Chicago, 1952, 1954, 1958).

sign which is the expression of a traditional value system modified by his unique self, there is less continuity in his self-awareness. In a sense, he is more keenly aware of himself than the inner-directed person, but it is not awareness of identity; he remains a constant puzzle to himself. Today he is this and tomorrow something else, not only in his occupation but in his own personality. The arduous job of fitting his own spontaneous impulses to his self, which he doesn't know very well, and to an ever-changing human environment consumes all of his energies. Consequently, there is little left for creativity, for solid object-relationships, for devotion to causes which lie outside of himself. His principal preoccupation is to get along with others. Neurotic or psychotic disintegration of personality is only one of the outcomes of this constant unsuccessful struggle to equilibrate between a loosely organized self and a changing environment. This is, however, by no means the most common outcome.

The most common escape from the permanent insecurity caused by lack of identity is joining a firmly established organization, a fraternity, a gang, a political party, characterized by a simple and emphatically stated ideology and value system. Instead of an arduously acquired internal identity, which is the result of an organic growth process, such a person obtains his identity by becoming a part of an organized group. Internal identity yields to group identification, to conformity. He knows himself and others know him mainly by his social role, by his occupation as in the guild system of the Middle Ages: Mr. Smith, Mr. Miller, Mr. Wheeler. In a stable immobile society this may serve as a basis of identity formation. Not so in our ever-changing society with its constantly shifting social roles.

Yet, in conforming to the group, the painful struggle for an internal identity is relieved. Even when he joins a non-conformist group, his non-conformism is not his; it is patterned by the group spirit. The man without internal identity sacrifices the uniqueness of his person—a uniqueness of which, to be sure, he never had active awareness—and finds his haven in becoming like everybody else. After maturation, he becomes a responsible member of society and his life consists of an unrelenting struggle for as complete as possible conformity achieved by the watchful observation of his peers. He must avoid any possible deviation, since this would require the internal task of including something different to his own internal structure, a task which is alien to him, which he gave up early in his life when he still had to cope with his own originality—an originality which is an inalienable property of childhood.

In a simple form, this can be stated by saying that contemporary youth loses the capacity for spontaneous learning and expects to be taught. There is in our days a tendency to overlook the difference between spontaneous learning and being taught or indoctrinated. Spontaneous learning is the essence of play and this type of learning retains always some of its playful character. It is a highly active process internally motivated. Groping experimentation, using one's own ingenuity, is its essence. The prevailing trend today is to rely more and more on imparting the ready-made results of previous learning to students. Such education relies fundamentally on the process of identification; the pupil incorporates *in toto* what was achieved by others. This appears an economical procedure; it saves the student from the struggle of discovering everything anew himself; it saves him from the struggles inherent in every spontaneous learning process. Yet, something is lost by this economy. To know something really requires that one repeat the original steps of discovery by one's own efforts. This is a most important principle so pitifully overlooked by the all-pervasive contemporary trend in education toward indoctrination, imparting knowledge in ready-made capsules.

The same is true for ego development. When it is based primarily on identifications, the patterns thus acquired never have the persistency and solidity of those acquired by playful experimentation. This is particularly true for *ad hoc* identifications with peers in an everchanging environment. The patterns which are incorporated wholesale by *ad hoc* identifications or indoctrination lack the original contributions of the person's unique qualities. Identity, based mainly on such identifications, is more brittle and is constantly in danger of being destroyed by the pressures of those highly individual aspirations of a person which have been neglected and suppressed. They were, of necessity, suppressed because no formula found by others precisely fits all the idiosyncratic qualities of an individual person. Partial identifications, of course, are always present, but these in healthy development become assembled and organically assimilated according to the person's own unique formula.

Identification is too comprehensive a term. It includes

different processes such as superficial imitation, wholesale identification with another person's external behavior, attitudes and values, and finally, selection of certain aspects, attitudes and values of another person and incorporation of them as an organic part of his own ego, reconciling these new additions with the already consolidated and harmoniously integrated portions of his personality. This is a kind of psychological form of "assimilation," analagous to its metabolic counterpart. The organism assimilates foreign proteins ingested in nutrition, it breaks them down into their component parts and builds up from these more elementary fragments its own protein. Also psychologically only this type of organically built up identifications can serve as a solid basis for the formation of an enduring ego identity. This is well illustrated by an anecdote which Kierkegaard tells in his *The Sickness unto Death*, published more than a hundred years ago.[5]

A peasant, having made some money, decided to urbanize himself. He went cleanly shaven to the capital, bought himself shoes and stockings and still had money left to get drunk. Trying to find his way home he lay down on the highway and fell asleep. A wagon came along and the driver yelled at him to get out of his way or he would run over his legs. The drunken peasant awoke, looked down at his legs but did not recognize them with shoes and stockings on. He said to the driver, "Drive on. They are not my legs."

The ego has a double function: to adjust itself to the internal unique combination of individual aspirations and instinctual pressures, to integrate them into a har-

[5] S. Kierkegaard, *The Sickness unto Death* (Princeton, 1946), p. 85.

monious unity, and at the same time to adjust this unity to a specific environment. The balance between these two kinds of adaptations—internal and external—may shift in either direction. The two extreme cases are: over-adjustment, that is to say, conformism, which sacrifices individuality and originality; and at the other pole, the lone wolf, the eccentric or the neurotic, who only by escaping into fantasy can realize his own desires.

There are, however, even in our own ever-changing era, always a few exceptional individuals who neither succumb to a neurotic withdrawal nor escape into conformity and become creative thinkers and artists. They succeed not only in fulfilling their own individual selves, but in creating a new world of ideas, and eventually, a new world.

There can be little doubt that our era, with the appearance of the masses on the social scene, favors the conformist solution. Previous more creative eras brought about radical advancements in basic knowledge, which eventually changed all aspects of our lives; in our era we are now preoccupied with catching up with these changes by adapting ourselves to this new world of our own creation. This seems a gigantic task; the growing social and international tensions demonstrate only too clearly that it is far from being solved. It appears inevitable that the internal task of cultivation of the individual features of the personality has to be postponed. Adjustment is the watchword of our times; creativity is felt as something which has to be postponed until our adjustment to what has been created in the past has been accomplished.

The vigorous growth of business enterprises and technological innovations which utilize creative discoveries of the past is often interpreted as creativity. One must not overlook, however, that they live on the great momentum of the past and of necessity will soon reach their natural limits if new advances in basic knowledge—the only true form of creativity—do not continue to give food for new technical applications. Such pioneering requires originality. At present, the other-directed person, the conformist, the communal man, dominates the social scene and the uniqueness of the individual recedes into the background. All this is further favored by increasing international tensions which threaten the survival of two great antagonistic world powers. This threat necessitates further organization, education for practical purposes, preparation for immediate action. There is no time for play, the source of real learning and creativity.

Much lip service is being given today to creativity and "individuality," particularly among college students. But in reality it is considered a disturbing factor, something which only increases the difficulties of adjustment, something which interferes with conformity.

The American tradition of rugged individualism lingers on more as a folklore than as something actually practiced, except by the marginal group of neurotic delinquents and eccentrics. It appears in hackneyed success stories and moving-picture plots. They provide a kind of vicarious satisfaction for those masses who in their actual life no longer dare or even seriously desire to live up to the heroic heritage of the past. Here is the key to the growing popularity of wild west scenarios. Literature, religion and art, just like dreams, often express those things which cannot be realized in actual life. At the same time, the stream of historical evolution relentlessly progresses toward increasing organization.

Contemporary man's struggle for his identity results then from the exceptional greatness of his adaptive tasks: adaptation to an everchanging cultural environment, which does not allow time for the crystallization of values to serve as guiding principles for behavior.

Under a stable system of values, adaptation to the social climate is easier. Rapidly changing conditions do not allow stable value systems to prevail for long. Living according to values sanctioned by tradition relieves the person of the arduous task of continuous readaptations. In slowly changing times man receives the patterns of adjustment from his predecessors. He can use his energies thus saved for creativeness. And yet, it is not possible to express in a simple quantitative formula the reciprocal relation between adaptation and creativity. No doubt, it is true that the greater the adaptive tasks, the less energy is left for creative activity, which requires freedom for playful experimentation with ideas which are not rigidly prescribed by immediate necessities. There are, however, considerations which contradict the validity of such a simple correlation between adaptation and creativity. Adaptive challenges, both internal and external, if not overwhelming, seem to stimulate the living organism to experiment to find solutions. Stable conditions to which the organism is well adjusted favor a kind of laziness, the preservation of a status quo.

The quantitative correlation between these two basic principles of life—adaptation and creative change—can be best represented by a curve with a peak which corresponds to an optimal amount of adaptive challenge. Such a theory was advanced by Toynbee on the basis of historical consideration. If the adaptive task (cultural challenge) does not exceed this optimal amount, it stimulates the culture-building creative functions of man. If the adaptational task becomes excessive, greater than the optimal peak of the curve, the problem-solving activities also decline. If the challenges man faces in his struggle for survival nearly transcend his faculty to deal with them, all his energies of necessity are consumed in the desperate struggle for adaptation, as, for example, in the case of the Eskimos. Creativity and playfulness go parallel. Extreme challenges interfere with playful experimentation.

This principle holds true both for external adaptation to existing conditions and for internal adaptation as represented by ego integration, the building of an harmonious internal identity. In our present days, the rapidity of social change and the absence of stable principles of conduct has reached a degree beyond that optimal amount of challenge which is stimulating without being paralyzing.

The weakness of this appealing formulation lies in its indefiniteness. What is an optimal amount of challenge? It is true that in static societies, where social change is slow and life is routinized, there is little incentive for individual creativity except in such restricted areas as decorative carvings of weapons or household utensils. On the other hand, periods of rapid cultural change are not always creative. In the absence of quantitative measurements, we can only make the unsatisfactory statement that cultural change may either stimulate creativity (as during the Renaissance) or may paralyze creative activities (as in the present, when each individual is struggling to orient himself in the everchanging currents of the social climate).

One factor, however, seems to be of outstanding significance, and this is *immediacy*. The need for an immediate solution of a challenge, be it external or internal, prevents that type of detached penetration and playful experimentation which are needed for truly creative accomplishments. Immediate necessities may stimulate the solution of some circumscribed technological problems when previously acquired knowledge can be applied to a restricted goal. We are witnessing this in a spectacular fashion today in the field of atomic research as applied to war technology and to ballistics. This is often confused with creativeness. True, we are producing spectacular new technical devices. And it is also true that such technical inventions can be employed for new basic research. But in themselves they do not represent new fundamental knowledge. All the experiences of the last three hundred years indicate that acquisition of new basic knowledge which can serve as the foundation for new practical applications requires the detached attitude of the scientist, who is not pressed to find answers for immediate needs but is allowed to follow his own curiosities in a leisurely fashion.

The Cold War is a good example of such a situation of immediacy. The permanent state of pending war is not a favorable climate for truly creative thought, either in the natural or the social and psychological sciences. In the natural sciences it promotes war technology, in the psychological and social sciences brainwashing and the more subtle manipulative devices toward making people conform. The imperative need of our times, the detached study of social dynamics and of personality integration, requires mutual trust, patience, and freedom of the spirit. The perpetual preparation for war is a fateful anachronism; it belongs to an era of colonialism when the prosperity of nations depended on subjugation and exploitation of the weak. Today it means fixation to conditions which no longer exist. Today prosperity can be better achieved by peaceful cooperation between nations. This is primarily a psychological problem, a question of political reorientation on the international scene. Such a reorientation alone can promote a cultural climate which allows for detachment, absence of the pressure of immediate survival problems and time for reflection. And only in such a free cultural climate can the luxury of the cultivation of the uniqueness of personality flourish—the source of all creativeness.

CHAPTER XIII

Reflections on Organization

> "Man must never be judged according to the category to which he belongs. The category is the most barbarous and diabolical aberration ever begotten by the human mind."
>
> G. V. GEÓRGHIU

There is no other part of the world where one of the most fundamental phenomena of nature—organization—can be better studied on the basis of direct observation than the United States. In fact, I became actively involved in it over a period of twenty-five years through my efforts to organize psychoanalytic teaching and research in Chicago.

In every organized system the individual components of the system lose the freedom of their own orbits. Organization—no matter what type of organization it may be—means certain fixed relationships between the constituent parts. This is true for all organized systems, be it molecules in a chemical compound, cells integrated in an organism, members of a group organized in a social system. In non-living systems we can precisely measure the degree of organization according to the second law of thermodynamics. The yardstick is given in the concept of entropy. Any system left on its own without external interference has the tendency to become less and less organized—while its entropy increases—as if the constituent parts would tend to free themselves from those forces which brought about their organization into a system. It appears that organization is always forced upon a system by external influences. Therefore, in a closed system which is not exposed to external influences, the elementary particles tend to free themselves from being organized and resume their random behavior.

Living organisms seem to contradict this general principle inasmuch as in the course of phylogenetic development more and more complex organisms appear. This exception from the second law of thermodynamics, which is considered the most universal principle valid for all events in nature, however, is only a seeming contradiction because organisms are not closed systems and their tendency toward increasing organization occurs at the cost of energy which they absorb from outside sources. This energy is used for the expenditure which every organization requires.

There cannot be any doubt that the same principle can also be applied to social organization. In social development, too, a trend toward increasing organization can be observed, if not as a universal phenomenon, at least during definite historical periods. Eventually, however, all cultures have disintegrated in known history.

There is good evidence that external pressures—threat of war, for example—increase the need for social organization. The same principle obtains also for social animals which become organized into social systems under the pressure of competition in the struggle for survival. Darwin considered the development of the social qualities of insects and man as a principal weapon in the struggle for survival.

Our present industrial era, more than any other known era in history, displays this trend toward increasing organization. The progress of the organizational process manifests itself primarily in the principle of "division of labor." This leads to specialization of social functions which are coördinated and integrated into a system. The functions needed for biological survival become divided between different social groups which, because of these specializations of functions, become more and more interdependent. This principle can be best observed in the social organization of insects, in which specialization of function has gone much farther than in present human societies, the different survival functions being divided among anatomically distinct groups—the workers, the soldiers and the sexual types. Their activities are closely coördinated, which makes secure the existence of each individual member as well as that of the organized system itself. The members can only exist together; they ceased to be biological jacks-of-all-trades and became specialists who depend upon each other almost as much as the different tissues of an organism do.

In human societies the totalitarian states come nearest to insect societies, although the specialization of functions in human society does not manifest itself on the biological level. A member of a totalitarian society, whose social function is restricted to pushing a lever of a machine, under pressing need—for example, if marooned on a deserted island—can still, theoretically at least, survive. This is no longer true for cells of a complex living organism, whose functions are so highly specialized that their survival requires a contribution from other cells. Detached from the organism they cannot survive. Such highly differentiated units in a complex organism have highly specialized functions; a liver cell, for example, can only secrete certain substances and loses the capacity for many of the diversified survival functions which monocellular organisms still possess. It receives its oxygen supply from the blood stream, which receives it from the lungs. It requires for its survival the contribution of other tissues. Such a highly differentiated particle of a total system has lost the capacity of and freedom for diversified functions and individual independent existence; its activities are highly circumscribed and routinized.

In studying human society we are in the unique position of looking at this problem from the point of view of the individual member of a system. We do not know how a molecule feels when its orbit of action becomes restricted within an organized system because self-awareness is not a property of molecules. We do not know the subjective reaction of a cell toward being a member of an organism. Only human beings are aware of their own existence and can communicate their subjective reactions to each other.

Our industrial era, particularly during the last half of a century, provides a unique opportunity to scrutinize the individual person's reactions to the rapidly progressing organization in western societies. In fact, we have here one of those experiments of nature in which a particular phenomenon can be best studied because of the peculiar circumstances which make the phenomenon accessible to observation. Astronomers often have to wait for certain constellations—for example, when a heavenly body happens to be nearest to the earth—to make certain critical observations. The present historical era, because of the unprecedented speed of progressive social organization, offers an exceptional opportunity to observe how it feels for a human being to become progressively swallowed up in an intricate, highly interdependent social system.

The most suitable object for studying this subjective reaction of man toward social organization is the transitional generation which has experienced two historical eras, distinguishable by different degrees of social differentiation and organization. Equally suited for such a study are persons who have changed their cultural habitat by immigration from a less to a more differentiated culture. For example: a peasant who lived a part of his life on a farm—where he produced his own food, wove his own cloth, built his own hut, repaired the wheel of his cart—and then emigrated to an industrial country where his functions are reduced to serving a single machine (more precisely one partial function of a complex machine), where he lives in a prefabricated tenement house and is dependent on stores which he can reach only by vehicles he has learned how to use but is incapable of repairing. To study such experiments of nature as the case of a member of an agricultural society which suddenly within a few years becomes industrialized is a task for sociologists, anthropologists, and social psychologists.

The first type of experiment of nature, however, the transitional generation within our own western civilization, is a natural object of study for the psychoanalyst. The phenomenon which confronts him when he undertakes such a study is precisely the one which has been in the focus of our interest: the loss of personal identity, the same phenomenon which existential writers call the loss of the authentic self or the "existential despair." The emergence of the other-directed person of Riesman refers basically to the same natural phenomenon.

Erikson's pathographic studies deal with such cases, where particular identification problems exaggerate the difficulty of ego integration, which, to some degree are well-nigh universal for the generation in transition.[1] These are the persons who partly still are rooted in older traditions, if for nothing else than for the fact that their parents' orientation belongs to a previous era. Erikson correctly maintains that every new suddenly arising integrative task, caused by biological growth, such as occurs in adolescence, threatens the feeling of identity. The rapidly progressing differentiation and organization of social functions, the change of social value, entail similar difficulties for personality integrations.

The differentiation of social functions favors an organization within the ego in which social roles replace ego identity which reflects the uniqueness of every individual. The advancing specialization of social functions and social roles leads to an atrophy of that ego function which has the task to bring into an harmonious unit the individual idiosyncratic features of a person. It leads to a hypertrophy of schematized roles. The integration within

[1] Erik Erikson, "Ego Development and Historical Change," *The Psychoanalytic Study of the Child, Vol. II* (New York, 1946).

the individual is reduced to integration of large categories, such as roles, and not highly distinct individual propensities. Social integration gradually replaces integration within the person's internal domain. For the communal man, the "organization man," it is preferable to become identical with those who share the same function. Organized mass society cannot bother with many prima donnas; it needs chorus girls. To be different, to have a distinct personality, becomes not only superfluous but disturbing. Mass society pressures the individual to lose his unique identity; those who still struggle to preserve it react with that phenomenon which contemporary social philosophers, sociologists and psychoanalysts recognize as a struggle for personal identity.

This perspective offers a consistent picture of the cultural trend and the corresponding personality developments in our times. Yet it cannot be generalized because there are great segments of the population in which this trend is not quite as prominent.

The struggle for the preservation of individuality may not be quite as hopeless as would appear in the light of these generalizations. Is there no place even in a highly organized society for a private life outside of social roles ? Theoretically, at least, the automation of production should liberate energy and time for every person, to be used for the expression of his own highly personal inclinations. Is conformity an unavoidable consequence of the growing crystallization of social functions ? Can a person not preserve and cultivate his own unique self and still fulfill his social role adequately? No doubt in his social function he will and should become like those others who fill the same place in the social organism. But does this preclude his freedom to express his own uniqueness in his personal life ?

Twenty-eight years ago, when I came to this country, my new friends soon bombarded me with the question, "What do you find most characteristic of the United States in contrast to Europe ?" I gave an answer which came to me spontaneously without any intervening deductive reasoning. "In Europe my professional life was an appendix of my personal life. Here I find that the opposite is true, my private life has become an appendix." I soon found in the tyranny of public opinion the enforcer of this condition.

One of my first American patients insisted on coming at an early hour so that he could be in his office at nine o'clock. He was his own master and actually had very little to do in his office. Yet, he could not afford, he explained to me, to create the impression of a man of leisure. It took me several months of similar experiences with patients to understand the tyrannical power of public opinion, requiring conformity with current value judgments. I found that in some respects public opinion, "the voice of the people," is a more effective tyrant, though more intangible and anonymous, than dictators and monarchs. Soon it became impossible for me to make as clear a distinction between private and public life as I had been accustomed to make in my earlier days. American society wanted all of you and did not tolerate any subordination to private affairs of your socially required and assigned activities. American society appeared a more serious society—one which meant business and would not tolerate any foolish or eccentric indulgence even in your private time. In fact, private life also was standardized to a higher degree than I had ever experienced before. Engaging in activities or interests which did not correspond to an accepted pattern, even though these patterns often changed capriciously according to current fads and fashions, put a person outside the group. You were not a good mixer, but a peculiar or asocial person, and later, when psychiatry became popular, a "schizoid" individual. This tyranny of public opinion extended not only to behavior but even to literary taste. Industrial mass production requires conformity in consumption. Strangely, this is true not only for industrial but also for cultural productions. Soon I became suspicious of best sellers; I found that as a whole their literary merits did not always run parallel with their popularity. I found this the clue for the sudden changes in the popularity of certain trends in art and literature, which closely resembled the changing popularity of industrial products. Also, in industrial products the discrepancy between quality and popularity was only too evident. The powerful influence of advertising is only possible when people are afraid of their own private tastes and opinions and find it more conducive to their social acceptability to follow the trend. The current revulsion against oversized automobiles is a hopeful indication that the public is not quite such a flock of sheep as industry would like to have it.

One conclusion appears inevitable: our social system is in the process of increasing organization. Social functions and roles become more and more specialized and man is drawn more and more into the web of a complex social machinery. The individual responds to this by replacing his internal unique personal identity with group identity. This shift goes hand in hand with a loss of spontaneous creative originality. In its place routine behavior patterns appear, which no longer express personal inclinations and values, but group patterns which all members having the same social role share with each other. All this amounts to a growing emphasis on adaptation to a complex social system with its routinized roles. The non-adaptive creative genius of man, his most human quality, must decline in such a climate.

This appears most visibly in the orientation of our educational system toward an increasing emphasis upon preparing the youth for a specialized social role in the framework of a highly routinized curriculum at the cost of a liberal non-specialized basic education, which exposes the student to the creative accomplishments of the past and present and which gives him greater opportunity to follow his own interests and to choose his own subjects and teachers.

The generation of transition, which experienced the freer atmosphere of the pre-war period, is most affected by this trend. These persons experience these changes as a threat to their individual identities and often respond to it with various psychopathological sequelae.

The growing organization and routinization of the social system, together with the advancing automation of production which reduces the time and energy needed for social functions, will eventually make the problem of leisure a central concern. Leisure which cannot be filled is a deadly serious issue.

Leisure, however, can have a saving social function. It allows for private life and thus may save individuality from the social juggernaut. It may, however, become a source of neurotic discontent. Only a society which does not succeed in reducing the individual solely to a performer of a useful social function can use leisure to its advantage. For a person whose whole personality is in the service of fulfilling his role in society, leisure means a void which can only be filled with the most primitive instinctual gratifications as the only means of combating lethal boredom, which, together with loneliness, represents the most common source of unhappiness. Without a meaningful private life, the progressing deterioration of entertainment in mass media performances (if a further movement below today's standards is still possible), the gradual dwindling away of sportsmanship from commercialized sports activities, the growing resentment against intellectual accomplishment and against sophistication, the cosmetic, uniform, factory-produced concept of feminine attractiveness, and the growing deterioration of social gatherings into chemically produced hilarity will remain a continuing trend towards the dehumanization of western man.

And yet, all this cannot be considered an unavoidable consequence of the far-reaching organization and standardization of social functions. Rather, the trend toward conformity is a secondary consequence of vanishing ego identity, which could be saved by granting the person in his private life the privilege of being different even if this is no longer possible to the same degree in his social functions as it was in times of a less closely knit society.

Conformity, which has its place in certain aspects of life, has become a general requirement. With the gradual decline of the influence of religious sentiments, the spiritual privacy of a person has become defenseless against public opinion, which is in the process of usurping the function of individual conscience. All this is not restricted to the United States. With justification one speaks of the growing Americanization of Europe. There, too, the same trend is conspicuously present though it has not reached the same degree as in the United States.

Life need not consist only of obligations to contribute to society; perhaps it becomes most meaningful in the obligation everyone has toward the cultivation and development of his own unique endowments. Man, through the cultivation of his unique self, although indirectly, advances human welfare more effectively than by merely accepting his share in those standardized assignments open to him in different social roles. The latter makes him a useful member of society in maintaining the status quo. Creative change, however, can only come from the not immediately useful realization of individual strivings, curiosities—sometimes even oddities—which may appear idle, playful and non-utilitarian at the moment.

Paradoxically and luckily, the utilitarian pragmatic orientation offers a remedy against its inherent sterility by its very achievements. Routinization, rationalization and automation of social functions relieve man from the pressures of immediate needs and scarcity; they open up unlimited possibilities for a coming age of creative leisure.

CHAPTER XIV

Play and the Serious Business of Living

> "Civilization is, in its earliest phases, played. It does not come from play like a babe detaching itself from the womb: it arises in and as play, and never leaves it."
>
> JOHAN HUIZINGA

"The child creates a world for himself; he feels he made it—it is his. He can destroy it, break it, throw it away. This is a form of creation. This is a different world—not like the real one, which is stubborn, unyielding, full of secrets and surprises; it is hard and resistant. The play world is comfortable, obedient and magic: hippity-hop, and I am where I want to be and I am what I want to be—a king, a fairy, a dog, a bear, a policeman, a coachman. The world of the artist is also a separate world, a self-created world, also without causality and also without serving arid purposes.

"There are brides who say farewell to their dolls with tears in their eyes. The tears are justified; they never will be as happy in the real world dominated by goals. The bride can still play with her dolls; the woman in love, never again. And for the man who falls in love, this will become the only serious matter. It is not true that love makes the artist; it is, rather, his failure in love. It is then that, exasperated by the real world, he seeks consolation in art.

"As long as these two powers (the serious goals of life and love) do not get hold of man, what a source of happiness is the world of play! Of real play, because when fame or money is the stake, there is an end of happiness. To win money or to make the headlines is not compatible with happiness. This is why only children are happy in this world of ours. It is a miracle how happy they can be. The artist, too, can partake in this happiness, at least occasionally. Work does not make one happy, only if it serves play. One can say all kinds of laudatory things about work, that it makes you alive, that gives you peace of mind, that it promotes your welfare, that it strengthens your morality, that it maintains the world and makes for progress; but it does not make the soul happy, does not liberate it, does not give it wings, does not render it carefree, does not refresh it. All this we can expect from play. From play and art. In art, however, great forces are in ambush: ambition, the thirst for fame and glory, envy, which turn against us and by which Satan entraps us. But mainly business—to make a trade of art—who can withstand this mighty temptation? There are some, but they are rare. You find them in the desert, as in bygone days, the anchorets. Only one who can escape into the desert, or who can create a desert around himself, can save his art in our days. There are those foolish childlike adults, for whom the wise ones, the experienced ones, those familiar with the ways of life, have a pitying smile. These are the ones who brag that they never played, not even as children. Poor fellows ! They do not know what a testimony they bear against themselves. These are the ones who never laugh. And if they ever laugh, it sounds horrible; a child crying is more pleasant than the laugh of these 'bearded' ones."

I quote this from Bernard Alexander's essay on play written in the second decade of this century.[1] It reflects the spirit of my early years, a spirit which yielded more and more to a serious, less hedonistic outlook on life. I quote it because I could not express all this quite as uninhibitedly as he could.

We have become more serious within the last fifty years because we have had to become more serious. We have become, more than ever before, like cells of a biological organism, and cells have to accomplish useful and serious functions and have no time for play.

Human and animal behavior is traditionally divided into two categories, one serving the survival of the individual and one serving the preservation of the species through propagation. Freud made this classification the original basis of the theory of instincts. He soon discovered, however, that much of the young animal's or child's behavior does not serve directly either survival or propagation. He called these "pregenital" erotic activities, including, among others, thumb-sucking, anal stimulation, the pleasurable excitation of the skin, aimless muscular activity, curiosity for its own sake—all of which have playful, pleasure-seeking connotations within the broad

[1] Bernard Alexander, *Müvészet* (Art) *Pantheon* (Budapest, 1926). (Translated by the author)

category of sexuality. He characterized these activities, which subjectively have erotic connotations, as immature, pregenital manifestations of the instinctual drive which in its mature genital form leads to reproduction. Greek mythology intuitively recognized this affinity between playfulness and sexuality in representing Eros, the god of both love and play, as a child.

Despite the volume of attention, both precisely descriptive and theoretical, which psychoanalysis has given to these aimless manifestations of sex, authors of our increasingly rationalistic Twentieth Century, including animal psychologists, have remarkably neglected these non-utilitarian aspects of human and animal behavior. In contrast, Nineteenth-Century philosophers had a great deal to say about play. Outstanding among these are Friedrich Schiller, Herbert Spencer, Jean Paul, Wilhelm Preyer, and particularly Karl Groos.

A profound theory of play was advanced in Schiller's *On the Esthetic Education of Mankind.* The essence of his view is in a quotation taken from Karl Groos:

> Nature has indeed granted, even to the creature devoid of reason, more than the mere necessities of existence, and into the darkness of animal life has allowed a gleam of freedom to penetrate here and there. When hunger no longer torments the lion, and no beast of prey appears for him to fight, then his unemployed powers find another outlet. He fills the wilderness with his wild roars, and his exuberant strength spends itself in aimless activity. In the mere joy of existence, insects swarm in the sunshine, and it is certainly not always the cry of want that we hear in the melodious rhythm of bird songs. There is evidently

> freedom in these manifestations, but no freedom from all necessity, only from a definite external necessity. The animal works when some want is the motive for its activity, and plays when a superabundance of energy forms this motive—when overflowing life itself urges it to action.[2]

Jean Paul also referred to play as the "expression of mental and physical exuberance."

Best known and most influential is Spencer's theory,[3] essentially identical with Schiller's, that "play is the expression of superfluous energy." He reasoned that inferior animals need all their energy for their maintenance. Higher types are more efficiently organized, and their strength is not entirely needed for survival. There remains a surplus of "vigor" no longer demanded by immediate emergencies. This excess of energy seeks pathways of discharge. The various functions of adaptation to basic biological requirements are mobilized at times; otherwise they remain unexercised for considerable periods. These unexercised nonessential energies find discharge in playfulness. Spencer in addition to the "principle of surplus" adduced imitation and repetition as important factors which determine the kind of play activity chosen by the animal.

Karl Groos critically analyzed the Schiller-Spencer theories.[4] He preferred Schiller's formulation and questioned Spencer's addition of imitation and repetition.[5] He accepted the basic concept that in play surplus energy

[2] Karl Groos, *The Play of Animals* (New York, 1898).
[3] Herbert Spencer, *Principles of Psychology*, Vol. II (New York, 1873).
[4] Karl Groos, *The Play of Animals* (New York, 1898), and *The Play of Man* (New York, 1908).
[5] Herbert Spencer, *loc. cit.*

is discharged, but he maintained that neither Schiller nor Spencer accounted for the specific kind of play which is characteristic of a species. He believed that the nature of play is determined by heredity. "The activity of all living beings is in the highest degree influenced by hereditary instincts—that is, the way an animal of a particular species controls his members and uses his voice, the way he moves about in his natural element, supplies himself with food, fights with other animals, or avoids them—his manner of doing all these things is governed fundamentally by inherited instincts. When the potential of psychic instinctual energy is not consumed, and there is a surplus of nervous excitation . . . then such instincts find expression even without serious occasion. The kitten treats a scrap of paper as its prey, the young bear wrestles with his brothers, the dog which after long confinement is set free hunts aimlessly about, etc. But such actions are exactly what we mean by the word play."

Groos gave an exhaustive description of the most diversified playful activities, beginning with the infant's unmistakeable happiness with contact which serves no other purpose except the pleasure it provides. In handling every object which comes within its reach, the infant not only exercises its motor faculties in a playful way but also the sensual stimulus of touching. Groos quoted Preyer,[6] who anticipated the Freudian explanation of the oral pleasures derived from thumb-sucking: "The child enjoys the mere contact." It gives the child pleasure to test with its mouth everything that offers an occasion for the use of its nerves and muscles. Preyer traced the enjoyment of deli-

[6] Karl Groos, *The Play of Man.*

cate food to this early, purely sensual, excitation of the oral region. More thoroughly he demonstrated that all sensory gratifications can yield playful pleasure—the sensation of warmth afforded by a bath; the sensations of smell, hearing, and sight which he elaborates in sensations of brightness, of perception of color and form, and of movement—all of which yield opportunities for playful gratifications. Similarly he described the playful use of the motor apparatus in destructive and constructive movements.

It is interesting from the psychoanalytic point of view that in spite of his painstaking and exhaustive descriptions of practically all known playful activities of the body and mind, Preyer did not sense their kinship with sexuality. He did clearly recognize and emphasize that these playful activities are not in the service of the serious tasks of life.

In a recent article McBride and Hebb[7] give a vivid description of the play of young dolphins.

> The partly grown porpoise, as with other mammals, is more playful than the fully mature; but all porpoises, mature and immature, do a good deal of playing with no aggressive element in it.
>
> The individual porpoise finding a feather from one of the pelicans that inhabit the surface of the tank may come up, balance it on its nose out of water, flip it backward, try to catch it, and so on. Another is likely to come rushing up also and catch the feather as it falls and race off, pursued by others who try to take it from it. One may catch it out

[7] A. F. McBride and D. O. Hebb, "Behavior of the Captive Bottle-Nose Dolphin *Tursiops Truncatus*," *J. Comparative & Physiological Psychology*, XLI, No. 2, 1948.

> of the side of its mouth, the rest pursuing the new owner of the prize. Such play among two or three of the porpoises may last an hour or more. The porpoises frequently catch small fish and let them go, apparently in play since they could easily kill them but do not—although the play is rough and the fish may get injured and die. . . . One young porpoise was often seen to get its nose under a large turtle, stand it on edge and push it all the way across the tank and up against the opposite wall.

The erotic stimulation is clearly demonstrated in the play of one dolphin which was "seen swimming upside down at the top of the tank, catching and towing a feather with its penis erect."

Prior to my discovery of Schiller's, Spencer's, and Groos's observations, I had advanced a similar theory of play as the exercise of surplus libidinal energy not required for the grim task of survival.[8] I had expanded this theory to apply not only to play but to all erotic phenomena, following Freud in considering play as one of the many manifestations of sexuality. I advanced the view that life is governed by three fundamental dynamic processes: the principle of stability, the principle of economy, and the principle of surplus energy.

Life is a dynamic equilibrium which requires certain constant conditions. In every organism there are biologically inherited self-controlling mechanisms by which stability is maintained, a state which makes the life process possible. It is assumed that these conditions are

[8] Franz Alexander, *Our Age of Unreason* (Philadelphia, 1942); "Three Fundamental Dynamic Principles of the Mental Apparatus and of the Behavior of Living Organisms," *Dialectica*, V, No. 3–4, 1951; and *Fundamentals of Psychoanalysis* (New York, 1948).

optimal for the life process. Among higher animals the basic function of the central nervous system consists in sustaining the homeostatic equilibrium which is continuously disturbed by the very process of life and by changing environmental influences. Freud called this the principle of stability and attributed it to Fechner, not cognizant of Claude Bernard's contribution. In man this homeostatic function can be studied by psychoanalytic methods, and therefore can justly be called by the name given to the apparatus which is the executor of it: the ego. This mental apparatus accomplishes its homeostatic task through four functions: first, internal sensory perceptions registering internal disturbances of the physicochemical equilibrium, perceiving them as needs and sensations; second, external sensory perceptions registering environmental conditions upon which the gratification of its needs depends; third, the integration of internal and external perceptions in a way that makes adequate coordinated voluntary execution possible; and finally, as the center of motor control, the ego performs its executive function in carrying out a behavior suited to the gratification of needs.

The second fundamental principle which governs the adaptive functions of the ego is called the principle of economy or inertia. Every organism is born with unconditioned reflexes which are useful for maintaining those constant internal conditions that are necessary for life. All the internal vegetative functions, such as digestion, circulation, and respiration, are such automatic self-regulatory mechanisms. They do not require conscious effort and, with the exception of eating and sphincter control, are not acquired by learning but belong to the hereditary equipment of the organism. Man, in contrast to animals, however, must learn through trial, error, and repetition the regulation of these functions which adapt the organism to its environment. Acquired habits adequate for maintaining biological and psychological homeostasis are repeated until they become automatic and are performed with minimum effort. Accordingly, learning consists first of groping experimentation through trial and error, and second of repetition of the successful trials that have proved useful.[9]

Next to the principle of stability the most basic tendency of the organism is to consolidate gradually by repetition newly acquired adaptations—which inherently require experimental efforts—and replace them by effortless automatic behavior. This tendency is of great importance in the genesis of psychopathology.

It is the second phase of learning which consolidates by repetition newly acquired knowledge. The stability principle expresses the tendency of the organism to maintain constant optimal conditions for life, but alone it is not sufficient to account for animal behavior. The tendency toward stability requires further definition by taking into account the principle of inertia: every organism tends to perform the homeostatic functions with a minimum expenditure of energy. This may interchangeably be called the "principle of (psychic) economy" or the "inertia principle." To a large degree, though not completely, it corresponds to Freud's "repetition compulsion." These two principles are the most universal dynamic principles of life.

[9] The gradual acquisition of conditioned responses constitutes a form of learning in which groping experimentation is not necessary.

The advantage to the organism of the principle of psychological economy is obvious. The energy saved by automatic behavior can be utilized to meet novel situations which might otherwise require strenuous trial-and-error experimentation. Bertalanffy refers to this as a progressive mechanization by which "the organism spares energy that can be put to better use.[10]

It is important to recognize inherent disadvantages in automatic behavior. Conditions change, and with growth the organism itself changes. Changed conditions require new adaptations. The adult cannot, like the infant, satisfy his needs by relying upon maternal help. He must learn to walk and eat and independently satisfy many other of his needs. Development requires continuous learning. The principle of psychological economy appears in this connection as inertia which impels the organism to cling to automatic behavior which was satisfactory in the past but which is no longer adequate. This is what Freud called "fixation." He also discovered that when conditions become difficult, novel, or threatening earlier patterns of behavior tend to reassert themselves. This disposition, which he called "regression," has proved to be one of the fundamental factors in psychopathology.

The ever-changing circumstances of human development require rapid, flexible *ad hoc* responses which are suitable adaptations at one moment but may be inappropriate at another. The capacity for such sudden shifts of conduct is the most highly developed function of the personality: the integrative functions of the ego. It rests on

[10] Ludwig Bertalanffy, *Problems of Life* (New York, 1952), pp. 46, 116 ff.; "An Outline of General Systems Theory," *British J. Philosophy of Science*, No. 1 (1950), p. 137.

the ability to learn from experience and to exercise abstract reasoning and differentiation. By memory and reason man is able to continue behaving in ways he has found useful and to alter his behavior as actual situations require. Life is thus a continuous struggle between the organism's tendency to retain old patterns, according to the principle of inertia, and to meet the challenge of development and changed circumstances by adopting new ones.

In spite of their universality, the principles of stability and inertia explain only those biological phenomena which assist in the preservation of life by useful adaptive responses. For understanding growth, propagation, and play I have introduced the principle of surplus energy.

Life can be viewed as a relationship between three vectors: one, intake of energy from nutritive substances and oxygen; two, their partial retention for use in growth; three, expenditure of energy to maintain the organism with a minimal functional homeostatic activity, involving loss in waste and heat, and expenditure represented by playful erotic activities and by propagation. The last occurs first in puberty as a new kind of eliminative function: the production of germ cells. Propagation is growth beyond the limits of the biological unit. It follows the pattern of propagation in monocellular organisms which occurs when the process of growth reaches a natural limit at maturity; thereafter reproduction occurs through the division of the cells. When a biological unit reaches a certain stage of development, addition of substance and energy becomes impossible because its capacity to organize living matter has reached a limit. Individual growth then stops and propagation serves as a means of releasing surplus energy; otherwise the homeostatic equilibrium would be disturbed.[11]

Energy which is not needed to maintain life I call surplus energy.[12] This is the source of all sexual activity. In the infant, whose needs are satisfied by adults, the incorporating and retentive vectors outweigh the eliminatory one; hence the rapidity of growth. Despite retention in the form of growth there is still much surplus which is neither stored nor used to maintain existence. This excess is released in erotic activities. This explains the preponderance of erotic behavior over self-preservative behavior in the child. Expending energy in play, the child discovers new uses for its organs and exercises them until mastery is achieved and their different functions become integrated in a utilitarian fashion for independent existence. The utility of this play is a secondary effect and has no motivational significance. The child does not exercise its faculties in play for an ultimate purpose; playing is an aim in itself. Erotic play for the sake of pleasure is the first phase, and the utilization of the functions acquired during erotic play is the second. This may appear paradoxical, but the prolonged dependence of the child upon the parents permits it the luxury of playful erotic activities. Thus the energy-saving principle and the creative use of surplus energy are interwoven and combine to maintain life and propagation. Repetition makes useful functions automatic, and saves energy which can be used for growth and procreation.

[11] Surplus, as well as lack of something that is needed, disturbs homeostasis. Discharge of surplus may therefore be a homeostatic factor.

[12] Energy here refers to an unmeasurable quantity or capacity and is not used in its limited physical sense.

According to this view, the erotic quality of an activity is predicated on the fact that it is not integrated in a complex utilitarian pattern but is pursued for its own sake. The quest for food, for example, is subservient to the goal of satisfying hunger. This is in contrast to a detached curiosity which is not subordinate to any specific goal but is an aim in itself.

All psychological motivational forces may become parts of more or less complex structures consisting of subsidiary goals which have to be reached before the final goal can be attained.[13] But they can also be expressed as aims in themselves without subserving any ultimate goals. Aggression, for example, can serve the aim of removing an obstacle that interferes with the gratification of a basic need. If a hungry man injures or kills a person to obtain food, he commits the aggressive act as an incidental means to another end. A child who tortures a small animal has no other aim than the pleasure derived from inflicting pain and from its mastery over something more helpless than it is. This is the erotic expression of aggression in the form of sadism. If this pleasurable sensation is sufficiently intensive, it may be accompanied by genital excitation which—in the instances in which it occurs—sufficiently testifies to its erotic nature. A tourist cheerfully endures the burden of a heavy knapsack for the gratification of his needs when he has arrived at his destination. The moral masochist unwittingly contrives to suffer defeat and disappointment. The erotized form of this striving requires physical pain for the achievement of sexual grat-

[13] Thomas French, "Goal, Mechanism, and Integrative Field," *Psychosomatic Medicine*, III (1941), p. 226.

ification. Curiosity is an overt means of sexual gratification in scoptophilia. Sublimated, it becomes the motivation for scientific research.

These samples suffice to define the thesis that all psychological motivation has two kinds of expression—utilitarian and erotic. Ferenczi anticipated this view by differentiating between the utilitarian and pleasurable functions of all bodily organs.[14] The practical, useful motivational forces are not isolated, as are the erotic strivings, but are parts of complex, structured patterns of behavior.

The relationship of play to utilitarian behavior becomes more complicated when we focus our attention on the playful, but most significant, exercise of man's mastery of both the internal and external exigencies of his existence. It has been demonstrated that many of those faculties which later become significant in adaptive, utilitarian behavior—such as the faculty of sense perception, muscular control—are perfected in playful activities, the aim of which is the activity itself. Waelder, referring to this phenomenon, designates it as "functional pleasure."[15] At first it seems somewhat confusing that mastery, the most utilitarian function—not only of the environment but also of internal instinctual conflicts—may become the content of activity in play.

Freud illustrated this phenomenon in describing the play of a child:

> The child had a wooden reel with a piece of string tied round it. It never occurred to him to pull it along the floor

[14] Sandor Ferenczi, *Thalassa: A Theory of Genitality* (New York, 1938).

[15] Robert Waelder, "The Psychoanalytic Theory of Play," *Psychoanalytic Quarterly*, II (1933), 208–224.

> behind him, for instance, and play at its being a carriage. What he did was to hold the reel by the string and very skillfully throw it over the edge of his curtained cot, so that it disappeared into it, at the same time uttering his expressive "o-o-o-o." He then pulled the reel out of the cot again by the string and hailed its reappearance with a joyful "Da" ("there").[16]

Freud evaluated this game as the child's impulse to gain mastery, by an active substitute, over his mother going away. By repeatedly throwing out and retrieving the object, the child gained an illusory control over the disappearance and reappearance of the mother. On a much more complex and intellectual level a game of chess may represent a similar phenomenon; a playful struggle for mastery.

This element of solving problems is essentially what is utilized with children in play therapy. The abreaction of "surplus tension" has been clearly recognized as one of the "orthotherapeutic" functions of children's play. The principle of subsequent mastery of traumatic (unresolved) conflictual experiences has been demonstrated in great detail in children's play by Erikson: "To the child especially the world of play affords opportunity to experiment with organ-modes in extrabodily arrangements which are physiologically safe, socially permissible, physically workable, and psychologically satisfying." Erikson concluded that the therapist's main function is to aid children in their playfulness to resolve their problems. When the game becomes unsuccessful the children transfer the "un-

[16] Sigmund Freud, *Beyond the Pleasure Principle* [1920] (New York, 1950), p. 13.

solvability of their problems into the play situation. The therapist accomplishes this by inducing the children by systematic interpretation to reconsider, on a more verbal level, the constellations which have overwhelmed them in the past and are apt to overwhelm them when reoccurring." [17]

Waelder, too, emphasized the function of mastery in play.[18] Pleasure derived from the playful exercise of different physiological functions is not sufficient to explain playful activities when a child conjures up traumatic situations which were anything but pleasurable when they originally occurred. If one includes in the category of functional pleasure the gratification derived from mastery of the unresolved threat of a past situation, the contradiction disappears. Not only does the child repeat simple performances of organ systems, such as the faculty of grabbing, locomotion, focusing with the eyes, deriving in a playful manner an erotic gratification from them, but it also experiments with its more complex faculty of successfully conquering dangerous situations. Erikson's examples show that not only experimentation with external dangers but also with internal conflicts becomes the content of children's play.

Lili Peller also considers that the solution of problems is the fundamental function of play.[19] She agrees with

[17] Erik H. Erikson, "Studies in the Interpretation of Play: 1. Clinical Observation of Play Disruption in Young Children," *Genetic Psychological Monographs,* XXII, 1940.

[18] Robert Waelder, *op. cit.*

[19] Lili E. Peller, "Libidinal Phases, Ego Development, and Play," in *The Psychoanalytic Study of the Child,* Vol. IX (New York, 1954), pp. 178–198.

Erikson that the child attempts to resolve internal conflicts by playful activity. It is important, however, to note that the essential feature of play is that during true playfulness the solution of a problem is not imperative. The young colt playfully romping in a meadow is engaged in pleasurably exercising his mastery of the problem of locomotion. Should he be threatened by an external danger, he may still appear to be romping, but this behavior can no longer in any sense be called play. The difference between these two outwardly similar activities is that in the first instance locomotion has a pleasurable aim in itself. In fleeing from a danger, locomotion is subordinated to the serious problem of survival.

All non-utilitarian forms of behavior which are classified as representing the broadest category of sexual (libidinal) gratification have two universal characteristics. They are: first, discharges of surplus energy which is not required for self-preservation; second, they discharge this surplus energy not in the attainment of a specific goal to which these activities are subordinated, but in the attainment of a pleasurable activity for its own sake. The playful erotic activity is a goal in itself.

In this connection it is of interest to refer to a phenomenon described by Groos. The playful activity, he has observed, has a tendency to persevere. He describes young animals that play until they are totally exhausted; also the ritual dances of primitive peoples which are continued to the point of complete collapse. This demonstrates clearly the principle of discharge for its own sake without regard for interest of the organism as a whole. These "playful" activities are not integrated into the total need of the organism, but are isolated phenomena of discharge, of blind activity pursued to exhaustion without consideration for anything but its intrinsic aims.

The implication of this view is that playful, erotic activities are primary in the ontogeny of each individual. They constitute the building stones which will be utilized later in integrated adult behavior. In playfulness, isolated faculties are practiced and perfected, although at the time they do not seem to serve any utilitarian function.

The observation of the early development of the child fully bears out this view. The limbs are moved only for the pleasurable sake of moving them. The thumb is sucked for the pleasure in sucking, not for gratifying hunger. The child's curiosity also has the quality of an interest detached from practical aims. Gradually, all these functions which have been perfected in playful, seemingly useless activities become integrated in the service of the preservation of the individual. In spite of the great advantages to the child from such experimental activities, it should not be overlooked that the motivation for such play activities is not their immediate usefulness. They are not performed to satisfy immediate survival needs. In such play, the ego practices its most essential function in a playful manner—its problem-solving tasks. This is clearly seen in such adult play activities as solving a chess problem or a crossword puzzle. Although more complex, they do not differ in principle from running around playfully or the common play of children of attempting to climb higher and higher trees, thus mastering their fear of falling. In such problem-solving play activities, the ego is practicing its basic function of mastery. It is stimulated by failures. The child tries to climb a tree again and again until finally it succeeds. All these activities are, at the moment, non-utilitarian discharges of surplus energy not needed for survival.

In the history of culture the creative significance of play was most convincingly expounded by Roheim. The most utilitarian inventions, such as agriculture, gardening, and cattle-raising, originated from playful activities and only secondarily became exploited for rational-economic purposes. Cattle-raising most probably came from totemistic rites in primitive religious practices. Domestic animals at first were objects of totemistic religious worship and their practical value for economic aims was only gradually formed. Primitive man stumbled upon these practical uses only after a period of playful preoccupation with digging the earth, and using animals for emotional (religious) outlets. Even recent technological inventions, such as flying, originate from the playful experimentation of adventurous dreamers who only vaguely visualized their possible practical significance. What motivated them was the primordial yearning to soar toward the skies, a common dream expressing aspirations for mastery, power, and freedom—and not a new means for passenger traffic and military destruction. Nothing demonstrates more convincingly that culture is the product of man's creative playfulness and fantasy and not of the sweat of his brow. His creativity is liberated when he is relieved of the immediate pressures of his survival needs. These immediate pressures can be relieved only by pinpointed goal-directed activities where the goal strictly determines the efforts by which it can be reached. Discovery of something new requires freedom for free playful experimentation which is not narrowed down by immediate necessities.

The genetic significance of play in cultural development was most comprehensively proposed by the Dutch historian Huizinga. He begins his book, *Homo Ludens*,[20] with the terse statement: "Play is older than culture, for culture, however adequately defined, always presupposes human society, and animals have not waited for men to teach them their play." He points out the similarity between play and ritual in support of his thesis that "culture arises in the form of play and in the twin union of play and culture, play is primary."

Huizinga emphasizes the function of contest in social institutions. Contest is a form of play and, "like all other forms of play, is largely devoid of purpose. That is to say, its action begins and ends in itself and the outcome does not contribute to the necessary life processes of the group." This, he notes, is well expressed in the Dutch saying, "It is not the marbles that matter, but the game." He considers contest as an essential feature of social life independently of its economic function. As a striking example, he adduces the Potlatch,[21] which among the Kwakiutl is "a great solemn feast during which one of . . . two groups with much pomp and ceremony makes gifts on a large scale to the other . . . for the express purpose of showing its superiority. The only return expected by the donors, but incumbent on the recipients, lies in the obligation of the

[20] J. Huizinga, *Homo Ludens* (London, 1949).

[21] Among the Chinook Indians of the northwestern coast of North America: the winter festival, celebrated by feasting, dancing and other ceremonies.

latter to reciprocate . . . within a certain period and if possible to surpass it. . . . In the Potlatch one proves one's superiority by the lavish prodigality of one's gifts, but what is even more striking, by the wholesale destruction of one's possessions just to show one can do without them." Huizinga finds that this ritual is not restricted to the Kwakiutl; it is "found all over the world in more or less obvious traces." In Melanesia the same customs exist; they also exist in Greek, Roman, old Germanic cultures, and there is evidence of them in ancient China. He quotes Malinowski that among the Trobriand Islanders foodstuffs are valued not only on account of their usefulness but also as a means of parading wealth. The important point is that in Potlatch the sole aim is of winning, of being superior, enhancing prestige. It is often clearly economically ruinous and as such strikingly non-utilitarian. That such originally playful contests may, in certain instances, become an integral part of the socio-economic structure (for instance, in the early phase of Western capitalism) and gradually lose their playful characteristics is not noted by Huizinga.

Huizinga puts special emphasis on the fact that every game has rules and restrictions which cannot be violated without destroying the playful character of its performance. His main objective is to discover the elements of play in all aspects of culture. He discovers the connection between legal justice and play even in the formal characteristics of the law: "The judicial contest is always subject to a system of restrictive rules which quite apart from the limitations of time and place set the lawsuit firmly and squarely in the domain of ordinary antithetical play." A lawsuit can be regarded as a game of chance, a contest, or a verbal battle.

From law, Huizinga turns to war and proposes the thesis that primitive war often was scarcely distinguishable from a playful exercise of personal courage. He qualifies this by adding that even archaic war "with its grimness and bitterness offers but scant occasion for this noble game to become a reality, and only in the distorted epical presentation is war played out in the ideal sphere of honor, virtue, and beauty."

To demonstrate the non-utilitarian, playful element in war, Huizinga quotes the instance of a Japanese prince, Kenchin, in his war against another prince, Shingen. When the former learned that inadvertently he had cut off the latter's supply of salt, he sent salt to his enemy expressing his contempt of such economic warfare by saying, "I fight not with salt but with the sword." Huizinga also quotes Ruskin, who maintained that in "the creative or foundational war the natural restlessness and love of contest among men are disciplined, by consent, into modes of beautiful—though it may be fatal—play."

In science, too, Huizinga demonstrates the riddle-solving motivation for the mere sake of finding a solution independent of its utility. Being fascinated by play, he deplores the fact that in the Nineteenth Century Western civilization was rapidly losing much of its playful character. He believes that all the creative achievements of previous centuries originated in non-utilitarian, playful practices. In our own age science particularly is in the process of becoming woven into the highly complex socio-economic structure of modern society. The most extreme expression of this, he says, is "the shameful misconception of Marxian doctrine that economic forces and material interests determine the course of the world. The grotesque overestimation of the economic factor was conditioned by our worship of technological progress which was itself the fruit of rationalism and utilitarianism." This shift comes to expression also in the rationalization of man's dress which sheds all the aesthetic, non-functional frills: "Work and production have become ideal, the idol of the age. All Europe has donned the boiler suit (overalls)."

The predominance of the practical technological applications of scientific knowledge which have been acquired in the previous two hundred years—while scientists were freely pursuing "pure" science—is another expression of this gradual rationalization of social life which lends to our own era its deadly seriousness. Its goals have become a statistical problem of securing food, shelter, and comforts for the masses. Play is now relegated to the special domain of sports—particularly spectator sports—in which it is more than less isolated from the essential fabric of modern industrial society. Huizinga finds some consolation in the observation that residues of play persist in such central events of modern society as American presidential elections.

The gradual rationalization and routinization of the functions of survival in society do not necessarily lead to the extinction of the playful creative activities of men. The efforts which are saved by the rationalization of basic economic processes can be utilized for the complex derivatives of play: for artistic, scientific creativeness, and for the embellishment of life by developing a more sophisticated art of living.

The affinity between play and creativity has long been recognized. Play emancipates itself from the grave exigencies of life. We call behavior rational when it is well adapted to given conditions and thus can serve the individual's survival. In play, the individual expresses his "non-adjusted" inclinations.

In playful experimentation with his own faculties, and without any consideration for utilitarian goals, man instead of "adjusting" himself to the world is able to shape it according to his own needs and desires. In building his own world, he furthers his survival and discovers the means for survival by creative acts while playfully exercising his abilities for their own sake. A truly creative act is, nevertheless, more complex than play. While play is mainly directed to self-gratification, in creativity communication with others becomes an important additional feature. The child expresses itself in play. The creative artist, writer, or scientist also expresses himself but at the same time attempts to convey this self-expression to others. Play though intimately related to the higher forms of creativity does not fully explain them. They are complex derivatives of play.

The creative nature of playing lies in greater freedom of choice in contrast to adaptive behavior. Adaptive behavior is closely determined by the adaptive goal; by the problem which the organism has to solve. As a rule there is only one or at most a few correct solutions.

In play, on the other hand, the freedom of choice is

practically unlimited which lends to it an experimental connotation. By contrast, utilitarian behavior is pedestrian. The goal is circumscribed and the procedure by which one may reach it is restricted by the goal itself as well as by the practical exigencies of a given situation.

Adaptation has a conserving and leveling function. It favors uniformity which is determined by the adaptive task that prescribes a certain solution. There is little choice. In play, however, and in his more complex creative activities when man is relieved from immediate tasks of adaptation, he reveals his individuality, building a world according to his own fantasy.

One is tempted to compare the relation between adaptive behavior and play with the relation between natural selection and mutation in biology. Mutation can be looked upon as a free and playful experimentation of nature with new, sometimes bizarre, combinations of genes which in themselves are not adaptive but produce individual variations in the species, some of which by chance may have a survival value. These successful experiments are preserved through heredity.

Play is one of the important sources (though not the only one) of man's culture-building faculty by which he changes the world according to his own image.

It is paradoxical that when man through scientific knowledge has become so efficient in securing with little effort the basic necessities of life, he becomes so deadly serious and looks nostalgically at the creative centuries of the past during which he still had the time and the detachment necessary for play and creativity. In this paradox lies the secret of the crisis of Western civilization.

CHAPTER XV

Retirement Neurosis or Malignant Boredom

"With all wish-fulfilling means at his command, he finds himself in the awkward situation of not knowing how to wish. At the bottom of his heart, he is aware, that he wishes nothing, that he himself is unable to direct his appetite and to choose among the innumerable things offered by his environment."

ORTEGA Y GASSET

The creative utilization of leisure requires lifelong preparation. While biological procreation is an inherited function, creativity on the cultural-symbolic level must be learned by every person during his own life, through all those complex processes to which we apply the term "education." Formal education provided by schools, however, is only one part of the highly complex and intangible process by which a person acquires the cultural heritage of past centuries.

Nothing shows this more clearly than the widespread American phenomenon which properly can be called "retirement neurosis." The victim as a rule is a man between sixty and seventy years, who, on the advice of his family, friends, or physician, consults the psychiatrist because of his despondency. It usually begins within a year after he retires from his business activities. Retirement—not having to work—presents him with a more formidable problem than he had ever had to face while struggling for financial success. One learns that he started with a newspaper route when he was eight or nine years old, and that, since then, he did nothing else but work continually for financial success. He never finished reading a book; he did not care nor had any time for the theater or for music. Everything in his life—his marriage, his children—was subordinated to his supreme goal of success. He tells the psychiatrist that what he really wanted was to give his children and his wife all the security he lacked in his own early years. Yet the fact is that twenty years ago he had already enough financial security for the rest of his life and for at least three successive generations. He could have given more time and attention to his family, if they were really as important to him as he claimed. Instead, with complete self-abandonment, he passionately built up his empire and subordinated everything else to this single purpose. For him, money, after he had more than enough, lost entirely its significance as a means for survival or even for a luxurious way of life—in which he never really indulged, having neither the time for it nor the inclination. Money became the symbol of his greatness. The enjoyment of life for its own sake, the art of living, was unknown to him. His home was planned by an architect and an interior decorator who never needed to consider their client's personality. His library was bought by the yard, his garden planned by a landscaper, his records bought according to best-seller lists; his wife was a mannequin on which to hang jewelry and furs; his children served to increase his social prestige by attending fashionable schools—all of which constantly reminded others and himself of his own success. Life for him consisted in making money, financial success being the measure of his self-esteem and the major organizing principle of his strivings. Now retired, he finds himself confronted by a never-before experienced void. Life suddenly loses all its meaning. His response is depression and a rapid deterioration of his physical health, as if he really wanted to die to escape boredom and humiliation.

It was most revealing when one of my patients, who after retirement developed depression with suicidal ideas, explained to me that the one thing which kept him alive was playing golf because he could in this continue endlessly the struggle for improving his handicap. Success at golf, he said, can be measured by numbers, just as a bank account can, and he could thus continue to approximate the only thing which gave him real pleasure in his earlier years.

This style of life does not have much room for "private life," and it does not prepare a person for retirement. It is in sharp contrast with the attitude of the typical pre-war philosophy of the Frenchman, who considered himself a failure if he could not retire as a "rentier" at forty to devote the rest of his years to the art of living, to the cultivation of his tastes, hobbies, and individual inclinations, all of which he approached with as much ingenuity and originality as his American counterpart did in improving his own and his nation's material and social standards.

American tourists, attracted every year to Europe in increasing numbers, intuitively feel—like Dodsworth of Sinclair Lewis—that they find something abroad which complements their existence and fills a void in their lives. Returning home, they console themselves with emphasizing that the large masses abroad have not the same material standards and often not even minimum comforts and security. They can only justify their way of life and measure its richness by the size and number of automobiles and television sets owned by the population. While they pridefully point out all their technical possessions, they forget that all these never would have come into being but for the impractical basic discoveries of men who were possessed by the desire to satisfy their idle curiosities about the nature of the universe.

These scientific dreamers never knew the problem of leisure. Their aims were unlimited, as boundless as the field of knowledge is and will ever remain to be. Work for them was play. From it they derived more pleasure than from any other form of play.

The problem of leisure today does not confront only the wealthy. It is not difficult to foresee that the advancing automation of production and the increase of national wealth, together with advancements in social security legislation, will further reduce working hours. The majority of the population will find itself more and more confronted with the problem of how to spend their free time. It is not difficult to foresee the time when a large proportion of people will be exposed to a more deadly disease than any caused by microörganisms: to malignant boredom, a disease which threatens not a specific organ of the body, but the organism as a whole. It deprives man of the meaning of life and undermines his wish to live. Leisure, we may forecast, in an affluent society will become one of the central problems of mental health, matching in significance the problems caused by economic substandards. It appears, indeed, that every advance, no matter how beneficial, creates new complications. Fortunately, these mechanistic-materialistic developments also contain the hidden solution of those problems they create.

The solution will not come from psychiatry. Psychiatry, by arduous prolonged and persistent work, may save a few individuals from their retirement neurosis. The answer lies in the field of education in the broadest sense, in a change in the whole ethos of society.

There are few contemporary Americans who recognize this problem more clearly than Robert Hutchins, who long ago began his valiant fight to introduce an emphasis on liberal education that would balance the prevailing trend toward preparing students merely for a trade or profession. This orientation may appear to the short-sighted as blatantly impractical. And yet, it is the most practical remedy for the impoverishment of life which is an inevitable result of our sterile and exclusively living-standard-oriented era. "Pragmatism is unpragmatic; it won't work in practice," writes Peter Viereck.[1] Only through liberal education can the contemporary youth regain his historical continuity with the past and absorb the ways of creative self-realization if he is to escape an abysmal void in his existence.

The more we succeed in reducing the energy and time

[1] Peter Viereck, "The Unadjusted Man," *Saturday Review*, November 1, 1958.

required to achieve high living standards, the more threateningly this void will appear before us. It is paradoxical but none the less true that the nearer man comes to his goal, to make his material life easy and abundant, the more he undermines the foundations of a meaningful existence in which materialistic objectives are not ultimate aims but only means by which he can remain human. Leisure, felt as an embarrassing void which cannot be meaningfully filled, is an irrefutable *reductio ad absurdum* of the presently prevailing orientation which considers the improvement of material standards to be the ultimate aim instead of the full development of one's unique self. Without having this explicitly in his mind every moment of his existence only two alternatives remain open for man: either to give up his human-ness and accept the role of a specialized cog in the complex social machine, and thus eventually be reduced to the state of a member of an insect society; or succumb to the prolonged sufferings of an unsuccessful neurotic struggle to retain his individuality in the fantasy world of neurotic symptoms or in delinquency, the only channels through which he can express his non-adjusted individual cravings, albeit only on a regressive level.

Similar considerations must have influenced Peter Viereck when, in a recent article, he voiced our desperate need for the unadjusted man, "Why not for once have the moral courage to be unadjusted, a bad mixer and shockingly devoid of leadership qualities ?" [2] Viereck, when he speaks of the "unadjusted" man, does not mean "maladjusted." He fights for the right of private life. "Every

[2] *Loc. cit.*

overadjusted society swallows up the diversities of private bailiwicks, private eccentricities, private inner life, and the creativity inherent in concrete personal loyalties and in loving attachments to unique local roots and their rich historical accretions."

CHAPTER XVI

Reflections on the Past, the Present and the Future

> **"If you base society on the idea of technique and economic gains then you lose not only freedom but the economic gains. Without spiritual know-why you lose even your technical know-how."**
>
> PETER VIERECK

It is time to summarize our reflections.

A person who has lived during the past fifty years of rapid cultural change, who in his early years has experienced the last phases of a more individualistic and creative era, and who later has been exposed to the advent of the statistical man, will naturally look back nostalgically to the good old days. He is likely to react to this change as to something destructive; he is likely to evaluate the present trend as dehumanization, a degeneration of those values he absorbed as integral parts of his self, the governing principles of his behavior. Only after detached reflection will he be ready to question of the universal validity of this reaction.

The existential despair is a particularly European disease alien to the average American. The beat generation is a ripple compared to the existentialist wave currently sweeping over Europe.

The American developments did not have to contend with the cultural heritage of the past. American individualism asserted itself, in the main, on the economic level. The nation was until recently absorbed in the application and further development of modern technology for the conquest of a vast wilderness. This preoccupation with technology and economic advancement became the most powerful organizing principle also within the personality. The basic existential dilemma—"What is the purpose and sense of existence ?"—did not become a pressing issue for a nation which had a vital and concrete answer: to build a technically efficient world with a steadily rising material standard of living for everyone. Such a concrete and timely goal appropriate to the life situation of the population did not leave room for idle contemplation about the meaning of existence. Every able-bodied and able-minded person could freely participate in the pursuit of highly practical goals and find full outlet in advancing his individual economic interests. The problem of finding new emotional outlets and new inspirations has become an issue only recently, with the advancing organization of big industry and big business, which has reduced the opportunities for exciting individual ventures, has favored conformity and routine, and has at the same time secured comfortable economic standards for the majority of people. For the majority, individualistic aspirations are no longer realizable in the arena of action and can be satisfied only by watching western films and criminal dramas or by participating passively in sports events as spectators.

While these outlets seem to secure the emotional equilibrium of the majority, at the fringes of society the growing juvenile delinquency reveals its precariousness. The emotionally and economically underprivileged youth, needing more than vicarious gratification, attempts to act out in life the traditional patterns of bravado, adventure and enterprise, the only ideals he knows but cannot live up to as a member of a large organization.

The growing organization of economic production, however, is not the only factor in these developments. The progressive automation of production deprives the worker of any personal gratification in performing his job. Man has become an extension of the machine, which no longer serves him; he has become its slave. Moreover, automation reduces working hours, creates leisure which man is not able to utilize in any creative fashion. Initiative and fantasy wither away; a bland stereotyped personality who does not aspire to form his own destiny emerges, who does not want to be different, to be himself, since none of his individual characteristics are needed or encouraged. All this is but the adaptation of the personality to the existing socio-economic structure. The plasticity of human nature seems to be immense; it appears possible that such a gradual transformation of personality structure can be accomplished without provoking internal revolt. A new species, the mass man, is in the making.

Primarily the generation in transition who (or whose parents) had experienced the previous era, are likely to show conflict. They are those who particularly feel this process of depersonalization as a loss of identity. Those of the pre-war generation who consider their unique selves as a capital entrusted to them to develop and to enrich by absorbing the cultural accomplishments of the past, those to whom a full life means self-realization and not merely filling a social role—only for these the present solution appears unacceptable, equivalent to living death.

And yet, some general considerations may throw a ray of hope on this bleak picture. The study of personality development as well as history points to two fundamental trends in human behavior: on the one hand, to adapt, and on the other, to grow and create. Adaptation seeks stability and security, the preservation of the status quo. Growth and creativity seek change, bringing into being something not there before. Man is a restless animal who is not satisfied by adapting himself to his environment. He succeeded spectacularly in changing his environment by creating civilization; instead of adapting himself to nature, he adapted nature not only to his needs but to his fantasy. As long as this basic human trait—creativity—not only on the biological but also on the symbolic (cultural) level persists—in other words, as long as man remains human—the merely security-seeking conforming mass man is not likely to stay here forever.

Technological advancement, automation, is making the struggle for existence, the gratification of basic biological needs less and less energy-consuming. This is precisely the function of the machine. Human energies thus liberated must find outlets. It seems we have forgotten the aim, concentrating only on the means, on technical advancement, and neglecting the main issue: how to use constructively our energies liberated by technology.

It is not probable that man for long will remain satisfied only with the comfort afforded by technology. He will build, as he always did in the past, on this abundant economic foundation second and third stories of civilization on the symbolic level. Eventually he will again seek new expressions for his creative mind, in new art, in scientific curiosity for its own sake, in basic research, in playful exercise of his potentialities beyond the immediate needs of survival, in the art of living which goes beyond material standards. All this, of course, can happen only if he can survive the present crisis.

This book is devoted to diagnosis and not to treatment. How the higher faculties of man can and should be cultivated, encouraged and developed is the province of public education. Education for creativity, however, can only flourish in a society which has grown out of its present, almost exclusive preoccupation with material standards of living. It can only be hoped that western humanity will not need the further spread of juvenile delinquency and neurosis, cold and hot wars, to be awakened from its present torpor and to be convinced of the sterility of its current ideals.

It is customary to say that Greek culture never could have come into being without a slave caste to which the basic economic functions were entrusted and which made it possible for others to indulge in the luxury of creative leisure. The serf during the Middle Ages and the industrial worker during the Nineteenth Century took over this lowly function. At present we are witnessing the age of automation, in which ingenious machine robots are taking over the function of slaves. This, together with liberal social legislation, will free the whole population from the excessive chores of existence. This movement toward liberation finds the masses unprepared for making constructive and enjoyable use of their newly acquired free time and energy. Leisure, it can be safely predicted, will increasingly become a central problem, just as scarcity and economic needs were in the not-too-remote past. This prediction, of course, is based on the hope that the Cold War will not remain with us for long and will not lead to mutual destruction.

Preparation for leisure essentially consists in the education of man in the use of his creative faculties. Man shares biological creativity with animals and it does not require learning. Creativity on the cultural level, on the other hand, can only be acquired during and after maturation. It has a cultural history, it transcends individual existence, it is molded by tradition even when it challenges tradition. This type of education enriches man's tastes and his ability to enjoy his existence beyond physical well-being; it opens up for him the unlimited frontiers of the mind.

The surplus energies saved by the machine, if not channeled toward creative goals, will be spent in crude physical indulgences and in sterile competition only for the sake of competition. Eventually they will be used for mutual destruction. Our highly mechanized society can survive only if the economic-material achievements are considered merely as a basis for the development of higher sublimated forms of creative interests.

A survey of the socio-economic trends of the last decades contains a few hopeful signs. A statistical table compiled by the U.S. Department of Commerce shows, for example, that in 1951 people spent almost three times as much for higher learning as in 1940; the same is true of expenditures for elementary and secondary school education. Amounts spent for magazines, books and sheet music have increased two and a half times since 1940. The Audit Bureau of Circulation shows that in 1901 when our population was 76,000,000, there were 223 magazines with a circulation totaling 436,000,000. By 1951, with our population doubled, there were 579 magazines with a total circulation of 3,822,000,000.

According to the Community Concerts Association of New York, 130% more classical music concerts were held out of New York City in 1950 than in 1940. According to the National Association of Concert Managers, the last decade saw an increase of 80% in the number of symphony orchestras and of 550% in the number of local opera companies. Twice as many towns now provide serious music regularly for their population.

At first glance these figures do not appear particularly significant if one compares them with similar increases in expenditures for such basic necessities of life as food, clothing, housing and household operation during the same period. Considering the fact that food prices increased more than 200% in the same period, increased expenditures for such basic necessities can be explained to a large degree by changes in prices. The same changes in cost, however, do not obtain in the cultural fields mentioned above.

The conclusion, therefore, may be justified that during these ten years interest in cultural and creative activities of the mind not only kept pace with interest in improving basic living standards, but was definitely growing. In other words, growth in national wealth in these ten years has manifested itself not only in improving the basic standards of living, but even more in an expansion of cultural aspirations and activities.

These statistical figures appear hopeful, but they do not allow definite conclusions. The meaning of statistical figures always remains uncertain as long as the phenomena to which they pertain are not fully understood. Can we conclude from them that the ideological trend in this country is taking a hopeful turn, that after the consolidation of our economic structure the creative interests of youth will be gradually diverted toward the unlimited frontiers of the mind?

Does the increased consumption of non-material goods really mean an increase of interest in non-economic pursuits? The fateful question is whether or not these figures reflect anything more than one facet of the universal conformist orientation, which induces persons who can afford it—and more and more people are becoming able to afford it—to acquire the external insignia of being up to date, well-educated and sophisticated. I am not in a position to confirm or challenge this pessimistic interpretation. Yet, the mere fact that these non-material interests are conspicuously displayed parallel to conspicuous consumption on the material level—the fact that attendance at concerts and theaters, presence of literary magazines on the drawing-room table, acquirement of a college education and ownership of objects of art are taking their place beside the ownership of technical devices as a means of increasing one's social prestige—all this could be interpreted more hopefully as a sign of a changing orientation. Even more important than the growing social prestige value of intellectual and artistic pursuits is the fact that the government and the general public is beginning to realize the significance of higher learning for national security.

Yet all this is not equivalent to real devotion and dedication. This type of interest in art and knowledge is still subordinated to other aims, to vanity and the more practical aim of national security, and it does not constitute genuine dedication to all these things for their own sake. Particularly, the recent wave of competition with Russia in the field of education for engineering careers entails the danger of further subordinating knowledge to utility and is not at all conducive to the development of a sense for the intrinsic value of knowledge, independent of its practical usefulness. On the contrary, this competitive spirit now introduced even into learning perpetuates those very objectives which undermine free societies and free scientific research. If the struggle for military supremacy and for increased material wealth, ease and comfort will remain the ultimate values, there will be no place for the higher aspirations of man. The first of these two scourges, striving for military strength, can be justified and excused as something imposed upon us by necessity, by world political circumstances which we cannot modify. They are dictated by self-preservation. There is no such excuse for the second evil, namely, the continued blind obsession with material advancement as an aim in itself and not merely as something which should promote the development of man's higher esthetic and intellectual faculties. This is a fateful anachronism, a cultural lag, a residue of the pioneering past which now in an era of affluence necessarily leads to deterioration of those qualities which are specifically human. The new slogan "Atoms for Peace" in itself is not the answer. If it only means further advancement of wealth, ease and comfort as ultimate goals, it will not change the sterility of our outlook.

By now we should be wise to the fact that technical advancement in itself does not mean much. We are witnessing how such marvelous technical innovations as television can be debased for corrupting the mind and promoting the atrophy of the child's most valuable possession, his creative fantasy, and thus add to the spiritual sterility of our age.

At the moment of this writing, all this talk about saving individuality and creativeness may strike the reader as untimely and quite Utopian. It seems to overlook the stark fact that the increasing competition with Russia for economic and military supremacy constitutes a permanent situation, will perpetuate the necessity for stricter organization of social functions, will further curtail private life, will confine the activities of scientists to immediate problems, will restrict educational goals to preparation for technology and economy, and will make the cultivation of individual growth, knowledge and erudition, the art of living, appear as luxuries, dreams of impractical fools. If this gigantic irrational race for supremacy continues and the competing powers do not reach a peaceful plan of coexistence and cooperation, the current increase of interest in aesthetic and intellectual achievements will wither away, the emphasis on technological know-how will persist and the hope remain very dim that this country after it has so far advanced the economic standard of life and general health will build a high spiritual culture upon its abundant material foundation. The desperate struggle for survival will of necessity overshadow all other aspirations of man.

The crucial question is: Can free institutions within a nation survive if fierce international competition continues and forces all free nations toward increasing organization of their economic, educational and research activities ? If they cannot survive, we might just as well give up our efforts to preserve our type of social system. This, however, is too sweeping a conclusion. Even during cold war rigid organization does not need to extend to all fields of social activities; education, research and art may remain relatively unregimented sanctuaries of freedom. Organization is only one of the factors in human progress. Creation is the other one. Only the creative accomplishment of individual minds can be organized. But first comes creation, which requires freedom and absence of pressure of immediate necessities. One can organize efforts toward pinpointed goals only after the knowledge necessary to reach the goal has been acquired. Acquisition of new basic knowledge is a creative act which cannot be regimented. That this is true is clearly suggested by the fact that Russia found it necessary to give to its leading scientists a greater amount of freedom than to any other of its citizens. It is not clear what type of freedom this is, how far it goes. Is it a freedom which allows the scientist to pursue his own particular interest ? In any case, it appears to be a concession to the principle of freedom, and not enthusiasm for freedom. It is a coldly calculated concession. It is a paradoxical attempt to organize freedom, to give it a definite and highly restricted place within the system.

One hears voices saying that this competition we call the Cold War has a beneficial aspect; it stimulates inventiveness and technological advancement. One should not fail to observe that, at the same time, it slowly destroys all those values which make life worth living. Should it continue long enough there will not be much left to be destroyed by an atomic war. This would be the logical conclusion of an era which worshiped the machine and was exterminated by its own idol.

Bibliographical Notes

Chapter I. Foundations

Among the books which made a deep impression upon the author, Ernst Mach's writings, *The History of the Theory of Heat* [Principien der Warmelehre] (Leipzig: Barth, 1923), and *The Analysis of Sensations and the Relation of the Physical to Psychical* (Trans. from the 1st German Edition by C. M. Williams, Revised and Supplemented from the 5th German Edition by Sidney Waterlow, Chicago: The Open Court Publishing Co., 1914), are outstanding. Mach's theory of the economy of thought processes remained a guiding principle for the author in his theoretical writings: the formulation of a minimum number of independent statements which account for the variety of phenomena observed.

Chapter II. First Acquaintance with Radicals

So far as it is possible for the author to reconstruct early influences upon his thought development, the reading of Ibsen's *A Doll's House* introduced into him the first reservations about the absoluteness of the contemporary standards of family life. This was reinforced by reading the plays of George Bernard Shaw and Frank Wedekind, particularly the latter's tragedy, *Frühlingserwachen* (Spring's Awakening).

Chapter III. Freud Enters My Life

Freud's *Interpretation of Dreams* was first read by the author when he was deeply steeped in physiological research in Franz Tangl's laboratory. The book initially bewildered him. It did not fit into anything he learned during his medical curriculum, nor did his readings about philosophy and academic psychology prepare him for the appreciation of this book. He re-read the book as a young assistant in the Psychiatric Institute of the University of Budapest, prompted by a schizophrenic patient who persistently told him his dreams. He then began to realize—at first only vaguely—that the type of reasoning Freud adopted might contain the clue for the understanding of mental disturbances. He also began to recognize the similarity between the reasoning of theoretical physicists and Freud's approach to mental phenomena.

Chapter VII. Psychoanalysis Comes of Age

A book, written by the author in collaboration with the lawyer, Hugo Staub, *The Criminal, The Judge and The Public,* originally published in German under the title *Der Verbrecher und Seine Richter* (Vienna: Int. Psychoan. Verlag, 1927), translated into English by Dr. Gregory Zilboorg (New York: MacMillan, 1931), and republished with new chapters (Glencoe, Illinois: The Free Press, 1956), played an important role in the author's career. It was instrumental in his being invited to the International Congress of Mental Hygiene in Washington, D. C., in April, 1930. The book aroused the interest of William Healy, a pioneer American criminologist, who suggested to the organizers of this Congress that the author should be invited to present his views on criminal psychology.

Chapter VIII. The Role of the Scientist in Society

The author's interest in the psychological motivations of the scientist in his research work goes far back into his youth. This interest, however, was particularly stimulated in reading an article by Michael Polanyi, his childhood friend, "The Rights and Duties of Science," *Manchester Economist* (October, 1939), which challenged J. D. Bernal's book, *The Social Function of Science* (London: Routledge & Kegan Paul, 1939). Polanyi was one of the founders of the English "Freedom of Science" movement, which insisted upon the autonomy of basic research and its independence of practical goals. The author earlier independently came to the same conviction as Polanyi that the subordination to practical aims of the pure quest for knowledge for its own sake is contradictory to the development of scientific knowledge. The English controversy, in which Polanyi played such an important role, gave a new impetus to the author's thinking about this problem, which is possibly one of the most fundamental issues of our age. Similar ideas have been expounded also by J. R. Baker in *Science and the Planned State* (New York: MacMillan, 1945). Reading autobiographical statements of creative scientists, among them Kekule's account of his discovering the carbon ring (Alfred Winterstein, *Autistisches Erleben im Schopferischem Vorgang Die Psychoanalytische Bewegung* Jahrgang I, 1929 Vienna: Intern. Psychoan. Verlag) further confirmed the author's conviction about the inspirational nature of fundamental discoveries.

Chapter IX. The Scientific Revolution

The author's interest in theoretical physics, which started with the reading—still in his high school days—of Ernst Mach's, Planck's and Boltzman's books on thermodynamics, continued up to the present age. The changes in physical theory, and particularly in the basic orientation of physicists toward nature, helped him greatly to understand the changes in outlook of Western man toward the world in the last fifty years. More recently, Norbert Wiener, *The Human Use of Human Beings* (Boston: Houghton Mifflin, 1954), Arthur S. Eddington, *New Pathways in Science* (London: Cambridge Univ. Press, 1935), Ernest Cassirer, *Einstein's Theory of Relativity, Substance and Function* (New York: Dover, 1953), Sir James Jeans, *Physics & Philosophy* (New York: MacMillan, 1943), George Gamow, *One two three . . . infinity* (New York: Viking, 1949), Louis de Broglie, *Revolution in Physics* (New York: Noonday Press, 1953), Neils Bohr, "On Adams & Human Knowledge," *Daedalus,* Vol. 87 (Spring, 1958), pp. 164–175, Werner Heisenberg, "Representation of Nature in Contemporary Physics," *Daedalus,* Vol. 87 (Summer, 1958), pp. 95–108, Werner Heisenberg, *Physics and Philosophy* (New York: Harper, 1958), deepened the author's understanding of the nature of the scientific revolution of our days.

Chapter X. Revolution in Art

For the understanding of the revolution in modern art, the author gained most from his continued exposure to classical and modern paintings. However, he found Arnold Hauser's *The Social History of Art* (New York: Knopf, 1951), particularly revealing concerning the nature of this revolution.

Chapter XI. Existentialism and Psychoanalysis

The author knew from his early interest in philosophy the works of Kierkegaard and Nietzsche. The present re-discovery of Kierkegaard by existentialist philosophers was one of those cultural historical phenomena which confirmed his belief that the conformist trend inherent in our industrial era constitutes a threat to the individual. The writings of Soren Kierkegaard, *The Sickness Unto Death* (Princeton: Princeton Univ. Press, 1946), and Nietzsche's *Uber Wahrheit und Lüge Im Ausser Moralischen Sinn, Unzeitgemässe Betrachtungen, Zur Geneologie der Moral,* and *Die Geburt der Tragodie* (all Leipzig: C. G. Nauman, Verlag, 1906), illuminate this danger most impressively. Edmund Husserl's *Ideas: General Introduction to Pure Phenomenology* (New York: MacMillan), and Martin Heidegger's *Existence and Being* (Chicago: Henry Regnery, 1950), are more methodical writings, yet, in the author's opinion less revealing for the cultural historical significance of the existentialist movement.

Chapter XII. The Struggle for Ego Identity

Among psychoanalytic writings, Erik H. Erikson's *Childhood and Society* (New York: Norton, 1950), *Das Problem der Identitat Entfaltung* der *Psychoanalyse* (Stuttgart: Ernst Klett Verlag, 1956), "Ego Development and Historical Change" in *The Psychoanalytic Study of the Child, Vol. II* (New York: International Univ. Press, 1946), Allan Wheelis's *The Quest for Identity* (New York: Norton, 1958), are most representative of the attempts to deal with a focal phenomenon of our era: the struggle for the preservation of a waning ego identity. Among the social scientists, David Reisman in his *The Lonely Crowd* (New Haven: Yale University Press, 1953), approached the same phenomenon from an even broader perspective, differentiating between the inner-directed and the other-directed person.

Chapter XIV. Play and the Serious Business of Living

The study of the psychology of play is of major significance for the understanding of both biological and cultural development, and in particular of creativity. The writings which the author found most illuminating on this subject are those of Friedrich Schiller, *On the Aesthetic Education of Mankind;* Karl Groos, *The Play of Animals* (New York: D. Appleton Co., 1898) and his *The Play of Man* (New York: D. Appleton Co., 1908); A. F. McBride and D. O. Hebb, "Behavior of the Captive Bottle-Nose *Dolphin Tursiops Truncatus,*" *J. Comparative & Physiological Psychology,* XLI, No. 2, 1948; Herbert Spencer, *Principles of Psychology,* Vol. II (New York: D. Appleton Co., 1873); Ludwig Bertelanffy, *Problems of Life* (New York: Wiley, 1952), pp. 46, 116; "An Outline of General Systems Theory," *British J. Philosophy of Science,* 1, 1950, p. 137; Bernard Alexander, *Müveszet* (*Art*) *Pantheon* (Budapest, 1927); Thomas M. French, *The Integration of Behavior, Vols. I, II, III* (Chicago: The University of Chicago Press, 1952, 1954, 1958); Sandor Ferenczi, "Thalassa: A Theory of Genitality" (New York: The Psychoanalytic Quarterly, 1933); Sigmund Freud, *Beyond The Pleasure Principle* [1920], (New York: Liveright, 1950); Erik H. Erikson, *Studies in the Interpretation of Play: 1. Clinical Observation of Play Disruption in Young Children,* Genetic Psychological Monographs, XXII, 1940; Lili E. Peller, "Libidinal Phases, Ego Development and Play" in *The Psychoanalytic Study of the Child,* Vol. IX (New York: International Universities Press, 1954), pp. 178–198. The author's own contributions to this field were earlier presented in his *Our Age of Unreason* (New York, Lippincott, 1942), "Three Fundamental Dynamic Principles of the Mental Apparatus and of the Behavior of Living Organisms," *Dialectica,* International Review of Philosophy of Knowledge, V, 1951, "A Contribution to the Theory of Play," *The Psychoanalytic Quarterly,* Vol. XXVII, 1958, pp. 175–193.

The most comprehensive study mainly of the relationship of play to culture is Johan Huizinga's *Homo Ludens* (London: Routledge & Kegan Paul, 1949).

Chapter XV. Retirement Neurosis or Malignant Boredom

The thesis that affluence and technological advancement do not help human beings to choose among the "innumerable things" offered by their environment, that contemporary man does not know how to wish, was most forcefully expounded by Ortega y Gasset's *Toward A Philosophy of History* (New York: Norton, 1941). The levelizing influence of our present-day conformist philosophy was masterfully exposed in Peter Viereck's article, "The Unadjusted Man," *Saturday Review,* Nov. 1, 1958.

Chapter XVI. Reflections on the Past, the Present and the Future

The vanishing regard for man as an individual person and its replacement by a merely statistical concern for a person's "paper-form" is the topic of G. V. Georghiu's novel, *The Twenty-Fifth Hour* (New York: Knopf, 1950), a book which after its publication became a best seller in France, but was coldly received by American reviewers and the American public.

INDEX

3

Date Due
